Python Mastery Unleashed

Advanced Programming Techniques

JARREL E.

Contents

Acknowledgment

As the author, I stand at the forefront of this project, but it is essential to recognize the collective effort and support that has been instrumental in bringing this book to fruition. The world of Python programming is vast and ever-evolving, and it is with the combined expertise and dedication of numerous individuals that we present this comprehensive guide to advanced Python techniques.

The Unsung Heroes: Editors and Reviewers

First and foremost, I extend my heartfelt gratitude to the editorial team who diligently combed through the manuscript, ensuring that every word was carefully placed, every concept clearly explained, and every code example meticulously tested. Their keen eye for detail and their commitment to excellence have been indispensable in crafting this book.

The Python Community

The Python community is a vibrant and generous one, where knowledge is freely shared and open-source projects

1

flourish. I want to express my gratitude to the Python community at large, from developers to educators and enthusiasts, for fostering an environment of continuous learning and collaboration.

My Family and Supporters

I owe a profound debt of gratitude to my family and friends, who supported me throughout the writing process. Their patience, encouragement, and understanding were the pillars upon which this endeavor was built.

Forward

In the ever-evolving world of technology, Python stands as a beacon of innovation and efficiency. This book is dedicated to those who have already embraced the fundamentals of Python and are now poised to explore the deeper realms of this versatile programming language.

The Power of Python Unveiled

Python is not just a language; it's a tool for shaping the future of computing. As we delve into the advanced techniques and concepts within this book, you will find yourself equipped to tackle challenges and create solutions that were previously beyond your reach. Whether you are a professional developer seeking to optimize your code, a data scientist diving deeper into machine learning, or an enthusiast with a passion for programming, this book is your gateway to Python excellence.

The Journey Begins

Within the pages of "Python Mastery Unleashed," you will embark on a journey that takes you from proficiency to mastery. This book is designed to be your guiding light through the intricate paths of advanced Python programming. By the time you reach the final chapter, you will have acquired the skills and knowledge necessary to tackle complex projects, optimize your code, and explore domains like data science, web development, and more.

What to Expect

This book is not merely a collection of code snippets; it's a comprehensive exploration of the art and science of Python programming. I encourage you to approach this book with an open mind and a willingness to learn. Python's adaptability and power are at your disposal, but it's up to you to harness its full potential. "Python Mastery Unleashed" will be your trusted companion on this journey, providing insights and guidance that can elevate your programming skills to new heights.

Preface

It is with great pleasure and enthusiasm that I present to you "Python Mastery Unleashed: Advanced Programming Techniques." This book is the culmination of a diligent effort to provide a comprehensive guide for individuals who aspire to elevate their Python programming skills to an advanced level. As a professional author with a profound passion for Python, my mission is to empower you with the knowledge and techniques required to produce professional-grade Python applications.

Python has rapidly evolved from a beginner-friendly language to a versatile and robust tool employed by developers across the globe. Whether you are an experienced programmer or someone just setting foot on the path of Python, this book is meticulously crafted to cater to your needs.

This book is replete with real-world examples, hands-on exercises, and illuminating case studies designed to cement your comprehension. Our intent is not merely to transform you into a proficient Python programmer but to equip you with the capacity to surmount intricate programming challenges with unwavering confidence.

Python's journey into advanced programming territory may be arduous, yet it is profoundly gratifying. We invite you to interact with this book, explore the provided code, and employ the acquired knowledge in your projects. Python is a vast canvas for your programming ingenuity, and this book shall provide you with the tools to craft your digital masterpieces.

Thank you for entrusting us with your pursuit of knowledge in "Python Mastery Unleashed: Advanced Programming Techniques." Let's embark on this transformative journey together, with the aim of emerging as true Python masters.

Introduction

1.1 Introduction

I have heard many people over the years say that Python is an easy language to lean and that Python is also a simple language. To some extent both of these statements are true; but only to some extent. While the core of the Python language is easy to lean and relatively simple (in part thanks to its consistency); the sheer richness of the language constructs and flexibility available can be overwhelming. In addition the Python environment, its Eco system, the range of libraries available, the often competing options available etc., can make moving to the next level daunting.

Once you have learned the core elements of the language such as how classes and inheritance work, how functions work, what are protocol sand Abstract Base Classes etc. Where do you go next? The aim of this book is to delve into those next steps. The book is organized into eight different topics:

1. Computer Graphics. The book covers Computer Graphics and Computer Generated Art in Python as well as Graphical User Interfaces and Graphing/ Charting via MatPlotLib.
2. Games Programming. This topic is covered using the pygame library.
3. Testing and Mocking. Testing is an important aspect of any software development; this book introduces testing in general and the PyTest module in detail. It also considers mocking within testing including what and when to mock.
4. File Input/Output. The book covers text file reading and writing as well as reading and writing CSV and Excel files. Although not strictly related to file input, regulator expressions are included in this section as they can be used to process textual data held in files.
5. Database Access. The book introduces databases and relational database in particular. It then presents the Python DB-API database access standard and one implementation of this standard, the PyMySQL module used to access a MySQL database.
6. Logging. An often missed topic is that of logging.The book therefore introduces logging the need for logging, what to log and what not to log as well as the Python logging module.
7. Concurrency and Parallelism. The book provides extensive coverage of concurrency topics including Threads, Processes and inter thread or process synchronization. It also presents Futures and AsyncIO.
8. Reactive Programming. This section of the book introduces Reactive Programming using the PyRx

reactive programming library.

9. Network Programming. The book concludes by introducing socket and web service communications in Python.

Each section is introduced by a chapter providing the background and key concepts of that topic. Subsequent chapters then cover various aspects of the topic.

For example, the first topic covered is on Computer Graphics. This section has an introductory chapter on Computer Graphics in general. It then introduces the Turtle Graphics Python library which can be used to generate a graphical display.

The following chapter considers the subject of Computer Generated Art and uses the Turtle Graphics library to illustrate these ideas. Thus several examples are presented that might be considered art. The chapter concludes by presenting the well known Koch Snowflake and the Mandelbrot Fractal set.

This is followed by a chapter presenting the MatPlotLib library used for generating 2D and 3D charts and graphs (such as a line chart, bar chart or scatter graph). The section concludes with a chapter on Graphical User Interfaces (or GUIs) using the wxpython library. This chapter explores what we mean by a GUI and some of the alternatives available in Python for creating a GUI.

Subsequent topics follow a similar pattern.

Each programming or library oriented chapter also includes numerous sample programs that can be downloaded from the GutHub repository and executed. These chapters also include one or more end of chapter exercises(with sample solutions also in the GutHub repository).

The topics within the book can be read mostly independently of each other. This allows the reader to dip into subject areas as and when required. For example, the File Input/Output section and the Database Access section can be read independently of each other (although in this case assessing both technologies may be useful in selecting an appropriate approach to adopt for the long term persistent storage of data in a particular system).

Within each section there are usually dependencies, for example it is necessary to understand the pygame library from the 'Building Games with pygame' introductory chapter, before exploring the worked case study presented by the chapter on the Star ship Meteors game. Similarly it is necessary to have read the Threading and Multiprocessing chapters before reading the Inter Thread/Process Synchronization chapter.

Computer Graphics

Introduction to Computer Graphics

Computer Graphics are everywhere; they are on your TV, in cinema adverts,the core of many films, on your tablet or mobile phone and certainly on your PC or Mac as well as on the dashboard of your car, on your smart watch and in children's electronic toys.

However what do we mean by the term Computer Graphics? The term goes back to a time when many (most) computers were purely textual in terms of their input and output and very few computers could generate graphical displays let alone handle input via such a display. However, in terms of this book we take the term Computer Graphics to include the creation of Graphical User Interfaces (or GUIs), graphs and charts such as bar charts or line plots of data, graphics in computer games (such as Space Invaders or Flight Simulator) as well as the generation of 2D and 3D scenes or images.We also use the term to include Computer Generated Art.

The availability of Computer Graphics is very important for

the huge acceptance of computer systems by non computer scientists over the last 40 years. It is in part thanks to the accessibility of computer systems via computer graphic interfaces that almost everybody now uses some form of computer system (whether that is a PC, a tablet, a mobile phone or a smart TV).

A Graphical User Interface (GUI) can capture the essence of an idea or a situation, often avoiding the need for a long passage of text or textual commands. It is also because a picture can paint a thousand words; as long as it is the right picture.

In many situations where the relationships between large amounts of information must be conveyed, it is much easier for the user to assimilate this graphically than textually. Similarly, it is often easier to convey some meaning by manipulating some system entities on screen, than by combinations of text commands.

For example, a well chosen graph can make clear information that is hard to determine from a table of the same data. In turn an adventure style game can become engaging and immersive with computer graphics which is in marked contrast to the textual versions of the 1980s. This highlights the advantages of a visual presentation compared to a purely textual one.

Background

Every interactive software system has a Human Computer

Interface, whether it be a single text line system or an advanced graphic display. It is the vehicle used by developers for obtaining information from their user(s), and in turn, every user has to face some form of computer interface in order to perform any desired computer operation.

Historically computer systems did not have a Graphical User Interface and rarely generated a graphical view. These systems from the 60s, 70s and 80s typically focused on numerical or data processing tasks. They were accessed via green or grey screens on a text oriented terminal. There was little or no opportunity for graphical output.

However, during this period various researchers at laboratories such as Stanford, MIT, Bell Telephone Labs and Xerox were looking at the possibilities that graphic systems might offer to computers. Indeed even as far back as 1963 Ivan Sutherland showed that interactive computer graphics were feasible with his Ph.D. thesis on the Sketchpad system.

The Graphical Computer Era

Graphical computer displays and interactive graphical interfaces became a common means of human–computer interaction during the 1980s. Such interfaces can save a user from the need to learn complex commands. They are less likely to intimidate computer naives and can provide a large amount of information quickly in a form which can be easily assimilated by the user.

The widespread use of high quality graphical interfaces

(such as those provided by the Apple Macintosh and the early Windows interface) led many computer users to expect such interfaces to any software they use. Indeed these systems paved the way for the type of interface that is now omnipresent on PCs, Macs, Linux boxes, tablets and smart phones etc. This graphical user interface is based on the WIMP paradigm (Windows, Icons, Menus and Pointers) which is now the prevalent type of graphical user interface in use today.

The main advantage of any window-based system, and particularly of a WIMP environment, is that it requires only a small amount of user training. There is no need to learn complex commands, as most operations are available either as icons, operations on icons, user actions (such as swiping) or from menu options, and are easy to use. (An icon is a small graphic object that is usually symbolic of an operation or of a larger entity such as an application program or a file). In general, WIMP based systems are simple to learn, intuitive to use, easy to retain and straightforward to work with.

These WIMP systems are exemplified by the Apple Macintosh interface (see Goldberg and Robson as well as Tesler), which was influenced by the pioneering work done at the Palo Alto Research Center on the Xerox Star Machine. It was, however, the Macintosh which brought such interfaces to the mass market, and first gained acceptance for them as tools for business, home and industry.This interface transformed the way in which humans expected to interact with their computers, becoming a defacto standard,which forced other manufacturers to provide similar interfaces on their own machines, for example Microsoft Windows for the PC.

This type of interface can be augmented by providing direct manipulation graphics. These are graphics which can be grabbed and manipulated by the user, using a mouse, to perform some operation or action. Icons are a simple version of this, the "opening" of an icon causes either the associated application to execute or the associated window to be displayed.

Interactive and Non Interactive Graphics

Computer graphics can be broadly subdivided into two categories:

- Non Interactive Computer Graphics
- Interactive Computer Graphics.

In Non Interactive Computer Graphics (aka Passive Computer Graphics) an image is generated by a computer typically on a computer screen; this image can be viewed by the user (however they cannot interact with the image). Examples of non-interactive graphics presented later in this book include Computer Generated Art in which an image is generated using the Python Turtle Graphics library.Such an image can viewed by the user but not modified. Another example might be a basic bar chart generated using MatPlotLib which presents some set of data.

Interactive Computer Graphics by contrast, involve the user interacting with the image displayed in the screen in some way, this might be to modify the data being displayed or to change they way in which the image is being rendered etc. It is typified by interactive Graphical User Interfaces (GUIs) in which a user interacts with menus, buttons, input field, sliders,scroll bars etc. However, other visual displays can also be interactive. For example, a slider could be used with a MatplotLib chart. This display could present the number of sales made on a particular date; as the slider is moved so the data changes and the chart is modified to show different data sets.

Another example is represented by all computer games which are inherently interactive and most, if not all, update their visual display in response to some user inputs. For example in the classic flight simulator game, as the user moves the joystick or mouse, the simulated plane moves accordingly and the display presented to the user updates.

Pixels

A key concept for all computer graphics systems is the pixel. Pixel was originally a word formed from combining and shortening the words picture (or pix) and element.A pixel is a cell on the computer screen. Each cell represents a dot on the screen. The size of this dot or cell and the number of cells available will vary depending upon the type, size and resolution of the screen. For example, it was common for early Windows PCs to have a 640 by 480 resolution display (using a VGA graphics card). This relates to the number of pixels in terms of the width and height. This meant that there were 640 pixels across the screen with 480 rows of pixels down the screen. By contrast today's 4K TV displays have 4096 by 2160 pixels.

The size and number of pixels available affects the quality of the images presented to a user. With lower resolution displays (with fewer individual pixels) the image may appear blocky or poorly defined; where as with a higher resolution it may appear sharp and clear.

Each pixel can be referenced by its location in the display grid. By filling a pixels on the screen with different colors various images/displays can be created. For example, in the following picture a single pixel has been filled at position 4 by 4:

Pixel filled
with colour red

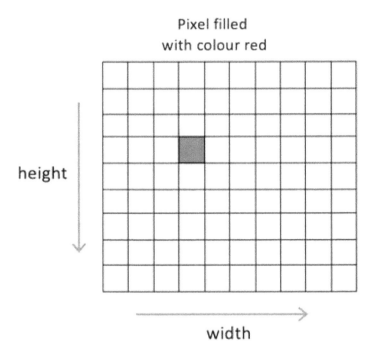

height

width

A sequence of pixels can form a line, a circle or any number of different shapes. However, since the grid of pixels is based on individual points, a diagonal line or a circle may need to utilize multiple pixels which when zoomed may have jagged edges. For example, the following picture shows part of a circle on which we have zoomed in:

Each pixel can have a color and a transparency associated with it. The range of colors available depends on the display system being used. For example, mono chrome displays only allow black and white, where as a grey scale display only allows various shades of grey to be displayed. On modern systems it is usually possible to represent a wide range of colors using the tradition RGB color codes (where R represents Red, G represents Green and B represents Blue). In this encoding solid Red is represented by a code such as [255, 0, 0] where as solid Green is represented by [0, 255, 0] and solid Blue by [0, 0, 255]. Based on this idea various shades can be represented by combination of these codes such as Orange which might be represented by [255, 150, 50]. This is illustrated below for a set of RGB colors using different red, green and blue values:

	RGB	Solid	75%	50%	25%
1	RGB(0, 0, 0)				
2	RGB(30, 0, 0)				
3	RGB(60, 0, 0)				
4	RGB(90, 0, 0)				
5	RGB(120, 0, 0)				
6	RGB(150, 0, 0)				
7	RGB(180, 0, 0)				
8	RGB(210, 0, 0)				
9	RGB(240, 0, 0)				
10	RGB(0, 30, 0)				
11	RGB(30, 60, 0)				
12	RGB(60, 90, 0)				
13	RGB(90, 120, 0)				
14	RGB(120, 150, 0)				
15	RGB(150, 180, 0)				
16	RGB(180, 210, 0)				
17	RGB(210, 240, 0)				
18	RGB(0, 0, 30)				
19	RGB(30, 30, 60)				
20	RGB(60, 60, 90)				
21	RGB(90, 90, 120)				
22	RGB(120, 120, 150)				
23	RGB(150, 150, 180)				
24	RGB(180, 180, 210)				
25	RGB(210, 210, 240)				

In addition it is possible to apply a transparency to a pixel. This is used to indicate how solid the fill color should be. The above grid illustrates the effect of applying a 75%, 50% and 25% transparency to colors displayed using the Python wxPython GUI library.In this library the transparency is referred to as the alpha opaque value. It can have values in the range 0–255 where 0 is completely trans- parent and 255 is completely solid.

Bit Map Versus Vector Graphics

There are two ways of generating an image/display across the pixels on the screen. One approach is known as bit mapped (or raster)graphics and the other is known as vector graphics. In the bit mapped approach each pixel is mapped to the values to be displayed to create the image. In the vector graphics approach geometric shapes are described (such as lines and points) and these are then rendered onto a display. Raster graphics are simpler but vector graphics provide much more flexibility and scalability.

Buffering

One issue for interactive graphical displays is the ability to change the display as smoothly and cleanly as possible. If a display is jerky or seems to jump from one image to another, then users will find it uncomfortable. It is therefore common to drawn the next display on some in memory structure; often referred to as a buffer. This buffer can then be rendered on the display once the whole image has been created. For example Turtle Graphics allows the user to define how many changes should be made to the display before it is rendered (or drawn) on to the screen. This can significantly speed up the performance of a graphic application.

In some cases systems will use two buffers; often referred to as double buffering. In this approach one buffer is being rendered or drawn onto the screen while the other buffer is being updated. This can significantly improve the overall performance of the system as modern computers can perform calculations and generate data much faster than it can typically be drawn onto a screen.

Python and Computer Graphics

In the remainder of this section of the book we will look at generating computer graphics using the Python Turtle Graphics library. We will also discuss using this library to create Computer Generated Art. Following this we will explore the MatPlotLib library used to generate charts and data plots such as bar charts, scatter graphs, line plots and heat maps etc. We will then explore the use of Python libraries to create GUIs using menus, fields, tables etc.

Python Turtle Graphics

Introduction

Python is very well supported in terms of graphics libraries. One of the most widely used graphics libraries is the Turtle Graphics library introduced in this chapter. This is partly because it is straight forward to use and partly because it is provided by default with the Python environment (and this you do not need to install any additional libraries to use it).

The chapter concludes by briefly considering a number of other graphic libraries including PyOpen GL. The PyOpenGL library can be used to create sophisticated 3D scenes.

The Turtle Graphics Library

The Turtle Module

This provides a library of features that allow what are known as vector graphics to be created. Vector graphics refers to the lines (or vectors) that can be drawn on the screen. The drawing area is often referred to as a drawing plane or drawing board and has the idea of x, y coordinates.

The Turtle Graphics library is intended just as a basic drawing tool; other libraries can be used for drawing two and three dimensional graphs (such as MatPlotLib) but those tend to focus on specific types of graphical displays.

The idea behind the Turtle module (and its name) derives from the Logo programming language from the 60s and 70s that was designed to introduce programming to children. It had an on screen turtle that could be controlled by commands such as forward (which would move the turtle forward), right (which would turn the turtle by a certain number of degrees), left (which turns the turtle left by a certain number of degrees) etc. This idea has continued into the current Python Turtle Graphics library where commands such as turtle.forward(10) moves the turtle (or cursor as it is now) forward 10 pixels etc. By combining together these apparently simple commands, it is possible to create intricate and quiet complex shapes.

Basic Turtle Graphics

Although the turtle module is built into Python 3 it is necessary to import the module before you use it:

```
import turtle
```

There are in fact two ways of working with the turtle module; one is to use the classes available with the library and the other is to use a simpler set of functions that hide the classes and objects.In this chapter we will focus on the set of functions you can use to create drawings with the Turtle Graphics library.

The first thing we will do is to set up the window we will use for our drawings; the TurtleScreen class is the parent of all screen implementations used for whatever operating system you are running on.

If you are using the functions provided by the turtle module, then the screen object is initialized as appropriate for your operating system. This means that you can just focus on the following functions to configure the layout/display such as this screen can have a title, a size, a starting location etc.

The key functions are:

- setup(width, height, startx, starty) Sets the size and position of the main window/screen. The parameters are:

– width—if an integer, a size in pixels, if a float, a fraction of the screen;
default is 50% of screen.

  – height—if an integer, the height in pixels, if a float, a fraction of the screen; default is 75% of screen.

  – startx—if positive, starting position in pixels from the left edge of the screen, if negative from the right edge, if None, center window horizontally.

  – starty—if positive, starting position in pixels from the top edge of the screen, if negative from the bottom edge, if None, center window vertically.

- title(title string) sets the title of the screen/window.
- exitonclick() shuts down the turtle graphics screen/window when the use clicks on the screen.
- bye() shuts down the turtle graphics screen/window.
- done() starts the main event loop; this must be the last statement in a turtle graphics program.
- speed(speed)the drawing speed to use, the default is 3. The higher the value the faster the drawing takes place, values in the range 0–10 are accepted.
- turtle.tracer(n = None) This can be used to batch updates to the turtle graphics screen. It is very useful when a drawing become large and complex. By setting the number (n) to a large number (say 600) then 600 elements will be drawn in memory before the actual screen is updated in one go; this can significantly speed up the generation of for example, a fractal picture.When called without arguments, returns the currently stored value of n.
- turtle.update() Perform an update of the turtle screen; this should be called at the end of a program when tracer() has been used as it will ensure that all elements have been drawn even if the tracer threshold has not yet been reached.
- pencolor(color) used to set the color used to draw lines on the screen; the color can be specified in numerous ways including using named colors set as 'red', 'blue', 'green' or using the RGB color codes or by specifying the color using hexadecimal numbers. For more information on the named colors and RGB color codes to use see https://www.tcl.tk/man/tcl/TkCmd/colors.htm. Note all color methods use American spellings for example

26

this method is pencolor (not pencolour).
· fillcolor(color) used to set the color to use to fill in closed areas within drawn lines. Again note the spelling of color!

The following code snippet illustrates some of these functions:

import turtle

```
#  set  a  title  for  your  canvas  window
turtle.title('My Turtle  Animation')
#  set  up  the  screen  size  (in  pixels)
#  set  the  starting  point  of  the  turtle
(0,  0)
turtle.setup(width=200,  height=200,  startx=0,
starty=0)
#  sets  the  pen  color  to  red
turtle.pencolor('red')
#  ...
#  Add  this  so  that  the  window  will  close
when  clicked  on turtle.exitonclick()
```

We can now look at how to actually draw a shape onto the screen.

The cursor on the screen has several properties; these include the current drawing color of the pen that the cursor moves, but also its current position (in the x, y coordinates of the screen) and the direction it is currently facing. We have already seen that you can control one of these properties using the pencolor() method, other methods are used to control the cursor (or turtle) and are presented below.

The direction in which the cursor is pointing can be altered using several functions including:

- right(angle) Turn cursor right by angle units.
- left(angle) Turn the cursor left by angle units.
- set heading(to_angle) Set the orientation of the cursor to to_angle.

Where 0 is east, 90 is north, 180 is west and 270 is south. You can move the cursor (and if the pen is down this will draw a line) using:

- forward(distance) move the cursor forward by the specified distance in the direction that the cursor is currently pointing. If the pen is down then draw a line.
- backward(distance)move the cursor backward by distance in the opposite direction that in which the cursor is pointing.

And you can also explicitly position the cursor:

- goto(x, y) move the cursor to the x, y location on the screen specified; if the pen is down draw a line. You can also use steps and set position to do the same thing.
- setx(x) sets the cursor's x coordinate, leaves the y coordinate unchanged.
- sety(y) sets the cursor's y coordinate, leaves the x

coordinate unchanged.

It is also possible to move the cursor without drawing by modifying whether the pen is up or down:

- penup() move the pen up—moving the cursor will no longer draw a line.
- pendown() move the pen down—moving the cursor will now draw a line in the current pen color.

The size of the pen can also be controlled:

- pensize(width) set the line thickness to width. The method width() is an alias for this method.

It is also possible to draw a circle or a dot:

- circle(radius, extent, steps) draws a circle using the given radius.

The extent determines how much of the circle is drawn; if the extent is not given then the whole circle is drawn.Steps indicates the number of steps to be used to drawn the circle (it can be used to draw regular polygons).

- dot(size, color) draws a filled circle with the diameter of size using the specified color.

You can now use some of the above methods to draw a shape on the screen.For this first example, we will keep it very simple, we will draw a simple square:

```
# Draw a square
turtle.forward(50)
turtle.right(90)
turtle.forward(50)
turtle.right(90)
turtle.forward(50)
turtle.right(90)
turtle.forward(50)
turtle.right(90)
```

The above moves the cursor forward 50 pixels then turns 90° before repeating these steps three times. The end result is that a square of 50 50 pixels is drawn on the screen:

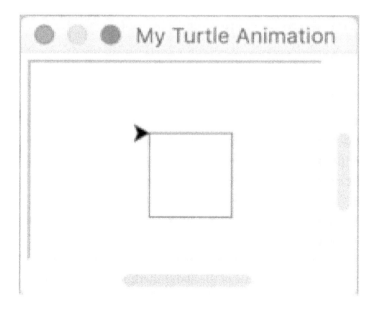

Note that the cursor is displayed during drawing (this can be turned off with turtle.hideturtle() as the cursor was originally referred to as the turtle).

Drawing Shapes

Of course you do not need to just use fixed values for the shapes you draw, you can use variables or calculate positions based on expressions etc.

For example, the following program creates a sequences of squares rotated around a central location to create an engaging image:

```python
import turtle
def setup():
""" Provide the config for the screen """
turtle.title('Multiple SquaresAnimation')
turtle.setup(100, 100, 0, 0)
turtle.hideturtle()
def draw_square(size):
""" Draw a squarein the currentdirection """
turtle.forward(size) turtle.right(90)
turtle.forward(size) turtle.right(90)
turtle.forward(size) turtle.right(90)
turtle.forward(size)
setup()
for _ in range(0, 12):
draw_square(50)
# Rotate the starting direction
turtle.right(120)
# Add this so that the window will close when
clickedon
turtle.exitonclick()
```

In this program two functions have been defined, one to setup the screen or window with a title and a size and to turn off the cursor display. The second function takes a size parameter and uses that to draw a square. The main part of the program then sets up the window and uses a for loop to draw 12 squares of 50 pixels each by continuously rotating 120° between each square. Note that as we do not need to reference the loop variable we are using the '_' format which is considered an anonymous loop variable in Python.

The image generated by this program is shown below:

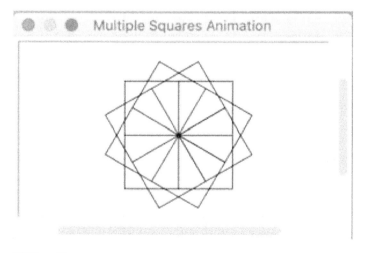

Filling Shapes

It is also possible to fill in the area within a drawn shape. For example, you might wish to fill in one of the squares we have drawn as shown below:

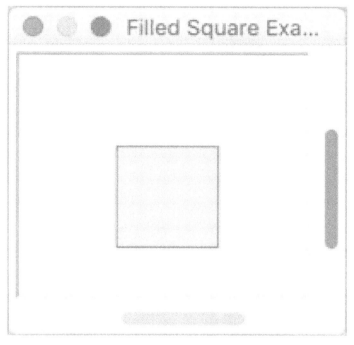

To do this we can use the begin_fill() and end_fill() functions:

- begin_fill() indicates that shapes should be filled with the current fill col- our,this function should be called just before drawing the shape to be filled.
- end_fill() called after the shape to be filled has been finished. This will cause the shape drawn since the last call to begin_fill() to be filled using the current fill

color.

- filling() Return the current fill state (True if filling, False if not).

The following program uses this (and the earlier draw_square()function) to draw the above filled square:

```
turtle.title('Filled Square Example')
turtle.setup(100, 100, 0, 0)
turtle.hideturtle()
turtle.pencolor('red') turtle.fillcolor('yellow')
turtle.begin_fill()
draw_square(60)
turtle.end_fill()
turtle.done()
```

Other Graphics Libraries

Of course Turtle Graphics is not the only graphics option available for Python; however other graphics libraries do not come prepacked with Python and must be downloaded using a tool such as Anaconda, PIP or PyCharm.

- PyQtGraph. The PyQtGraph library is pure Python library oriented towards mathematics, scientific and engineering graphic applications as well as GUI applications. For more information see http://www.pyqtgr aph.org.
- Pillow. Pillow is a Python imaging library (based on PIL the Python Imaging library) that provides image processing capabilities for use in Python. For more

information on Pillow see https://pillow.readthedocs.
io/en/stable.
· Pyglet. pyglet is another windowing and multimedia
library for Python. See https://bitbucket.org/pyglet/
pyglet/wiki/Home.

3D Graphics

Although it is certainly possible for a developer to create
convincing 3D images using Turtle Graphics; it is not the
primary aim of the library. This means that there is no
direct support for creating 3D images other than the basic
cursor moving facilities and the programmers skill.

However, there are 3D graphics libraries available for
Python.One such library is Panda3D (https://www.panda3d
.org) while another is VPython (https://vpython.org) while
a third is pi3d (https://pypi.org/project/pi3d). However we
will briefly look at the PyOpenGL library as this builds on
the very widely used OpenGL library.

PyOpenGL

PyOpenGL his an open source project that provides
a set of bindings (or wrappings around) the OpenGL
library.OpenGL is the Open Graphics Library which is a
cross language, cross platform API for rendering 2D and
3D vector graphics. OpenGL is used in a wide range of
applications from games, to virtual reality, through data
and information visualization systems to Computer Aided
Design (CAD) systems. PyOpenGL provides a set of Python

functions that call out from Python to the underlying OpenGL libraries. This makes it very easy to create 3D vector based images in Python using the industry standard OpenGL library. A very simple examples of an image created using PyOpenGL is given below:

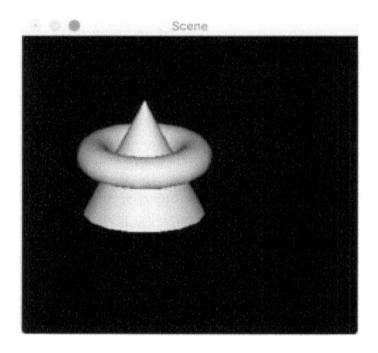

Computer Generated Art

Creating Computer Art

Computer Art is defined as any art that uses a computer. However, in the context of this book we mean it to be art that is generated by a computer or more specifically a computer program. The following example, illustrates how in a very few lines of Python code, using the Turtle graphics library, you can create images that might be considered to be computer art.

The following image is generated by a recursive function that draws a circle at a given x, y location of a specified size. This function recursively calls itself by modifying the parameters so that smaller and smaller circles are drawn at different locations until the size of the circles goes below 20 pixels.

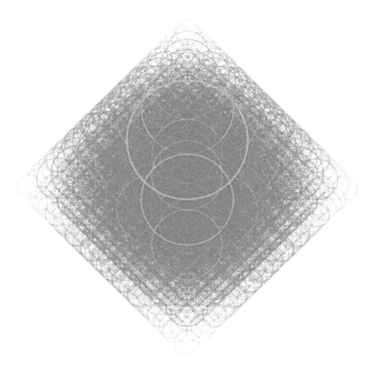

The program used to generate this picture is given below for reference:

import turtle

```
WIDTH = 640
HEIGHT = 360
def setup_window():
#Set up the window
turtle.title('Circles in My Mind')
turtle.setup(WIDTH, HEIGHT, 0, 0)
turtle.colormode(255)   # Indicates RGB numbers
will be in the range 0 to 255
```

```
turtle.hideturtle()  # Batch drawing to the
screen for faster rendering
turtle.tracer(2000)  # Speed up drawing process
turtle.speed(10)
turtle.penup()
def draw_circle(x,  y,  radius,  red=50,
green=255,  blue=10, width=7):
""" Draw a circle at a specific x, y location.
Then draw four smaller circles recursively"""
colour  =  (red,  green,  blue)
# Recursively drawn smaller circles
if radius  >  50:
# Calculatecolours and line width for smaller
circles
if red  <  216:
red  =  red  +  33 green  =  green  -  42 blue  =
 blue  +  10 width  -=  1
else:
red  =  0 green  =  255
# Calculate the radius for the smaller circles
new_radius  =  int(radius  /  1.3)
# Drawn four circles
draw_circle(int(x  +  new_radius),  y,
new_radius,  red, green,  blue,  width)
draw_circle(x  -  new_radius,  y,  new_radius,
red,  green, blue,  width)
draw_circle(x,  int(y  +  new_radius),
new_radius,  red, green,  blue,  width)
draw_circle(x,  int(y  -  new_radius),
new_radius,  red, green,  blue,  width)
#Draw the original circle turtle.goto(x,  y)
    turtle.color(colour)
    turtle.width(width)
    turtle.pendown()
    turtle.circle(radius)
    turtle.penup()
#Run the program print('Starting')
```

39

```
setup_window()
draw_circle(25,-100,200)
# Ensure that all the drawingis rendered
turtle.update() print('Done')
turtle.done()
```

There are a few points to note about this program. It uses recursion to draw the circles with smaller and smaller circles being drawn until the radius of the circles falls below a certain threshold (the termination point).

It also uses the turtle.tracer() function to speed up drawing the picture as 2000 changes will be buffered before the screen is updated.

Finally, the colors used for the circles are changed at each level of recession; a very simple approach is used so that the Red, Green and Blue codes are changed resulting in different color circles. Also a line width is used to reduce the size of the circle outline to add more interest to the image

A Computer Art Generator

As another example of how you can use Turtle graphics to create computer art, the following program randomly generates RGB colors to use for the lines being drawn which gives the pictures more interest. It also allows the user to input an angle to use when changing the direction in which the line is drawn. As the drawing happens within a loop even this simple change to the angle used to draw the lines can generate very different pictures.

```python
# Lets play with some colours
import turtle
from random  import randint
def get_input_angle():
""" Obtain input from user and convert to an
int"""
message  =  'Please provide an angle:'
value_as_string  =  input(message)
while not value_as_string.isnumeric(): print('The
input must be an integer!') value_as_string  =
input(message)
return int(value_as_string)
def generate_random_colour():
"""Generates an R,G,B values randomly in range
0 to 255 """
r  =  randint(0,
255)
g  =  randint(0,
255)
b  =  randint(0,
return r,  g,  b
255)
print('Set up Screen') turtle.title('Colourful
pattern') turtle.setup(640,  600)
turtle.hideturtle()
turtle.bgcolor('black')    # Set the background
colour of the screen
turtle.colormode(255)    # IndicatesRGB numbers
will be in the range 0 to 255
turtle.speed(10)
angle  =  get_input_angle()
print('Start the drawing')
for i  in range(0,  200):
```

```
turtle.color(generate_random_colour())
turtle.forward(i)
turtle.right(angle)
print('Done')
turtle.done()
```

Some sample images generated from this program are given below. The left most picture is generated by inputting an angle of 38 degrees, the picture on the right uses an angle of 68 degrees and the bottom picture an angle of 98 degrees.

The following pictures below use angles of 118, 138 and 168 degrees respectively.

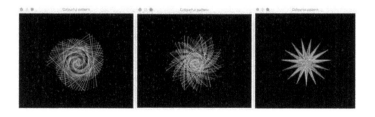

What is interesting about these images is how different each is; even though they use exactly the same program. This illustrates how algorithmic or computer generated art can be as subtle and flexible as any other art form. It also illustrates that even with such a process it is still up to the human to determine which image (if any) is the most aesthetically pleasing.

Fractals in Python

Within the arena of Computer Art fractals are a very well known art form. Fractals are recurring patterns that are calculated either using an iterative approach (such as a for loop) or a recursive approach (when a function calls itself but with modified parameters). One of the really interesting features of fractals is that they exhibit the same pattern (or nearly the same pattern)at successive levels of granularity. That is, if you magnified a fractal image you would find that the same pattern is being repeated at successively smaller and smaller magnifications. This is known as expanding symmetry or unfolding symmetry; if this replication is exactly the same at every scale, then it is called affine self-similar.

Fractals have their roots in the world of mathematics starting in the 17th century, with the term fractal being coined in the 20th century by mathematical Benoit Mandelbrot in 1975. One often cited description that Mandelbrot published to describe geometric fractals is a rough or fragmented geometric shape that can be split into parts,each of which is (at least approximately) a reduced-size copy of the whole.

Since the later part of the 20th century fractals have been a commonly used way of creating computer art. One example of a fractal often used in computer art is the Koch snowflake, while another is the Mandelbrot set. Both of these are used in this chapter as examples to illustrate how Python and the Turtle graphics library can be used to create fractal based art.

The Koch Snowflake

The Koch snowflake is a fractal that begins with equilateral triangle and then replaces the middle third of every line segment with a pair of line segments that form an equilateral bump. This replacement can be performed to any depth generating finer and finer grained (smaller and smaller) triangles until the overall shape resembles a snow flake.

The following program can be used to generate a Koch snowflake with different levels of recursion. The larger the number of levels of recursion the more times each line segment is dissected.

```
import turtle
# Set up Constants
ANGLES = [60, -120, 60, 0] SIZE_OF_SNOWFLAKE
 = 300
def get_input_depth():
""" Obtain input from user and convert to an
int"""
```

```
message  =  'Please provide the depth (0 or a
positive interger):'
value_as_string  =  input(message)
while not value_as_string.isnumeric(): print('The
input must be an integer!') value_as_string  =
input(message)
return int(value_as_string)
def setup_screen(title, background='white',
screen_size_x=640, screen_size_y=320,
tracer_size=800):
print('Set up Screen')
turtle.title(title) turtle.setup(screen_size_x,
screen_size_y) turtle.hideturtle()
turtle.penup()
turtle.backward(240)
# Batch drawing to the screen for faster rendering
turtle.tracer(tracer_size)
turtle.bgcolor(background)  # Set the background
colour of the screen
def draw_koch(size, depth):
if depth > 0:
for angle  in ANGLES:
draw_koch(size / 3, depth - 1)
turtle.left(angle)
else:
turtle.forward(size)
depth  =  get_input_depth()
setup_screen('Koch Snowflake (depth ' +
str(depth)  +  ')', background='black',
screen_size_x=420,  screen_size_y=420)
# Set foreground colours
turtle.color('sky blue')
# Ensure snowflake is centred turtle.penup()
turtle.setposition(-180,0) turtle.left(30)
turtle.pendown()
# Draw three sides of snowflake
for _  in range(3): draw_koch(SIZE_OF_SNOWFLAKE,
```

```
depth) turtle.right(120)
# Ensure that all the drawing is rendered
turtle.update() print('Done') turtle.done()
```

Several different runs of the program are shown below with the depth set at 0, 1, 3 and 7.

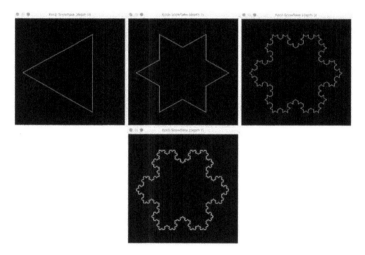

Running the simple draw_koch() function with different depths makes it easy to see the way in which each side of a triangle can be dissected into a further triangle like shape. This can be repeated to multiple depths giving a more detailed structured in which the same shape is repeated again and again.

Mandelbrot Set

Probably one of the most famous fractal images is based

on the Mandelbrot set. The Mandelbrot set is the set of complex numbers c for which the function z * z + c does not diverge when iterated from z = 0 for which the sequence of functions (func(0), func(func(0)) etc.) remains bounded by an absolute value. The definition of the Mandelbrot set and its name is down to the French mathematician Adrien Douady, who named it as a tribute to the mathematician Benoit Mandelbrot.

Mandelbrot set images may be created by sampling the complex numbers and testing, for each sample point c, whether the sequence func(0), func(func(0)) etc. ranges to infinity (in practice this means that a test is made to see if it leaves some predetermined bounded neighborhood of 0 after a predetermined number of iterations). Treating the real and imaginary parts of c as image coordinates on the complex plane, pixels may then be colored according to how soon the sequence crosses an arbitrarily chosen threshold, with a special color (usually black) used for the values of c for which the sequence has not crossed the threshold after the predetermined number of iterations (this is necessary to clearly distinguish the Mandelbrot set image from the image of its complement).

The following image was generated for the Mandelbrot set using Python and Turtle graphics.

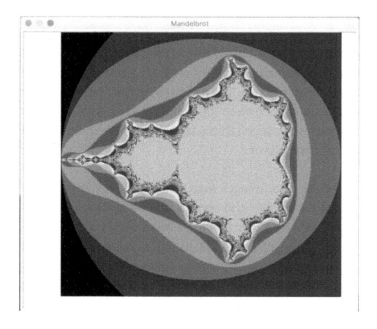

The program used to generate this image is given below:

```
for y  in range(IMAGE_SIZE_Y):
zy  = y  * (MAX_Y - MIN_Y) / (IMAGE_SIZE_Y
- 1)  + MIN_Y
for x  in range(IMAGE_SIZE_X):
zx  = x  * (MAX_X - MIN_X) / (IMAGE_SIZE_Y
- 1)  + MIN_X
z  = zx + zy * 1j c = z
for i  in range(MAX_ITERATIONS):
if abs(z)  > 2.0:
break
z  = z * z + c
turtle.color((i % 4 * 64, i % 8 * 32, i
% 16 * 16))
turtle.setposition(x - SCREEN_OFFSET_X,
```

```
                    y  -   SCREEN_OFFSET_Y)
turtle.pendown()
turtle.dot(1)
turtle.penup()
```

Introduction to Matplotlib

Introduction

Matplotlib is a Python graphing and plotting library that can generate a variety of different types of graph or chart in a variety of different formats. It can be used to generate line charts, scatter graphs, heat maps, bar charts, pie charts and 3D plots. It can even support animations and interactive displays.

An example of a graph generated using Matplotlib is given below. This shows a line chart used to plot a simple sign wave:

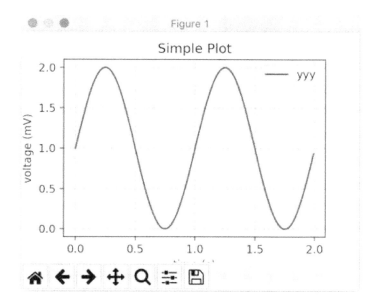

Matplotlib is a very flexible and powerful graphing library. It can support a variety of different Python graphics plat-forms and operating system windowing environments. It can also generate output graphics in a variety of different formats including PNG, JPEG, SVG and PDF etc.

Matplotlib can be used on its own or in conjunction with other libraries to provide a wide variety of facilities. One library that is often used in conjunction with Matplotlib is NumPy which is a library often used in Data Science applications that provides a variety of functions and data structures (such as n-dimensional arrays) that can be very useful when processing data for display within a chart.

However, Matplotlib does not come pre built into the Python environment; it is an optional module which must be added to your environment or IDE.

In this chapter we will introduce the Matplotlib library, its architecture, the components that comprise a chart and the pyplot API. The pyplot API is the simplest and most common way in which a programmer interacts with Matplotlib. We will then explore a variety of different types of chart and how they can be created using Matplotlib, from simple line charts, through scatter charts, to bar charts and pie charts. We will finish by looking at a simple 3D chart.

Matplotlib

Matplotlib is a graph plotting library for Python. For simple graphs Matplotlib is very easy to use, for example to create a simple line graph for a set of x and y coordinates you can use the matplotlib.pyplot.plot function:

```
import matplotlib.pyplot  as pyplot
# Plot a sequence of values
pyplot.plot([1,  0.25,  0.5,  2,  3,  3.75,  3.5])
# Displaythe chart in a window
pyplot.show()
```

This very simple program generates the following graph:

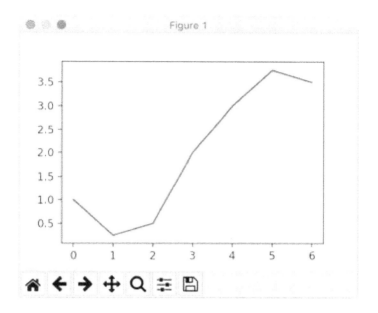

In this example, the plot() function takes a sequence of values which will be treated as the y axis values; the x axis values are implied by the position of the y values within the list. Thus as the list has six elements in it the x axis has the range 0–6. In turn as the maximum value contained in the list is 3.75, then the y axis ranges from 0 to 4.

Plot Components

Although they may seem simple, there are numerous elements that comprise a Matplotlib graph or plot. These elements can all be manipulated and modified independently.It is therefore useful to be familiar with the Matplotlib terminology associated with these elements, such as ticks, legends, labels etc.

The elements that make up a plot are illustrated below:

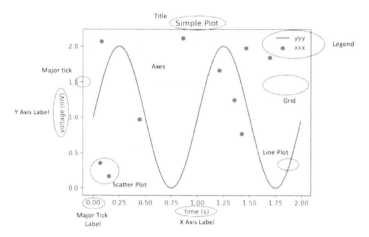

The diagram illustrates the following elements:

- Axes An Axes is defined by the matplotlib.axes.Axes class. It is used to maintain most of the elements of a figure namely the X and Y Axis, the Ticks, the Line plots, any text and any polygon shapes.
- Title This is the title of the whole figure.

Ticks (Major and Minor) The Ticks are represented by the class matplotlib.axis.Tick. A Tick is the mark on the Axis indicating a new value. There can be Major ticks which are larger and may be labeled. There are also minor ticks which can be smaller (and may also be labeled).

- Tick Labels (Major and Minor) This is a label on a Tick.
- Axis The maplotlib.axis.Axis class defines an Axis object(such as an X or Y axis) within a parent Axes instance. It can have for matters used to format the labels used for the major and minor ticks. It is also possible to set the locations of the major and minor ticks.
- Axis Labels (X, Y and in some cases Z) These are labels used to describe the Axis.
- Plot types such as line and scatter plots. Various types of plots and graphs are supported by Matplotlib including line plots, scatter graphs, bar charts and pie charts.
- Grid This is an optional grid displayed behind a plot, graph or chart. The grid can be displayed with a variety of different line styles (such as solid or dashed lines), colors and line widths.

Matplotlib Architecture

The Matplotlib library has a layered architecture that hides much of the complexity associated with different windowing systems and graphic outputs.This architecture has three main layers,the Scripting Layer, the Artist Layer and the Back end Layer. Each layer has specific responsibilities and components. For example,the Back end is responsible for reading and interacting with the graph or plot being generated. In turn the Artist Layer is responsible for creating the graph objects that will be rendered by the Back end Layer. Finally the Scripting Layer is used by the developer to create the graphs.

This architecture is illustrated below:

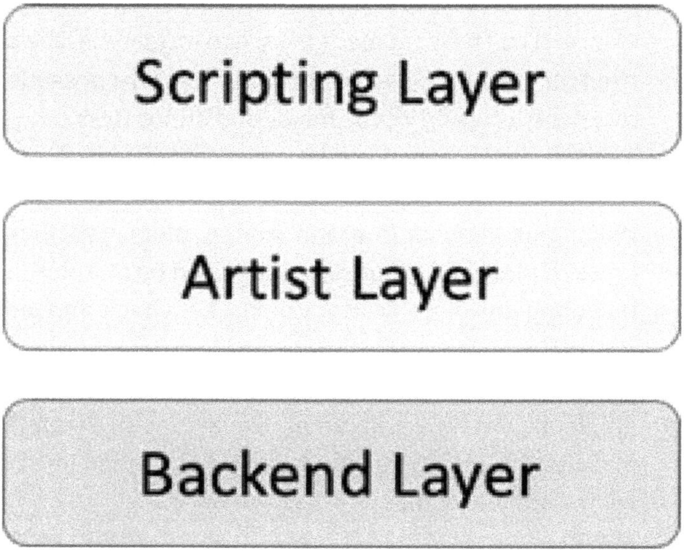

Back end Layer

The Matplotlib back end layer handles the generation of output to different target formats. Matplotlib itself can be used in many different ways to generate many different outputs.

Matplotlib can be used interactively, it can be embedded in an application (or graphical user interface), it may be used as part of a batch application with plots being stored as PNG, SVG, PDF or other images etc.

To support all of these use cases, Matplotlib can target different outputs, and each of these capabilities is called a back end; the "frontend" is the developer facing code. The Back end Layer maintains all the different back ends and the programmer can either use the default back end or select a different back end as required.

The back end to be used can be set via the matplotlib.use() function. For example, to set the back end to render Postscript use: matplotlib.use('PS') this is illustrated below:

```
import matplotlib
if 'matplotlib.backends'  not in sys.modules:
matplotlib.use('PS')
import matplotlib.pyplot  as pyplot
```

It should be noted that if you use the matplotlib.use() function, this must be done before importing matplotlib.pyplot. Calling matplotlib.use ()after matplotlib.pyplot has been imported will have no effect. Note that the argument passed to the matplotlib.use() function is case sensitive.

The default renderer is the 'Agg' which uses the Anti-Grain Geometry C++ library to make a raster (pixel) image of the figure. This produces high quality raster graphics based images of the data plots.

The 'Agg' back end was chosen as the default back end as it works on a broad selection of Linux systems as its supporting requirements are quite small; other back ends may run on one particular system, but may not work on another system. This occurs if a particular system does not have all the dependencies loaded that the specified Matplotlib back end relies on.

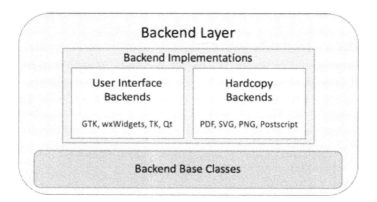

The Backend Layer can be divided into two categories:

- User interface back ends (interactive) that support various Python windowing systems such as wxWidgets (discussed in the next chapter), Qt, TK etc.
- Hard copy Back ends (non interactive) that support raster and vector graphic outputs.

The User Interface and Hard copy back ends are built upon common abstractions referred to as the Back end base classes.

The Artist Layer

The Artist layer provides the majority of the functionality that you might consider to be what Matplotlib actually does; that is the generation of the plots and graphs that are rendered/ displayed to the user (or output in a particular format).

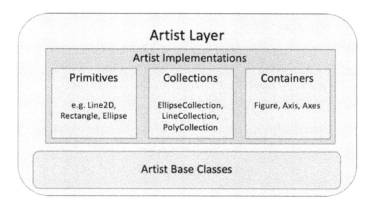

The artist layer is concerned with things such as the lines, shapes, axis, and axes, text etc. that comprise a plot.

The classes used by the Artist Layer can be classified into one of the following three groups; primitives, containers and collections:

- Primitives are classes used to represent graphical objects that will be drawn on to a figures canvas.
- Containers are objects that hold primitives. For example, typically a figure would be instantiated and used to create one or more Axes etc.
- Collections are used to efficiently handle large numbers

of similar types of objects.

Although it is useful to be aware of these classes; in many cases you will not need to work with them directly as the pyplot APIhides much of the detail. However, it is possible to work at the level of figures, axes, ticks etc. if required.

The Scripting Layer

The scripting layer is the developer facing interface that simplifies the task of working with the other layers.

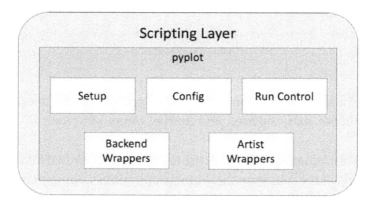

Note that from the programmers point of view, the Scripting Layer is represented by the pyplot module. Under the covers pyplot uses module-level objects to track the state of the data, handle drawing the graphs etc.

When imported pyplot selects either the default back end for the system or the one that has been configured; for example via the matplotlib.use() function.

It then calls a setup() function that:

- creates a figure manager factory function, which when called will create a new figure manager appropriate for the selected back end,
- prepares the drawing function that should be used with the selected back end,
- identifies the callable function that integrates with the back end main loop function,
- provides the module for the selected back end.

The pyplot interface simplifies interactions with the internal wrappers by providing methods such as plot(), pie(), bar(), title(), savefig(), draw() and figure() etc.

Most of the examples presented in the next chapter will use the functions provided by the pyplot module to create the required charts; thereby hiding the lower level details.

Graphing with Matplotlib pyplot

Introduction

In this chapter we will explore the Matplotlib pyplot API. This is the most common way in which developers generate different types of graphs or plots using Matplotlib.

The pyplot API

The purpose of the pyplot module and the API it presents is to simplify the generation and manipulation of Matplotlib plots and charts.As a whole the Matplotlib library tries to make simple things easy and complex things possible. The primary way in which it achieves the first of these aims is through the pyplot API as this API has high level functions such as bar(), plot(), scatter() and pie() that make it easy to create bar charts, line plots, scatter graphs and pie charts.

One point to note about the functions provided by the pyplot API is that they can often take very many parameters; however most of these parameters will have default values that in many situations will give you a reasonable default behavior/ default visual representation. You can therefore ignore most of the parameters available until such time as you actually need to do something different; at which point you should refer to the Matplotlib documentation as this has extensive material as well as numerous examples.

It is of course necessary to import the pyplot module;as it is a module within the Matplotlib (e.g. matplotlib.pyplot) library. It is often given an alias within a program to make it easier to reference. Common alias for this module are pyplot or plt.

A typical import for the pyplot module is given below:

```
import matplotlib.pyplot as pyplot
```

The plyplotAPI can be used to

- · construct the plot,
- · configure labels and axis,
- · manage color and line styles,
- · handles events/allows plots to be interactive,
- · display(show) the plot.

We will see examples of using the pyplot API in the following sections.

Line Graphs

A Line Graph or Line Plot is a graph with the points on the graph (often referred to as markers) connected by lines to show how something changes in value as some set of values (typically the x axis) changes; for example, over a series to time intervals (also known as a time series). Time Series line charts are typically drawn in chronological order; such charts are known as run charts.

The following chart is an example of a run chart;it charts time across the bottom (x axis) against speed (represented by the y axis).

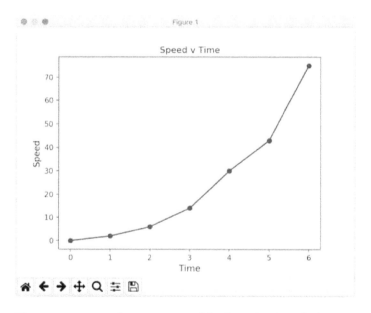

The program used to generate this chart is given below:

```
import matplotlib.pyplot as pyplot
```

```
# Set up the data
x = [0, 1, 2, 3, 4, 5, 6]
y = [0, 2, 6, 14, 30, 43, 75]

# Set the axes headings pyplot.ylabel('Speed',
fontsize=12) pyplot.xlabel('Time', fontsize=12)

# Set the title
pyplot.title("Speed v Time")

# Plot and display the graph
# Using blue circles for markers ('bo')
# and a solid line ('-') pyplot.plot(x, y, 'bo-')
pyplot.show()
```

The first thing that this program does is to import the matplotlib.pyplot module and give it an alias of pyplot (as this is a shorter name it makes the code easier to read).

Two lists of values are then created for the x and y coordinates of each marker or plot point.

The graph itself is then configured with labels being provided for the x and y axis (using the pyplot functions xlabel() and ylabel()). The title of the graph is then set (again using a pyplot function).

After this the x and y values are then plotted as a line chart on the graph. This is done using the pyplot.plot() function. This function can take a wide range of parameters, the only compulsory parameters being the data used to define the plot points. In the above example a third parameter is provided; this is a string 'bo-'. This is a coded format string in that each element of the string is meaningful to the pyplot.plot() function. The elements of the string are:

- b—this indicates the color to use when drawing the line; in this case the letter 'b' indicates the color blue (in the same way 'r' would indicate red and 'g' would indicate green).
- o—this indicates that each marker (each point being plotted) should be represented by a circle. The lines between the markers then create the line plot.
- '−'—This indicates the line style to use. A single dash ('-') indicates a solid line, where as a double dash ('−') indicates a dashed line.

Finally the program then uses the show() function to render the figure on the screen; alternatively savefig() could have been used to save the figure to a file.

Coded Format Strings

There are numerous options that can be provided via the format string, the following tables summarizes some of these:

The following color abbreviations are supported by the format string:C

Character	Color
'b'	blue
'g'	green
'r'	red
'c'	cyan
'm'	magenta
'y'	yellow
'k'	black
'w'	white

Different ways of representing the markers (points on the graph) connected by the lines are also supported including:

Character	Description
'.'	point marker
','	pixel marker
'o'	circle marker
'v'	triangle_down marker
'^'	triangle_up marker
'<'	triangle_left marker
'>'	triangle_right marker
's'	square marker
'p'	pentagon marker
'*'	star marker
'h'	hexagon1 marker
'+'	plus, marker
'x'	x marker
'D'	diamond marker

Finally, the format string supports different line styles:

Character	Description
'-'	solid line style
'--'	dashed line style
'-.'	dash-dot line style
':'	dotted line style

Some examples of formatting strings:

- 'r' red line with default markers and line style.
- 'g-' green solid line.
- '−' dashed line with the default color and default markers.
- 'yo:' yellow dotted line with circle markers.

Scatter Graph

A Scatter Graph or Scatter Plot is type of plot where individual values are indicated using Cartesian (or x and y) coordinates to display values. Each value is indicated via a mark (such as a circle or triangle)on the graph. They can be used to represent values obtained for two different variables; one plotted on the x axis and the other plotted on the y axis.

An example of a scatter chart with three sets of scatter values is given below

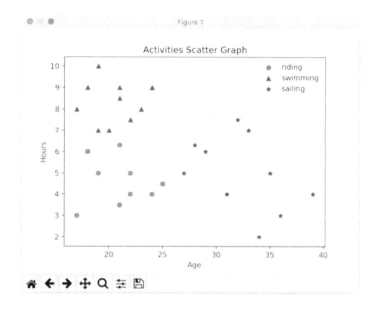

In this graph each dot represents the amount of time people of different ages spend on three different activities.

The program that was used to generate the above graph is shown below:

```
import matplotlib.pyplot as pyplot
# Create data
riding = ((17, 18, 21, 22, 19, 21, 25, 22, 25,
24), (3, 6, 3.5, 4, 5, 6.3, 4.5, 5, 4.5, 4))
swimming = ((17, 18, 20, 19, 22, 21, 23, 19, 21,
24), (8, 9, 7, 10, 7.5, 9, 8, 7, 8.5, 9))
sailing = ((31, 28, 29, 36, 27, 32, 34, 35, 33,
39), (4, 6.3, 6, 3, 5, 7.5, 2, 5, 7, 4))
# Plot the data
```

```
pyplot.scatter(x=riding[0], y=riding[1], c='red',
marker='o', label='riding')
pyplot.scatter(x=swimming[0], y=swimming[1],
c='green', marker='^', label='swimming')
pyplot.scatter(x=sailing[0], y=sailing[1],
c='blue', marker='*', label='sailing')
# Configuregraph pyplot.xlabel('Age')
pyplot.ylabel('Hours') pyplot.title('Activities
Scatter Graph') pyplot.legend()
# Display the chart
pyplot.show()
```

In the above example the plot.scatter() function is used to generate the scatter graph for the data defined by the riding, swimming and sailing tuples.

The colors of the markers have been specified using the named parameter c.

This parameter can take a string representing the name of a color or a two dimensional array with a single row in which each value in the row represents an RGB color code. The marker Indicates the marker style such as 'o' for a circle, a '∧' for a triangle and '*' for a star shape. The label is used in the chart legend for the marker.

Other options available on the pyplot.scatter() function include:

- alpha : indicates the alpha blending value, between 0 (transparent) and 1 (opaque).
- linewidths : which is used to indicate the line width of

the marker edges.

- edgecolors : indicates the color to use for the marker edges if different from the fill color used for the marker (indicates by the parameter 'c').

When to Use Scatter Graphs

A useful question to consider is when should a scatter plot be used? In general scatter plats are used when it is necessary to show the relationship between two variables. Scatter plots are sometimes called correlation plots because they show how two variables are correlated.

In many cases a trend can be discerned between the points plotted on a scatter chart (although there may be outlying values). To help visualize the trend it can be useful to draw a trend line along with the scatter graph. The trend line helps to make the relationship of the scatter plots to the general trend clearer.

The following chart represents a set of values as a scatter graph and draws the trend line of this scatter graph. As can be seen some values are closer to the trend line than others.

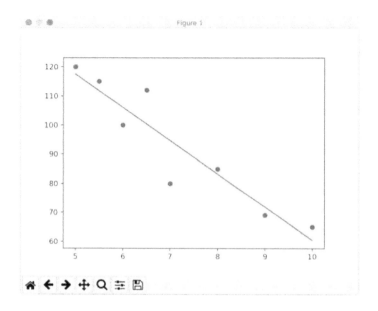

The trend line has been created in this case using the numpy function polyfit().

The polyfit() function performs a least squares polynomial fit for the data it is given. A poly1d class is then created based on the array returned by polyfit(). This class is a one-dimensional polynomial class. It is a convenience class, used to encapsulate "natural" operations on polynomials.The poly1d object is then used to generate a set of values for use with the set of x values for the function pyplot.plot().

```
import numpy as np
import matplotlib.pyplot as pyplot
x = (5, 5.5, 6, 6.5, 7, 8, 9, 10)
y = (120, 115, 100, 112, 80, 85, 69, 65)
# Generate the scatter plot
pyplot.scatter(x, y)
# Generate the trend line
z = np.polyfit(x, y, 1) p = np.poly1d(z)
pyplot.plot(x, p(x), 'r')
# Display the figure
pyplot.show()
```

Pie Charts

A Pie Chart is a type of graph in which a circle is divided into sectors (or wedges) that each represent a proportion of the whole. A wedge of the circle represents a category's contribution to the overall total. As such the graph resembles a pie that has been cut into different sized slices.

Typically, the different sectors of the pie chart are presented in different colors and are arranged clockwise around the chart in order of magnitude. However, if there is a slice that does not contain a unique category of data but summarizes several, for example "other types" or "other answers", then even if it is not the smallest category, it is usual to display it last in order that it does not detract from the named categories of interest.

The following chart illustrates a pie chart used to represent programming language usage within a particular organization.

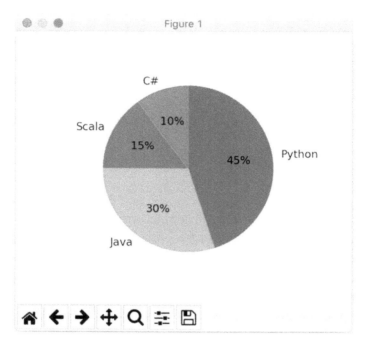

The pie chart is created using the pyplot.pie() function.

```
import matplotlib.pyplot as pyplot

labels = ('Python','Java','Scala','C#')
sizes = [45, 30, 15, 10]

pyplot.pie(sizes, labels=labels,
autopct='%1.f%%', counterclock=False,
startangle=90)
```

```
pyplot.show()
```

The pyplot.pie() function takes several parameters, most of which are optional. The only required parameter is the first one that provides the values to be used for the wedge or segment sizes.The following optional parameters are used in the above example:

- The labels parameter is an optional parameter that can take a sequence of strings that are used to provide labels for each wedge.
- The auto pct parameter takes a string (or function) to be used to format the numeric values used with each wedge.
- The counterclockwise parameter. By default wedges are plotted counter clockwise in pyplot and so to ensure that the layout is more like the traditional clockwise approach the counter clock parameter is set to False.
- The start angle parameter. The starting angle has also been moved 90° using the start angle parameter so that the first segment starts at the top of the chart.

Expanding Segments

It can be useful to emphasis a particular segment of the pie chart by exploding it; that is separating it out from the rest of the pie chart. This can be done using the explode parameter of the pie() function that takes a sequence of values indicating how much a segment should be exploded by.

The visual impact of the pie chart can also be enhanced in this case by adding a shadow to the segments using the named shadow boolean parameter. The effect of these are shown below:

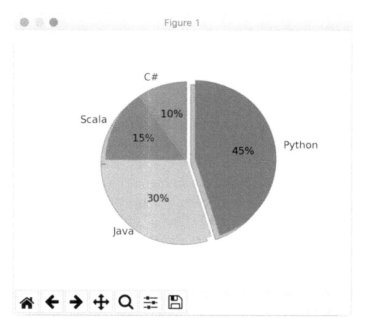

The program that generated this modified chart is given below for reference:

```
import matplotlib.pyplot as pyplot
labels = ('Python','Java','Scala','C#')
sizes = [45, 30, 15, 10]
# only "explode" the 1st slice (i.e. 'Python')
explode = (0.1, 0, 0, 0)
pyplot.pie(sizes, explode=explode, labels=labels,
```

```
autopct='%1.f%%', shadow=True,
counterclock=False, startangle=90)
pyplot.show()
```

When to Use Pie Charts

It is useful to consider what data can be/should be presented using a pie chart. In general pie charts are useful for displaying data that can be classified into nominal or ordinal categories. Nominal data is categorized according to descriptive or qualitative information such as program languages, type of car, country of birth etc. Ordinal data is similar but the categories can also be ranked,for example in a survey people may be asked to say whether they classed something as very poor, poor, fair, good, very good.

Pie charts can also be used to show percentage or proportional data and usually the percentage represented by each category is provided next to the corresponding slice of pie.

Pie charts are also typically limited to presenting data for six or less categories. When there are more categories it is difficult for the eye to distinguish between the relative sizes of the different sectors and so the chart becomes difficult to interpret.

Bar Charts

A Bar Chart is a type of chart or graph that is used to present different discrete categories of data. The data is usually presented vertically although in some cases horizontal bar charts may be used. Each category is represented by a bar whose height (or length) represents the data for that category.

Because it is easy to interpret bar charts, and how each category relates to another, they are one of the most commonly used types of chart. There are also several different common variations such as grouped bar charts and stacked bar charts.

The following is an example of a typical bar chart. Five categories of programming languages are presented along the x axis while the y axis indicates percentage usage. Each bar then represents the usage percentage associated with each programming language.

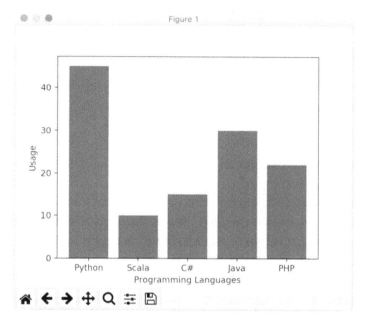

The program used to generate the above figure is given below:

```
import matplotlib.pyplot as pyplot
# Set up the data
labels = ('Python','Scala','C#','Java','PHP')
index = (1, 2, 3, 4, 5) # provideslocations on x
axis sizes= [45, 10, 15, 30, 22]
# Set up the bar chart
pyplot.bar(index, sizes, tick_label=labels)
# Configure the layout pyplot.ylabel('Usage')
pyplot.xlabel('Programming Languages')
# Display the chart
pyplot.show()
```

The chart is constructed such that the lengths of the differ-ent bars are proportional to the size of the category they represent. The x-axis represents the different categories and so has no scale. In order to emphasize the fact that the categories are discrete, a gap is left between the bars on the x-axis. The y-axis does have a scale and this indicates the units of measurement.

Horizontal Bar Charts

Bar charts are normally drawn so that the bars are vertical which means that the taller the bar, the larger the category. However, it is also possible to draw bar charts so that the bars are horizontal which means that the longer the bar, the larger the category. This is a particularly effective way of presenting a large number of different categories when there is insufficient space to fit all the columns required for a vertical bar chart across the page.

In Matplotlib the pyplot.barh() function can be used to generate a horizontal bar chart:

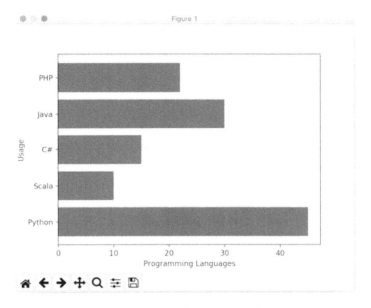

In this case the only line of code to change from the previous example is:

```
pyplot.barh(x_values, sizes, tick_label = labels)
```

Colored Bars

It is also common to color different bars in the chart in different colors or using different shades. This can help to distinguish one bar from another. An example is given below:

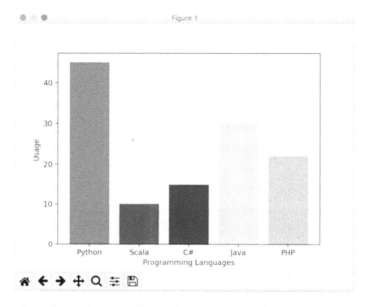

The color to be used for each category can be provided via the color parameter to the bar() (and barh()) function.This is a sequence of the colors to apply. For example, the above colored bar chart can be generated using:

```
pyplot.bar(x_values, sizes, tick_label=labels,
color=('red',
'green', 'blue', 'yellow', 'orange'))
```

Stacked Bar Charts

Bar Charts can also be stacked. This can be a way of showing total values (and what contributes to those total values) across several categories. That is, it is a way of viewing overall totals, for several different categories based on how different elements contribute to those totals.

Different colors are used for the different sub-groups that contribute to the overall bar. In such cases, a legend or key is usually provided to indicate what sub-group each of the shadings/colors represent. The legend can be placed in the plot area or may be located below the chart.

For example, in the following chart the total usage of a particular programming language is composed of its use in games and web development as well as data science analytics.

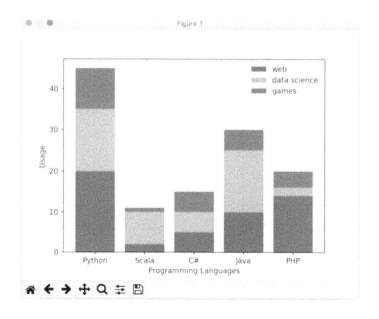

From this figure we can see how much each use of a programming language contributes to the overall usage of that language. The program that generated this chart is given below:

```
import matplotlib.pyplot as pyplot
# Set up the data
labels = ('Python', 'Scala', 'C#', 'Java', 'PHP')
index = (1, 2, 3, 4, 5) web_usage = [20, 2, 5,
10, 14] data_science_usage = [15, 8, 5, 15, 2]
games_usage = [10, 1, 5, 5, 4]
# Set up the bar chart
pyplot.bar(index, web_usage,tick_label=labels,
label='web') pyplot.bar(index,
data_science_usage, tick_label=labels,
label='data science', bottom=web_usage)
web_and_games_usage = [web_usage[i] +
data_science_usage[i]
for i in range(0,len(web_usage))]
pyplot.bar(index, games_usage, tick_label=labels,
label='games', bottom=web_and_games_usage)
# Configurethe layout pyplot.ylabel('Usage')
pyplot.xlabel('Programming Languages')
pyplot.legend()
# Display the chart
pyplot.show()
```

One thing to note from this example is that after the first set of values are added using the pyplot.bar()function, it is necessary to specify the bottom locations for the next set of bars using the bottom parameter. We can do this just using the values already used for web_usage for the second bar chart; however for the third bar chart we must add the values used for web_usage and data_- science_usage together (in this case using a for list comprehension).

Grouped Bar Charts

Finally, Grouped Bar Charts are a way of showing information about different sub-groups of the main categories. In such cases, a legend or key is usually provided to indicate what sub-group each of the shadings/colors represent. The legend can be placed in the plot area or may be located below the chart.

For a particular category separate bar charts are drawn for each of the subgroups. For example, in the following chart the results obtained for two sets of teams across a series of lab exercises are displayed. Thus each team has a bar for lab1, lab2, lab3 etc. A space is left between each category to make it easier to compare the sub categories.

The following program generates the grouped bar chart for the lab exercises example:

```
import matplotlib.pyplot as pyplot
BAR_WIDTH = 0.35
# set up groupedbar charts teama_results = (60,
75, 56, 62, 58) teamb_results = (55, 68, 80, 73,
55)
# Set up the index for each bar
index_teama = (1, 2, 3, 4, 5)
index_teamb = [i + BAR_WIDTH for i in index_teama]
# Determine the mid point for the ticks
ticks = [i + BAR_WIDTH / 2 for i in index_teama]
```

```
tick_labels = ('Lab 1', 'Lab 2', 'Lab 3', 'Lab
4', 'Lab 5')
# Plot the bar charts
pyplot.bar(index_teama, teama_results, BAR_WIDTH,
color='b', label='Team A')
pyplot.bar(index_teamb, teamb_results, BAR_WIDTH,
color='g', label='Team B')
# Set up the graph pyplot.xlabel('Labs')
pyplot.ylabel('Scores') pyplot.title('Scores by
Lab') pyplot.xticks(ticks, tick_labels)
pyplot.legend()
# Display the graph
pyplot.show()
```

Notice in the above program that it has been necessary to calculate the index for the second team as we want the bars presented next to each other. Thus the index for the teams includes the width of the bar for each index point, thus the first bar is at index position 1.35, the second at index position 2.35 etc. Finally the tick positions must therefore be between the two bars and thus is calculated by taking into account the bar widths.

This program generates the following grouped bar chart:

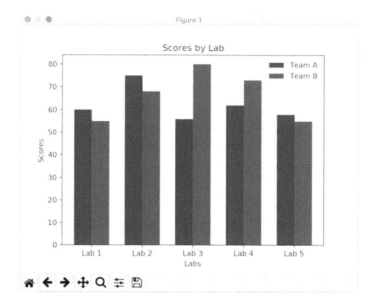

Figure sand Subplots

A Matplotlib figure is the object that contains all the graphical elements displayed on a plot. That is the axes, the legend, the title as well as the line plot or bar chart itself. It thus represents the overall window or page and is the top, out graphical component.

In many cases the figure is implicit as the developer interacts with the pyplot API; however the figure can be accessed directly if required.

Thematplotlib.pyplot.figure() function generates a figure object. This function returns a matplotlib.figure.Figure object. It is then possible to interact directly with the figure object. For example it is possible to add axes to the figure, to add sub plots to a graph etc.

Working directly with the figure is necessary if you want to add multiple sub- plots to a figure. This can be useful if what is required is to be able to compare different views of the same data side by side. Each subplot has its own axes which can coexist within the figure.

One or more subplots can be added to a figure using the figure.addsubplot() method. This method adds an Axes to the figure as one of a set of one or more subplots. A subplot can be added using a 3-digit integer(or three separate integers) describing the position of the subplot.The digits represent the number of rows, columns and the index of the sub plot within the resulting matrix.

Thus 2, 2, 1 (and 221) all indicate that the subplot will take the 1st index within a two by two grid of plots. In turn 2, 2, 3 (223) indicates that the sub plot will be at index 3 which will be row 2 and column 1 within the 2 by 2 grid of plots. Where as 2, 2, 4 (or 224) indicates that the plot should be added as at index 4 or the fourth subplot within the grid (so position 2 by 2) etc.

For example, the following figure illustrates four subplots presented within a single figure. Each subplot is added via the figure.add_subplot() method.

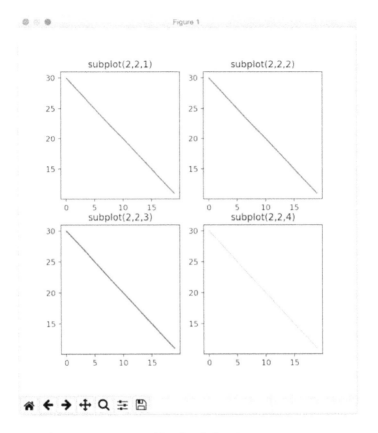

This figure is generated by the following program:

```
import matplotlib.pyplot as pyplot
t = range(0,20)
s = range(30,10, -1)
# Set up the grid of subplots to be 2 by 2
grid_size='22'
# Initialize a Figure
figure = pyplot.figure()
```

```python
# Add first subplot
position = grid_size + '1'
print('Adding first subplot to position',
position) axis1 = figure.add_subplot(position)
axis1.set(title='subplot(2,2,1)')
axis1.plot(t, s)
# Add second subplot
position = grid_size + '2'
print('Adding second subplot to position',
position) axis2 = figure.add_subplot(position)
axis2.set(title='subplot(2,2,2)')
axis2.plot(t, s, 'r-')
# Add third subplot
position = grid_size + '3'
print('Adding third subplot to position',
position) axis3 = figure.add_subplot(position)
axis3.set(title='subplot(2,2,3)')
axis3.plot(t, s, 'g-')
# Add fourth subplot
position = grid_size + '4'
print('Adding fourth subplot to position',
position) axis4 = figure.add_subplot(position)
axis4.set(title='subplot(2,2,4)')
axis4.plot(t, s, 'y-')
# Display the chart
pyplot.show()
```

The console output from this program is given below:

   Adding first subplot to position221
   Adding second subplot to position222
   Adding third subplot to position223
   Adding fourth subplot to position224

Graphs

A three dimensional graph is used to plot the relationships between three sets of values(instead of the two used in the examples presented so far in this chapter). In a three dimensional graph as well as the x and y axis there is also a z axis.

The following program creates a simple 3D graph using two sets of values generated using the numpy range function. These are then converted into a coordinate matrices using the numpy meshgrid() function. The z axis values are created using the numpy sin() function. The 3D graph surface is plotted using the plot_surface() function of the futures axes object. This takes the x, y and z coordinates. The function is also given a color map to use when rendering the surface (in this case the Matplotlib cool to warm color map is used).

```
import matplotlib.pyplot as pyplot
# Import matplotlib colour map
from matplotlib import cm as colourmap
# Required for £D Projections
from mpl_toolkits.mplot3d import Axes3D
# Provide access to numpy functions
import numpy as np
# Make the data to be displayed x_values =
np.arange(-6, 6, 0.3) y_values = np.arange(-6, 6,
0.3)
# Generate coordinate matrices from coordinate
vectors
x_values, y_values= np.meshgrid(x_values,
y_values)
# Generate Z valuesas sin of x plus y values
z_values = np.sin(x_values + y_values)
```

```
# Obtain the figure object
figure = pyplot.figure()
# Get the axes object for the 3D graph
axes = figure.gca(projection='3d')
# Plot the surface.
surf = axes.plot_surface(x_values, y_values,
z_values,
cmap=colourmap.coolwarm)
# Add a color bar which maps values to colors.
figure.colorbar(surf)
# Add labels to the graph pyplot.title("3D
Graph") axes.set_ylabel('y values', fontsize=8)
axes.set_xlabel('x values', fontsize=8)
axes.set_zlabel('z values', fontsize=8)
# Display the graph
pyplot.show()
```

This program generates the following 3D graph:

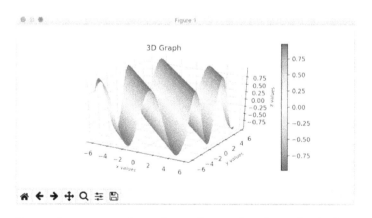

One point to note about three dimensional graphs is that they are not universally accepted as being a good way to present data. One of the maxims of data visualization is keep it simple/keep it clean. Many consider that a three dimensional chart does not do this and that it can be difficult to see what is really being shown or that it can be hard to interpret the data appropriately. For example, in the above chart what are the values associated with any of the peaks? This is difficult to determine as it is hard to see where the peaks are relative to the X, Y and Z axis. Many consider such 3D charts to be eye candy; pretty to look at but not providing much information. As such the use of a 3D chart should be minimized and only used when actually necessary.

Graphical User Interfaces

A Graphical User Interface can capture the essence of an idea or a situation, often avoiding the need for a long passage of text. Such interfaces can save a user from the need to learn complex commands. They are less likely to intimidate computer users and can provide a large amount of information quickly in a form which can be easily assimilated by the user.

The widespread use of high quality graphical interfaces has led many computer users to expect such interfaces to any software they use. Most programming languages either incorporate a Graphical User Interface (GUI) library or have third party libraries available.

Python is of course a cross platform programming language and this brings in additional complexities as the underlying operating system may provide different windowing facilities depending upon whether the program is running on Unix, Linux, Mac OS or Windows operating systems.

In this chapter we will first introduce what we mean by a GUI and by WIMP based UIs in particular. We will then consider the range of libraries available for Python before selecting one to use. This chapter will then describe how to create rich client graphical displays(desktop application)using one of these GUI libraries. Thus in this chapter we consider how windows, buttons, text fields and labels etc. are created,added to windows, positioned and organized.

GUIs and WIMPS

GUIs (Graphical User Interfaces) and WIMP (Windows, Icons, Mice and Pop-up Menus) style interfaces have been available within computer systems for many years but they are still one of the most significant developments to have occurred. These interfaces were originally developed out of a desire to address many of the perceived weaknesses of purely textual interfaces.

The textual interface to an operating system was typified by a peremptory prompt. In Unix/Linux systems for example, the prompt is often merely a single character such as %, > or $, which can be intimidating. This is true even for experienced computer users if they are not familiar with the Unix/Linux family of operating systems.

For example, a user wishing to copy a file from one directory to another might have to type something like:

```
> cp file.pdf
~otheruser/projdir/srcdir/newfile.pdf
```

This long sequence needs to be entered with no mistakes in order to be accepted. Any error in this command will cause the system to generate an error message which might or might not be enlightening. Even where systems attempt to be more "user friendly" through features like command histories, much typing of arrow keys and file names is typically needed.

The main issue on both input and output is one of band-width. For example, in situations where the relationships between large amounts of information must be described, it is much easier to assimilate this if output is displayed graphically than if it is displayed as a tables of figures. On input, combinations of mouse actions can be given a meaning that could otherwise only be conveyed by several lines of text.

WIMP stands for Windows (or Window Managers), Icons, Mice and Pop-up menus. WIMP interfaces allow the user to overcome at least some of the weaknesses of their textual counterparts—it is possible to provide a pictorial image of the operating system which can be based on a concept the user can relate to, menus can be used instead of textual commands and information in general can be displayed graphically.

The fundamental concepts presented via a WIMP interface were originally developed at XEROX's Palo Alto Research Center and used on the Xerox Star machine, but gained much wider acceptance through first the Apple Macintosh and then IBM PC implementations of WIMP interfaces.

Most WIMP style environments use a desktop analogy (although this is less true of mobile devices such as phones and tablets):

- the whole screen represents a working surface (a desk-top),
- graphic windows that can overlap represent sheets of paper on that desktop,
- graphic objects are used for specific concepts, for example filing cabinets for disks or a waste bin for file disposal (these could be regarded as desk accessories),
- various application programs are displayed on the screen, these stand for tools that you might use on your desktop.

In order to interact with this display, the WIMP user is provided with a mouse (or alight pen or a touch sensitive screen), which can be used to select icons and menus or to manipulate windows.

The software basis of any WIMP style environment is the window manager. It controls the multiple, possibly overlapping windows and icons displayed on the screen. It also handles the transfer of information about events which occur in those windows to the appropriate application and generates the various menus and prompts used.

A window is an area of the graphic screen in which a page or piece of a page of information may be displayed; it may display text, graphics or a combination of both. These windows may be overlapping,and associated with the same process, or they may be associated with separate processes. Windows can generally be created, opened, closed, moved and resized.

An icon is a small graphic object that is usually symbolic of an operation or of a larger entity such as an application program or a file. The opening of an icon causes either the associated application to execute or the associated window to be displayed.

At the heart of the users ability to interact with such WIMP based programs is the event loop. This loop listens for events such as the user clicking a button or selecting a menu item or entering a text field. When such an event occurs it triggers the associated behavior (such as running a function linked with a button).

Windowing Frameworks for Python

Python is a cross platform programming language. As such Python programs can be written on one platform (such as a Linux box) and then run on that platform or another operating system platform(such as Windows or Mac OS). This can however generate issues for libraries that need to be available across multiple operating system platforms. The area of GUIs is particularly an issue as a library written to exploit features available in the Microsoft Windows system may not be available (or may look different) on Mac OS or Linux systems.

Each operating system that Python runs on may have one or more windowing systems written for it and these systems may or may not be available on other operating systems. This makes the job of providing a GUI library for Python that much more difficult.

Developers of Python GUIs have taken one of two approaches to handle this:

- One approach is to write a wrapper that abstracts the underlying GUI facilities so that the developer works at a level above a specific windowing system's facilities. The Python library then maps (as best it can) the facilities to the underlying system that is currently being used.
- The other approach is to provide a closer wrapping to a particular set of facilities on the underlying GUI system and to only target systems that support those facilities.

Some of the libraries available for Python are listed below and have been categorized into platform-independent libraries and platform specific libraries:

Platform-Independent GUI Libraries

- Tkinter. This is the standard built-in Python GUI library.It is built on top of the Tcl/Tk widget set that has been around for very many years for many different operating systems. Tcl stands for Tool Command Language while Tk is the graphical user interface toolkit for Tcl.

- wxPython. wxWidgets is a free, highly portable GUI library. Its is written in C++ and it can provide a native look and feel on operating systems such as Windows, Mac OS, Linux etc.wxPython is a set of Python bindings for wxWidgets. This is the library that we will be using in this chapter.
- PyQT or PySide both of these libraries wrap the Qt toolkit facilities. Qt is a cross platform software development system for the implementation of GUIs and applications.

Platform-Specific GUI Libraries

- PyObjc is a Mac OS specific library that provides an Objective-C bridge too the Apple Mac Cocoa GUI libraries.
- PythonWin provides a set of wrappings around the Microsoft Windows foundation classes and can be used to create Windows based GUIs.

The wxPython GUI Library

The wxPython Library

The wxPython library is a cross platform GUI library (or toolkit) for Python. It allows programmers to develop highly graphical user interfaces for their programs using common concepts such as menu bars, menus, buttons, fields, panels and frames.

In wxPython all the elements of a GUI are contained within top level windows such as a wx.Frame or a wx.Dialog. These windows contain graphical components known as widgets or controls. These widgets/controls may be grouped together into Panels (which may or may not have a visible representation).

Thus in wxPython we might construct a GUI from:

- Frames which provide the basic structure for a window: borders, a label and some basic functionality (e.g. resizing).
- Dialogs which are like Frames but provide fewer border controls.

- Widgets/Controls that are graphical objects displayed in a frame. Some other languages refer to them as UI components. Examples of widgets are buttons, checkboxes, selection lists, labels and text fields.
- Containers are component that are made up of one or more other components (or containers). All the components within a container (such as a panel) can be treated as a single entity.

Thus a GUI is constructed hierarchically from a set of widgets, containers and one or more Frames (or in the case of a pop up dialog then Dialogs). This is illustrated below for a window containing several panels and widgets:

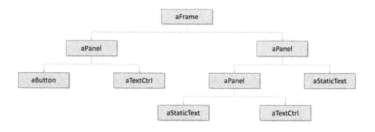

Windows such as Frames and Dialogs have a component hierarchy that is used (amongst other things) to determine how and when elements of the window are drawn and redrawn. The component hierarchy is rooted with the frame, within which components and containers can be added.

The above figure illustrates a component hierarchy for a

frame, with two container Panels and a few basic widgets/ui components held within the Panels. Note that a panel can contain another sub panel with different widgets in.

wxPython Modules

The wxPython library is comprised of many different modules. These modules provide different features from the core wx module to the html oriented wx.html and wx.html2 modules. These modules include:

- wx which holds the core widgets and classes in the wx library.
- wx.adv that provides less commonly used or more advanced widgets and classes.
- wx.grid contains widgets and classes supporting the display and editing of tabular data.
- wx.richtext consists of widgets and classes used for displaying multiple text styles and images.
- wx.html comprises widgets and supporting classes for a generic html renderer.
- wx.html2 provides further widget and supporting classes for a native html renderer, with CSS and javascript support.

Windows as Objects

In wxPython, Frames and Dialogs as well as their contents are instances of appropriate classes (such as Frame, Dialog, Panel, Button or Static Text). Thus when you create a window, you create an object that knows how to display itself on the computer screen. You must tell it what to display and then tell it to show its contents to the user.

You should bear the following points in mind during your reading of this chapter; they will help you understand what you are required to do:

- You create a window by instantiating a Frame or Dialog object.
- You define what the window displays by creating a widget that has an appropriate parent component. This adds the widget to a container, such as a type of panel or a frame.
- You can send messages to the window to change its state, perform an operation, and display a graphic object.
- The window, or components within the window, can send messages to other objects in response to user (or program)actions.
- Everything displayed by a window is an instance of a class and is potentially subject to all of the above.
- wx.App handles the main event loop of the GUI application.

A Simple Example

An example of creating a very simple window using wx-Python is given below. The result of running this short program is shown here for both a Mac and a Windows PC:

This program creates a top level window (the wx.Frame) and gives it a title. It also creates a label (a wx.StaticText object) to be displayed within the frame.

To use the wxPythonlibrary it is necessary to import the wx module.

```
import wx
# Createthe Application Object
app  =  wx.App()
# Now createa Frame (representingthe window)
frame  =  wx.Frame(parent=None,  title='Simple
Hello World')
# And add a text label to it
text  =  wx.StaticText(parent=frame,  label=
'Hello Python')
# Displaythe window (frame)
frame.Show()
# Start the event loop
app.MainLoop()
```

The program also creates a new instance of the Application Object called wx. App().

Every wxPython GUI program must have one Application

Object. It is the equivalent of the main() function in many non-GUI applications as it will run the GUI application for you. It also provides default facilities for defining startup and shutdown operations and can be sub classed to create custom behavior.

Thewx.StaticText class is used to create a single (or multiple) line label. In this case the label shows the string 'Hello Python'. The StaticText object is constructed with reference to its parent container. This is the container within which the text will be displayed. In this case the StaticText is being displayed directly within the Frame and thus the frame object is its containing parent object. In contrast the Frame which is a top level window, does not have a parent container.

Also notice that the frame must be shown (displayed) for the user to see it. This is because there might be multiple different windows that need to be shown (or hidden) in different situations for an application.

Finally the program starts the applications' main event loop; within this loop the program listens for any user input (such as requesting that the window is closed).

The wx.App Class

The wx.App class represents the application and is used to:

- start up the wxPython system and initialize the underlying GUI toolkit,

- set and get application-wide properties,
- implement the native windowing system main message or event loop, and to dispatch events to window instances.

Every wxPython application must have a single wx.App instance. The creation of all of the UI objects should be delayed until after the wx.App object has been created in order to ensure that the GUI platform and wxWidgets have been fully initialized.

It is common to subclass the wx.App class and override methods such as OnPreInit and OnExit to provide custom behavior. This ensures that the required behavior is run at appropriate times. The methods that can be overridden for this purpose are:

- OnPreInit, This method can be overridden to define behavior that should be run once the application object is created, but before the OnInit method has been called.
- OnInit This is expected to create the applications main window, display that window etc.
- OnRun, This is the method used to start the execution of the main program.
- OnExit, This can be overridden to provide any behavior that should be called just before the application exits.

As an example, if we wish to set up a GUI application such that the main frame is initialized and shown after the wx.App has been instantiated then the safest way is to override the OnInit() method of the wx.App class in a suitable subclass. The method should return True of False; where True is used to indicate that processing of the application should continue and False indicates that the application should terminate immediately (usually as the result of some unexpected issue).

An example wx.App subclass is shown below:

```
class MainApp(wx.App):
def OnInit(self):
"""Initialise the main GUI Application"""
frame  =  WelcomeFrame()
frame.Show()
# Indicatewhether processing should continue or
not
return True
This class can now be instantiated and the
MainLoop started, for example:
# Run the GUI application app  =  MainApp()
app.MainLoop()
```

It is also possible to override the OnExit() to clean up anything initialized in the OnInit() method.

Window Classes

The window or widget container classes that are commonly used within a wxPython application are:

- wx.Dialog A Dialog is a top level window used for popups where the user has limited ability to interact

with the window. In many cases the user can only input
some data and/or accept or decline an option.

· wx.Frame A Frame is a top level window whose size and
position can be set and can (usually) be controlled by
the user.

· wx.Panel Is a container (non top level window) on
which controls/widgets can be placed. This is often
used in conjunction with a Dialog or a Frame to manage
the positioning of widgets within the GUI.

The inheritance hierarchy for these classes is given below
for reference:

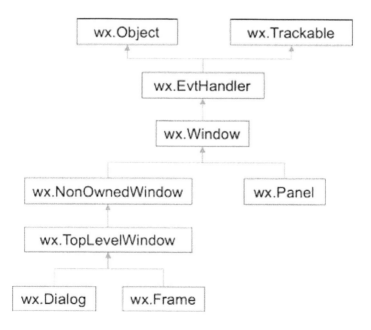

As an example of using a Frame and a Panel, the following application creates two Panels and displays them within a top level Frame. The background color of the Frame is the default grey; while the background color for the first Panel is blue and for the second Panel it is red. The resulting display is shown below:

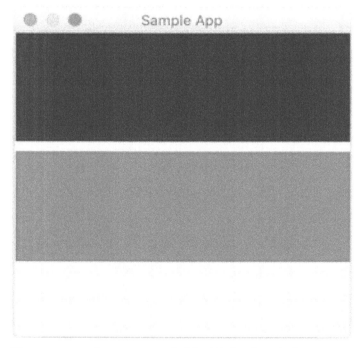

The program that generated this GUI is given below:

```
import wx
class SampleFrame(wx.Frame):
def    init    (self):
super().    init    (parent=None, title='Sample
```

```
App', size=(300, 300))
# Set up the first Panel to be at position 1, 1
# (The default)and of size 300 by 100
# with a blue background self.panel1 =
wx.Panel(self) self.panel1.SetSize(300, 100)
self.panel1.SetBackgroundColour(wx.Colour(0, 0,
255))
# Set up the second Panel to be at position1, 110
# and of size 300 by 100 with a red background
self.panel2 = wx.Panel(self)
self.panel2.SetSize(1, 110, 300, 100)
self.panel2.SetBackgroundColour(wx.Colour(255,
0, 0))
class MainApp(wx.App):
def OnInit(self):
""" Initialise the main GUI Application"""
frame = SampleFrame()
frame.Show()
return True
# Run the GUI application app = MainApp()
app.MainLoop()
```

The SampleFrame is a subclass of the wx.Frame class; it thus inherits all of the functionality of a Top Level Frame (window). Within the init() method of the SampleFrame the super classes init() method is called. This is used to set the size of the Frame and to give the Frame a title. Note that the Frame also indicates that it does not have a parent window.

When the Panel is created it is necessary to specify the window (or in this case Frame) within which it will be displayed. This is a common pattern within wxPython.

Also note that the SetSize method of the Panel class also allows the position to be specified and that the Color class is the wxPython Color class.

Widget/Control Classes

Although there are very many widgets/controls available to the developer, the most commonly used include:

- wx.Button/wx.ToggleButton/wx.RadioButton These are widgets that provide button like behavior within a GUI.
- wx.TextCtrl This widget allows text to be displayed and edited. I can be a single line or multiple line widget depending upon configuration.
- wx.StaticText Used to display one or more lines of read-only text. In many libraries this widgets is known as a label.
- wx.StaticLine A line used in dialogs to separate groups of widgets. The line may be vertical or horizontal.
- wx.ListBox This widget is used to allow a user to select one option from a list of options.
- wx.MenuBar/wx.Menu/wx.MenuItem. The components that can be used to construct a set of menus for a User Interface.
- wx.ToolBar This widget is used to display a bar of buttons and/or other widgets usually placed below the menu bar in a wx.Frame.

The inheritance hierarchy of these widgets is given below. Note that they all inherit from the class Control (hence why they are often referred to as Controls as well as Widgets or GUI components).

Whenever a widget is created it is necessary to provide the container window class that will hold it, such as a Frame or a Panel, for example:

enter_button = wx.Button(panel, label=**'Enter'**)

In this code snippet a wx.Button is being created that will have a label 'Enter' and will be displayed within the given Panel.

Dialogs

The generic wx.Dialog class can be used to build any custom dialog you require. It can be used to create modal and modeless dialogs:

- A modal dialog blocks program flow and user input on other windows until it is dismissed.
- A modeless dialog behaves more like a frame in that

program flow continues, and input in other windows is still possible.

- The wx.Dialog class provides two versions of the show method to support modal and modeless dialogs. The ShowModal() method is used to display a modal dialog, while the Show() is used to show a modeless dialog.

As well as the generic wx.Dialog class,the wxPython library provides numerous prebuilt dialogs for common situations. These pre built dialogs include:

- wx.ColourDialog This class is used to generate a color chooser dialog.
- wx.DirDialog This class provides a directory chooser dialog.
- wx.FileDialog This class provides a file chooser dialog.
- wx.FontDialog This class provides a font chooser dialog.
- wx.MessageDialog This class can be used to generate a single or multi-line message or information dialog. It can support Yes, No and Cancel options.It can be used for generic messages or for error messages.
- wx.MultiChoiceDialog This dialog can be used to display a lit of strings and allows the user to select one or more values for the list.
- wx.PasswordEntryDialog This class represents a dialog that allows a user to enter a one-line password string from the user.
- wx.ProgressDialog If supported by the GUI platform, then this class will provide the platforms native progress dialog, otherwise it will use the pure Python

wx.GenericProgressDialog. The wx. GenericProgressDi alog shows a short message and a progress bar.

· wx.TextEntryDialog This class provides a dialog that requests a one-line text string from the user.

Most of the dialogs that return a value follow the same pattern. This pattern returns a value from the ShowModel() method that indicates if the user selected OK or CANCEL (using the return value wx.ID_OK or wx.ID_CANCEL). The selected/entered value can then be obtained from a suitable get method such as GetColourData() for the ColourDialog or GetPath() for the DirDialog.

Arranging Widgets Within a Container

Widgets can be located within a window using specific coordinates (such as 10 pixels down and 5 pixels across). However, this can be a problem if you are considering cross platform applications, this is because how a button is rendered (drawn) on a Mac is different to Windows and different again from the windowing systems on Linux/Unix etc.

This means that different amount of spacing must be given on different plat- forms. In addition the fonts used with text boxes and labels differ between different platforms also requiring differences in the layout of widgets.

To overcome this wxPython provides Sizers. Sizers work with a container such as a Frame or a Panel to determine how the contained widgets should be laid out. Widgets are added to a sizer which is then set onto a container such as a Panel.

A Sizer is thus an object which works with a container and the host windowing platform to determine the best way to display the objects in the window. The developer does not need to worry about what happens if a user resizes a window or if the program is executed on a different windowing platform.

- Sizers therefore help to produce portable, presentable user interfaces. In fact one
- Sizer can be placed within another Sizer to create complex component layouts.

There are several sizers available including:

- wx.BoxSizer This sizer can be used to place several widgets into a row or column organization depending upon the orientation. When the BoxSizer is created the orientation can be specified using wx.VERTICAL or wx, HORIZONTAL.
- wx.GridSizer This sizer lays widgets out in a two dimensional grid.Each cell within the grid has the same size. When the GridSizer object is created it is possible to specify the number of rows and columns the grid has. It is also possible to specify the spacing between the cells both horizontally and vertically.
- wx.FlexGridSizer This sizer is a slightly more flexible version of the GridSizer. In this version not all columns

and rows need to be the same size (although all cells in the same column are the same width and all cells in the same row are the same height).

· wx.GridBagSizer is the most flexible sizer. It allows widgets to be positioned relative to the grid and also allows widgets to span multiple rows and/or columns.

To use a Sizer it must first be instantiated. When widgets are created they should be added to the sizer and then the sizer should be set on the container.

For example, the following code uses a GridSizer used with a Panel to layout out four widgets comprised of two buttons, a StaticText label and a TextCtrl input field:

```
# Create the panel
panel = wx.Panel(self)
# Create the sizer to use with 4 rows
and 1 column
# And 5 spacing around each cell grid =
wx.GridSizer(4, 1, 5, 5)
# Create the widgets
text = wx.TextCtrl(panel, size=(150, -1))
enter_button = wx.Button(panel, label='Enter')
label = wx.StaticText(panel,label='Welcome')
message_button = wx.Button(panel, label='Show
Message')
# Add the widgets to the grid sizer
grid.AddMany([text, enter_button, label,
message_button])
# Set the sizer on the panel
panel.SetSizer(grid)
```

The resulting display is shown below:

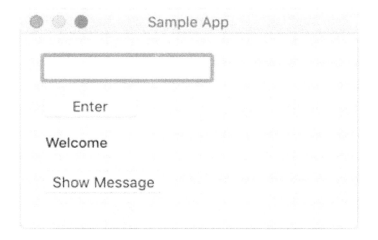

Drawing Graphics

In earlier chapters we looked at the Turtle graphics API for generating vector and raster graphics in Python. The wxPython library provides its own facilities for generating cross platform graphic displays using lines, squares, circles,text etc. This is provided via the Device Context.

A Device Context (often shortened to just DC) is an object on which graphics and text can be drawn. It is intended to allow different output devices to all have a common graphics API (also known as the GDI or Graphics Device Interface). Specific device contexts can be instantiate depending on whether the program is to use a window on a computer screen or some other output medium (such as a printer).

There are several Device Context types available such as wx.WindowDC, wx. PaintDC and wx.ClientDC:

- The wx.WindowDC is used if we want to paint on the whole window(Windows only). This includes window decorations.
- The wx.ClientDC is used to draw on the client area of a window. The client area is the area of a window without its decorations (title and border).
- The wx.PaintDC is used to draw on the client area as well but is intended to support the window refresh paint event handling mechanism.

Note that the wx.PaintDC should be used only from a wx.PaintEvent handler while the wx.ClientDC should never be used from a wx.PaintEvent handler.

Whichever Device Context is used, they all support a similar set of methods that are used to generate graphics, such as:

- DrawCircle (x, y, radius)Draws a circle with the given center and radius.
- DrawEllipse (x, y, width, height) Draws an ellipse contained in the rectangle specified either with the given top left corner and the given size or directly.
- DrawPoint (x, y) Draws a point using the color of the current pen.
- DrawRectangle (x, y, width, height) Draws a rectangle

with the given corner coordinate and size.

- DrawText (text, x, y) Draws a text string at the specified point, using the current text font, and the current text foreground and background colors.
- DrawLine (pt1, pt2)/DrawLine (x1, y1, x2, y2) This method draws a line from the first point to the second.

It is also important to understand when the device context is refreshed/redrawn. For example, if you resize a window, maximize it, minimize it, move it, or modify its contents the window is redrawn.This generates an event, a PaintEvent. You can bind a method to the PaintEvent (using wx.EVT_PAINT) that can be called each time the window is refreshed.

This method can be used to draw whatever the contents of the window should be. If you do not redraw the contents of the device context in such a method than whatever you previously drew will display when the window is refreshed.

The following simple program illustrates the use of some of the Draw methods listed above and how a method can be bound to the paint event so that the display is refreshed appropriately when using a device context:

```
import wx
class DrawingFrame(wx.Frame):
def    init    (self,  title):
super().    init    (None, title=title,
size=(300,  200))
self.Bind(wx.EVT_PAINT,  self.on_paint)
```

```
def on_paint(self,  event):
"""set up the device context (DC) for painting"""
dc  =  wx.PaintDC(self) dc.DrawLine(10,  10,  60,
 20) dc.DrawRectangle(20,  40,  40,  20)
dc.DrawText("Hello World",  30,
70)dc.DrawCircle(130,  40,  radius=15)
class GraphicApp(wx.App):
def OnInit(self):
""" Initialisethe GUI display""" frame  =
DrawingFrame(title='PyDraw') frame.Show()
return True
# Run the GUI application app  =  GraphicApp()
app.MainLoop()
```

When this program is run the following display is generated:

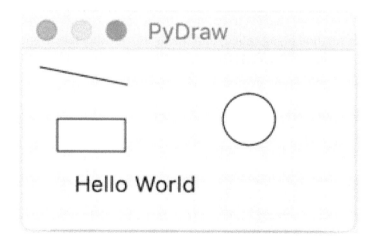

Events in wxPython User Interfaces

Event Handling

Events are an integral part of any GUI; they represent user interactions with the interface such as clicking on a button, entering text into a field, selecting a menu option etc.

The main event loop listens for an event; when one occurs it processes that event (which usually results in a function or method being called) and then waits for the next event to happen. This loop is initiated in wxPython via the call to the MainLoop() method on the wx.App object.

This raises the question 'what is an Event?'. An event object is a piece of information representing some interaction that occurred typically with the GUI (although an event can be generated by anything). An event is processed by an Event Handler. This is a method or function that is called when the event occurs. The event is passed to the handler as a parameter. An Event Binder is used to bind an event to an event handler.

Event Definitions

It is useful to summarize the definitions around events as the terminology used can be confusing and is very similar:

- Event represents information from the underlying GUI framework that describes something that has happened and any associated data. The specific data available will differ depending on what has occurred. For example, if a window has been moved then the associated data will relate to the window's new location. Where as a CommandEvent generated by a selection action from a ListBox provides the item index for the selection.
- Event Loop the main processing loop of the GUI that waits for an event to occur.When an event occurs the associated event handler is called.
- Event Handlers these are methods (or functions) that are called when an event occurs.
- EventBinders associate a type of event with an event handler. There are different event binders for different types of event.For example, the event binder associated with the wx.MoveEvent is named wx.EVT_MOVE.

The relationship between the Event, the Event Handler via the Event Binder is illustrated below:

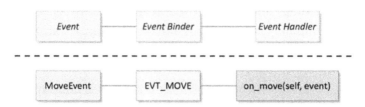

The top three boxes illustrate the concepts while the lower 3 boxes provide a concrete example of binding a Move_Event to an on_move() method via the EVT_MOVE binder.

Types of Events

There are numerous different types of event including:

- wx.CloseEvent used to indicate that a Frame or Dialog has been closed.The event binder for this event is named wx.EVT_CLOSE.
- wx.CommandEvent used with widgets such as buttons,list boxes, menu items, radio buttons, scroll bars, sliders etc.Depending upon the type of widget that generated the event different information may be provided. For example, for a Button a CommandEvent indicates that a button has been clicked where as for a ListBox it indicates that an option has been selected,etc. Different event binders are used for different event situations. For example, to bind a command event to a event handler for a button then the wx.EVT_BUTTON binder is used; while for a ListBox a wx.EVT_LISTBOXbinder can be used.
- wx.FocusEvent This event is sent when a window's focus changes (loses or gains focus). You can pick up a

window gaining focus using the wx. EVT_SET_FOCUS event binder. The wx.EVT_KILL_FOCUS is used to bind an event handler that will be called when a window loses focus.

- wx.KeyEvent This event contains information relating to a key press or release.
- wx.MaximizeEvent This event is generated when a top level window is maximized.
- wx.MenuEvent This event is used for menu oriented actions such as the menu being opened or closed; however it should be noted that this event is not used when a menu item is selected (MenuItems generate CommandEvents).
- wx.MouseEvent This event class contains information about the events generated by the mouse: this includes information on which mouse button was pressed (and released) and whether the mouse was double clicked etc.
- wx.WindowCreateEvent This event is sent just after the actual window is created.
- wx.WindowDestoryedEvent This event is sent as early as possible during the window destruction process.

Binding an Event to an Event Handler

An event is bound to an Event Handler using the Bind() method of an event generating object (such as a button, field, menu item etc.) via a named Event Binder.

For example:

```
button.Bind(wx.EVT_BUTTON,
self.event_handler_method)
```

Implementing Event Handling

There are four steps involved in implementing event handling for a widget or window, these are:

1. Identify the event of interest. Many widgets will
   generate different events in different situations; it
   may therefore be necessary to determine which event
   you are interested in.
2. Find the correct Event Binder name, e.g. wx.EVT_CLOSE,
   wx.EVT_MOVE or wx.EVT_BUTTON etc. Again you
   may find that the widget you are interested in supports
   numerous different event binders which may be used
   in different situations (even for the same event).
3. Implement an event handler (i.e. a suitable method or
   function) that will be called when the event occurs.
   The event handler will be supplied with the event
   object.
4. Bind the Event to the Event Handler via the Binder
   Name using the Bind() method of the widget or window.

To illustrate this we will use a simple example.

We will write a very simple event handling application. This
application will have a Frame containing a Panel. The Panel

will contain a label using the wx. StaticText class.

We will define an event handler called on_mouse_click() that will move the StaticText label to the current mouse location when the left mouse button is pressed. This means that we can move the label around the screen.

To do this we first need to determine the widget that will be used to generate the event. In this case it is the panel that contains the text label. Having done this we can look at the Panel class to see what events and Event Bindings it supports. It turns out that the Panel class only directly defines support for NavigationKeyEvents. This is not actually what we want; however the Panel class extends the Window class.

The Window class supports numerous event bindings, from those associated with setting the focus (wx.EVT_SET_FOCUS and wx.EVT_KILL_FOCUS) to key presses (wx.EVT_KEY_DOWN and wx.EVT_KEY_UP) as well as mouse events. There are however numerous different mouse event bindings. These allow left, middle and right mouse button clicks to be picked up, down clicks to be identified,situations such as the mouse entering or leaving the window etc. However, the binding we are interested in for a MouseEvent is the wx. EVT_LEFT_DOWNbinding; this picks up on the MoueEvent when the left mouse button is pressed (there is also the wx.EVT_LEFT_UP binding which can be used to pick up an event that occurs when the left mouse button is released).

We now know that we need to bind the on_mouse_click() event handler to the MouseEvent via the wx.EVT_LEFT_DOWN event binder, for example:

```
self.panel.Bind(wx.EVT_LEFT_DOWN,
self.on_mouse_click)
```

All event handler methods takes two parameters, self and the mouse event. Thus the signature of the on_mouse_click() method is:

```
def on_mouse_click(self, mouse_event):
```

The mouse event object has numerous methods defined that allow information about the mouse to be obtained such as the number of mouse clicks involved (GetClickCount()), which button was pressed (GetButton()) and the current mouse position within the containing widget or window (GetPosition ()). We can therefore use this last method to obtain the current mouse location and then use the SetPosition(x, y) method on the StaticText object to set its position.

The end result is the program shown below:

```
import wx
class WelcomeFrame(wx.Frame):
""" The Main Window / Frame of the application """
def   init (self):
super(). init (parent=None, title='Sample App',
size=(300, 200))
```

```
# Set up panel within the frame and text label
self.panel = wx.Panel(self)
self.text = wx.StaticText(self.panel,
label='Hello')
# Bind the on_mouse_clickmethod to the
# Mouse Event via the
# left mouse click binder
self.panel.Bind(wx.EVT_LEFT_DOWN,
self.on_mouse_click)
def on_mouse_click(self, mouse_event):
"""When the left mouse button is clicked This
method is called. It will obtain thecurrent mouse
coordinates, and reposition the text label
to this position. """
x, y = mouse_event.GetPosition() print(x, y)
self.text.SetPosition(wx.Point(x, y))
class MainApp(wx.App):
def OnInit(self):
""" Initialisethe main GUI Application"""
frame = WelcomeFrame()
frame.Show()
# Indicate that processingshould continue
return True
# Run the GUI application app = MainApp()
app.MainLoop()
```

When this program is run; the window is displayed with the 'Hello' StaticText label in the top left hand corner of the Frame(actually it is added to the Panel, however the Panel fills the Frame in this example). If the user then clicks the left mouse button anywhere within the Frame then the 'Hello'label jumps to that location.

This is shown below for the initial setup and then for two

locations within the window.

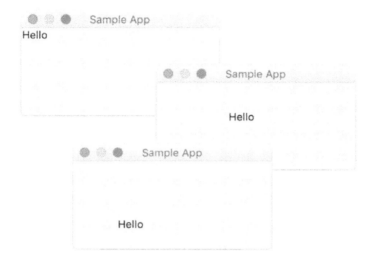

An Interactive wxPython GUI

An example of a slightly larger GUI application, that brings together many of the ideas presented in this chapter,is given below.

In this application we have a text input field (a wx.TextCtrl) that allows a user to enter their name. When they click on the Enter button (wx.Button) the welcome label (a wx.StaticText) is updated with their name.The 'Show Message' button is used to display a wx.MessageDialog which will also contain their name.

The initial display is shown below for both a Mac and a Windows PC, note that the default background color for a Frame is different on a Windows PC than on a Mac and thus although the GUI runs on both platforms, the look differs between the two:

The code used to implement this GUI application is given below:

```
import wx
class HelloFrame(wx.Frame):
def
  init    (self,  title):
super().    init    (None,  title=title,
size=(300,200))
self.name  =  '<unknown>'
# Create the BoxSizer to use for the Frame
vertical_box_sizer  =  wx.BoxSizer(wx.VERTICAL)
self.SetSizer(vertical_box_sizer)
# Createthe panel to contain the widgets
panel  =  wx.Panel(self)
# Add the Panel to the Frames Sizer
vertical_box_sizer.Add(panel,
wx.ID_ANY,
wx.EXPAND  |  wx.ALL,
20)
```

```python
# Create the GridSizerto use with the Panel
grid = wx.GridSizer(4, 1, 5, 5)
# Set up the input field
self.text = wx.TextCtrl(panel, size=(150, -1))
# Now configurethe enter button
enter_button = wx.Button(panel, label='Enter')
enter_button.Bind(wx.EVT_BUTTON, self.set_name)
# Next set up the text label
self.label = wx.StaticText(panel,
label='Welcome', style=wx.ALIGN_LEFT)
# Now configurethe Show Message button
message_button = wx.Button(panel, label='Show
Message')
message_button.Bind(wx.EVT_BUTTON,
self.show_message)
# Add the widgetsto the grid sizer to handle
layout
grid.AddMany([self.text, enter_button,
self.label, message_button])
# Set the sizer on the panel
panel.SetSizer(grid)
# Centre the Frame on the Computer Screen
self.Centre()
def show_message(self, event):
""" Event Handler to display the Message Dialog
using the current value of the name attribute.
""" dialog = wx.MessageDialog(None,
message='Welcome To Python ' + self.name,
caption='Hello',
style=wx.OK)
dialog.ShowModal()
def set_name(self, event):
"""Event Handler for the Enter button.
Retrieves the text entered into the input field
and sets the self.name attribute. This is then
used to set the text label """
self.name = self.text.GetLineText(0)
```

```
self.label.SetLabelText('Welcome ' + self.name)
class MainApp(wx.App):
def OnInit(self):
"""Initialise the GUI display"""
frame = HelloFrame(title='Sample App')
frame.Show()
# Indicatewhether processing should continueor not
return True
def OnExit(self):
"""Executes when the GUI application shuts down"""
print('Goodbye')
# Need to indicatesuccess or failure
return True
# Run the GUI application app = MainApp()
app.MainLoop()
```

If the user enters their name in the top TextCtrl field, for example 'Phoebe', then when they click on the 'Enter' button the welcome label changes to 'Welcome Phoebe':

If they now click on the 'Show Message' button then the wx. MessageDialog (a specific type of wx.Dialog) will display a welcome message to Phoebe:

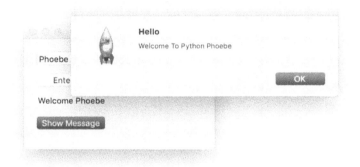

Online Resources

There are numerous online references that support the development of GUIs and of

Python GUIs in particular, including:

- https://docs.wxpython.org for documentation on wx-Python.
- https://www.wxpython.org wxPython home page.
- https://www.wxwidgets.org For information on the underlying wxWidgets

Cross platform GUI library.

Simple GUI Application

This exercise builds on the GUI you created in the last chapter.

The application should allow a user to enter their name and age. You will need to check that the value entered into the age field is a numeric value (for example using is numeric()). If the value is not a number then an error message dialog should be displayed.

A button should be provided labeled 'Birthday'; when clicked it should increment the age by one and display a Happy Birthday message. The age should be updated within the GUI.

An example of the user interface you created in the last chapter is given below:

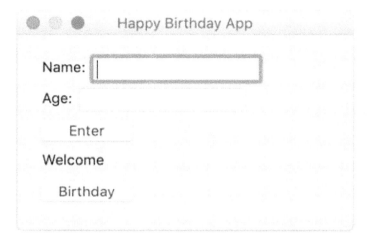

As an example,the user might enter their name and age as shown below:

When the user clicks on the 'birthday' button then the Happy Birthday message dialog is displayed:

GUI Interface to a Tic Tac Toe Game

The aim of this exercise is to implement a simple Tic Tac Toe game. The game should allow two users to play interactive using the same mouse. The first user will have play as the 'X' player and the second user as the 'o' player.

When each user selects a button you can set the label for the button to their symbol. You will need two check after each move to see if someone has won (or if the game is a draw).

You will still need an internal representation of the grid so that you can deter- mine who, if anyone, has won.

An example of how the GUI for the TicTacToe game might look is given below:

You can also add dialogs to obtain the players names and to notify them who won or whether there was a draw.

PyDraw wxPython Example Application

Introduction

This chapter builds on the GUI library presented in the last two chapters to illustrate how a larger application can be built. It presents a case study of a drawing tool akin to a tool such as Visio etc.

The PyDraw Application

The PyDraw application allows a user to draw diagrams using squares, circles, lines and text. At present there is no select, resize, reposition or delete option available (although these could be added if required). PyDraw is implemented using the wxPython set of components as defined in version 4.0.6.

When a user starts the PyDraw application, they see the interface shown above (for both the Microsoft Windows and Apple Mac operating systems). Depending on the operating system it has a menu bar across the top (on a Mac this menu bar is at the Top of the Mac display), a tool bar below the menu bar and a scrollable drawing area below that.

The first button on the tool bar clears the drawing area. The second and third buttons are only implemented so that they print out a message into the Python console, but are intended to allow a user to load and save drawings.

The tool bar buttons are duplicated on the menus defined for the application, along with a drawing tool selection menu, as shown below:

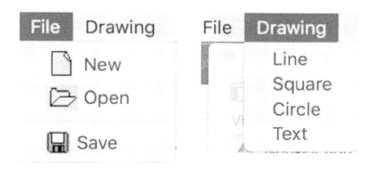

The Structure of the Application

The user interface created for the PyDraw application is made up of a number of elements (see below): the PyDrawMenuBar, the PyDrawToolbar containing a sequence of buttons across the top of the window, the drawing panel, and the window frame (implemented by the PyDrawFrame class).

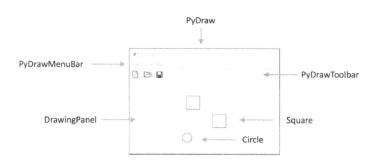

The following diagram shows the same information as that presented above, but as a containment hierarchy, this means that the diagram illustrates how one object is contained within another. The lower level objects are contained within the higher level objects.

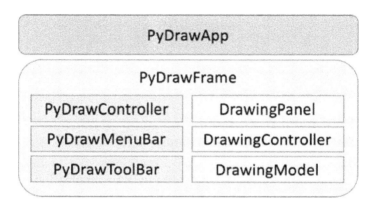

It is important to visualize this as the majority of wxPython interfaces are built up in this way, using containers and sizers.

The inheritance structure between the classes used in the PyDraw application is illustrated below. This class hierarchy is typical of an application which incorporates user interface features with graphical elements.

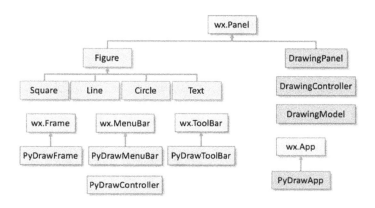

Model, View and Controller Architecture

The application adopts the well established Model-View-Controller(or MVC) design pattern for separating out the responsibilities between the view element (e.g. the Frame or Panel), the control element (for handling user input) and the model element (which holds the data to be displayed).

This separation of concerns is not a new idea and allows the construction of GUI applications that mirror the Model-View-Controller architecture. The intention of the MVC architecture is the separation of the user display, from the control of user input, from the underlying information model as illustrated below.

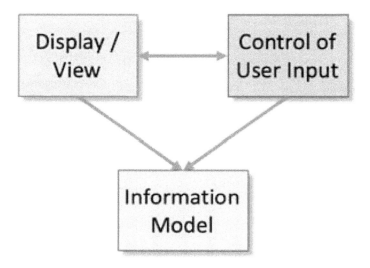

There are a number of reasons why this separation is useful:

- re-usability of application and/or user interface components,
- ability to develop the application and user interface separately,
- ability to inherit from different parts of the class hierarchy.
- ability to define control style classes which provide common features separately from how these features may be displayed.

This means that different interfaces can be used with the same application, without the application knowing about it. It also means that any part of the system can be changed without affecting the operation of the other. For example, the way that the graphical interface (the look) displays the information could be changed without modifying the actual application or how input is handled (the feel). Indeed the application need not know what type of interface is currently connected to it at all.

PyDraw MVC Architecture

The MVC structure of the PyDraw application has a top level controller class PyDrawController and a top level view class the PyDrawFrame (there is no model as the top level MVC triad does not hold any explicit data itself). This is shown below:

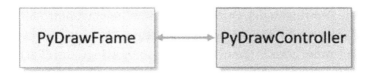

At the next level down there is another MVC structure; this time for the drawing element of the application. There is a DrawingController, with a DrawingModel and a Drawing-Panel (the view) as illustrated below:

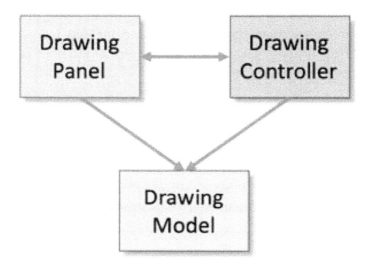

The DrawingModel, DrawingPanel and DrawingController classes exhibit the classic MVC structure. The view and the controller classes (DrawingPanel and DrawingController) know about each other and the drawing model, whereas the DrawingModel knows nothing about the view or the controller. The view is notified of changes in the drawing through the paint event.

Additional Classes

There are also four types of drawing object(of Figure): Circle, Line, Square and Text figures. The only difference between these classes is what is drawn on the graphic device context within the on_paint() method.The Figure class, from which they all inherit, defines the common attributes used by all objects within a Drawing (e.g. point representing an x and y location and size).

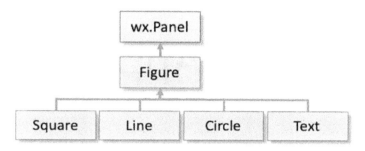

The PyDrawFrame class also uses a PyDrawMenuBar and a PyDrawToolBar class. The first of these extends the wx.MenuBar with menu items for use within the PyDraw application.In turn the PyDrawToolBar extends the wx.Tool-Bar and provides icons for use in PyDraw.

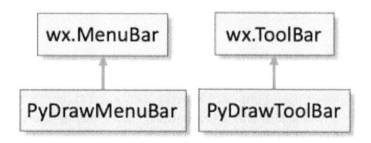

The final class is the PyDrawApp class that extends the wx.App class.

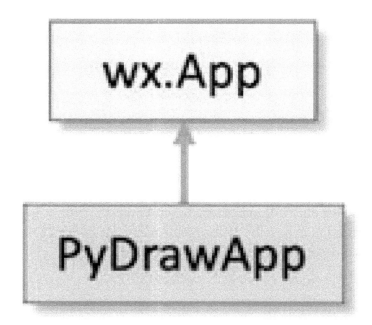

Object Relationships

However, the inheritance hierarchy is only part of the story for any object oriented application. The following figure illustrates how the objects relate to one another within the working application.

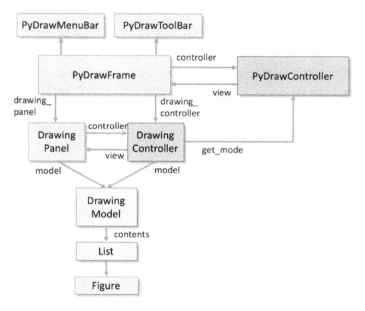

The PyDrawFrame is responsible for setting up the con-troller and the DrawingPanel. The PyDrawController is responsible for handling menu and tool bar user interac-tions. This separates graphical elements from the behavior triggered by the user.

TheDrawingPanel is responsible for displaying any figures held by the DrawingModel. TheDrawingController man-ages all user interactions with the DrawingPanel including adding figures and clearing all figures from the model. The DrawingModel holds list of figures to be displayed.

The Interactions Between Objects

We have now examined the physical structure of the application but not how the objects within that application interact. In many situations this can be extracted from the source code of the application (with varying degrees of difficulty). However, in the case of an application such as PyDraw, which is made up of a number of different interacting components, it is useful to describe the system interactions explicitly.

The diagrams illustrating the interactions between the objects use the following conventions:

- a solid arrow indicates a message send,
- a square box indicates a class,
- a name in brackets indicates the type of instance,
- numbers indicate the sequence of message sends.

These diagrams are based on the collaboration diagrams found in the UML (Unified Modelling Language) notation.

The PyDrawApp

When the PyDrawApp is instantiated the PyDrawFrame in created and displayed using the OnInit() method. The MainLoop() method is then invoked. This is shown below:

```
class PyDrawApp(wx.App):
def OnInit(self):
""" Initialisethe GUI display""" frame  =
PyDrawFrame(title='PyDraw') frame.Show()
return True
# Run the GUI application app  =  PyDrawApp()
```

```
app.MainLoop()
```

The PyDrawFrame Constructor

The PyDrawFrame constructor method sets up the main display of the UI application and also initializes the controllers and drawing elements. This is shown below using a collaboration diagram:

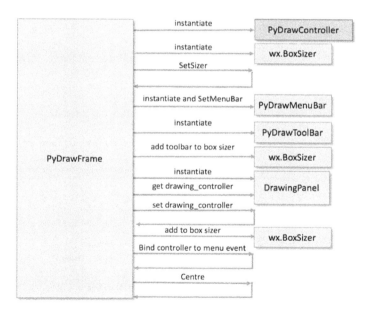

ThePyDrawFrame constructor sets up the environment for the application. It creates the top level PyDrawController. It creates the DrawingPanel and initializes the display layout. It initializes the menu bar and tool bar. It binds the controllers menu handler to the menus and centers itself.

Changing the Application Mode

One interesting thing to note is what happens when the user selects an option from the Drawing menu. This allows the mode to be changed to a square, circle,line or text. The interactions involved are shown below for the situation where a user selects the 'Circle' menu item on the Drawing menu (using a collaboration diagram):

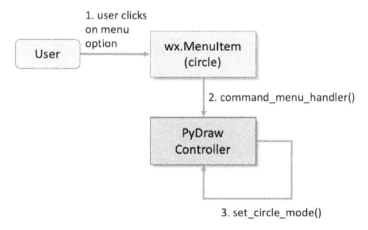

When the user selects one of the menu items the command_menu_handler () method of the PyDrawController is invoked. This method determines which menu item has been selected; it then calls an appropriate setter method (such as set_circle_mode() or set_line_mode() etc.). These methods set the mode attribute of the controller to an appropriate value.

Adding a Graphic Object

A user adds a graphic object to the drawing displayed by
the DrawingPanel by pressing the mouse button. When the
user clicks on the drawing panel, the DrawingController
responds as shown below:

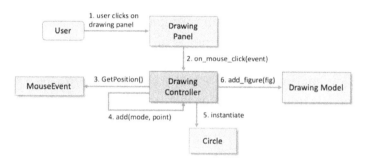

The above illustrates what happens when the user presses
and releases a mouse button over the drawing panel, to create a new figure. When the user presses the mouse button,
a mouse clicked message is sent to the DrawingController,
which decides what action to perform in response (see
above). In PyDraw, it obtains the cursor point at which the
event was generated by calling the GetPosition() method
on the mouse_event.

The controller then calls its own add() method passing
in the current mode and the current mouse location.The
controller obtains the current mode (from the PyDrawCon-

troller using the method callback provided when the DrawingController is instantiated) and adds the appropriate type
of figure to the DrawingModel.

The add() method then adds a new figure to the drawing
model based on the specified mode.

The Classes

This section presents the classes in the PyDraw application.
As these classes build on concepts already presented in
the last few chapters, they shall be presented in their
entirety with comments highlighting specific points of
their implementations. Note that the code imports the wx
module from the wxPython library, e.g.

```
import  wx
```

The PyDrawConstants Class

The purpose of this class is to provide a set of constants
that can be referenced in the remainder of the application.
It is used to provide constants for the IDs used with menu
items and toolbar tools. It also provides constants used
to represent the current mode (to indicate whether a line,
square, circle or test should be added to the display).

```
class PyDrawConstants: LINE_ID  =  100
 SQUARE_ID  =  102
 CIRCLE_ID  =  103
 TEXT_ID  =  104
```

```
SQUARE_MODE  =  'square'
LINE_MODE   =  'line'
CIRCLE_MODE  =  'circle'
TEXT_MODE   =  'Text'
```

The PyDrawFrame Class

The PyDrawFrame class provides the main window for the
application. Note that due to the separation of concerns
introduced via the MVC architecture, the view class is only
concerned with the layout of the components:

```
class PyDrawFrame(wx.Frame):
""" Main Frame responsible for the layout of the
UI."""
def  init   (self, title):
super().  init   (None, title=title,
size=(300, 200))
# Set up the controller
self.controller = PyDrawController(self)
# Set up the layout fo the UI
self.vertical_box_sizer =
wx.BoxSizer(wx.VERTICAL)
self.SetSizer(self.vertical_box_sizer)
# Set up the menu bar
self.SetMenuBar(PyDrawMenuBar())
# Set up the toolbar
self.vertical_box_sizer.Add(PyDrawToolBar(self),
wx.ID_ANY,
wx.EXPAND  |  wx.ALL, )
# Setup drawing panel
self.drawing_panel = DrawingPanel(self,
self.controller.get_mode)
```

```
self.drawing_controller =
self.drawing_panel.controller
# Add the Panel to the Frames Sizer
self.vertical_box_sizer.Add(self.drawing_panel,
wx.ID_ANY,
wx.EXPAND  |  wx.ALL)
# Set up the command event handling for the menu
bar and tool bar
self.Bind(wx.EVT_MENU,
self.controller.command_menu_handler)
self.Centre()
```

The PyDrawMenuBar Class

The PyDrawMenuBar class is a subclass of the wx.MenuBar class which defines the contents of the menu bar for the PyDraw application. It does this by creating two wx.Menu objects and adding them to the menu bar. Each wx.Menu implements a drop down menu from the menu bar. To add individual menu items the wx. MenuItem class is used. These menu items are appended to the menu. The menus are themselves appended to the menu bar. Note that each menu item has an id that can be used to identify the source of a command event in an event handler. This allows a single event handler to deal with events generated by multiple menu items.

```
class PyDrawMenuBar(wx.MenuBar):
def   init   (self): super().   init    ()
fileMenu  =  wx.Menu()
newMenuItem  =  wx.MenuItem(fileMenu, wx.ID_NEW,
text="New",  kind=wx.ITEM_NORMAL)
```

```
newMenuItem.SetBitmap(wx.Bitmap("new.gif"))
fileMenu.Append(newMenuItem)
loadMenuItem = wx.MenuItem(fileMenu,
wx.ID_OPEN, text="Open", kind=wx.ITEM_NORMAL)
loadMenuItem.SetBitmap(wx.Bitmap("load.gif"))
fileMenu.Append(loadMenuItem)
fileMenu.AppendSeparator()
saveMenuItem = wx.MenuItem(fileMenu,
wx.ID_SAVE, text="Save", kind=wx.ITEM_NORMAL)
saveMenuItem.SetBitmap(wx.Bitmap("save.gif"))
fileMenu.Append(saveMenuItem)
fileMenu.AppendSeparator()
quit = wx.MenuItem(fileMenu, wx.ID_EXIT,
'&Quit\tCtrl+Q')
fileMenu.Append(quit)
self.Append(fileMenu, '&File')
drawingMenu = wx.Menu()
lineMenuItem = wx.MenuItem(drawingMenu,
PyDraw_Constants.LINE_ID, text="Line",
kind=wx.ITEM_NORMAL)
drawingMenu.Append(lineMenuItem)
squareMenuItem = wx.MenuItem(drawingMenu,
PyDraw_Constants.SQUARE_ID, text="Square",
kind=wx.ITEM_NORMAL)
drawingMenu.Append(squareMenuItem)
circleMenuItem = wx.MenuItem(drawingMenu,
PyDraw_Constants.CIRCLE_ID, text="Circle",
kind=wx.ITEM_NORMAL)
drawingMenu.Append(circleMenuItem)
textMenuItem = wx.MenuItem(drawingMenu,
PyDraw_Constants.TEXT_ID, text="Text",
kind=wx.ITEM_NORMAL)
drawingMenu.Append(textMenuItem)
self.Append(drawingMenu, '&Drawing')
```

The PyDrawToolBar Class

The DrawToolBar class is a subclass of wx.ToolBar. The classes constructor initializes three tools that are displayed within the toolbar. The Realize() method is used to ensure that the tools are rendered appropriately. Note that appropriate ids have been used to allow an event handler to identify which tools generated a particular command event. By reusing the same ids for related menu items and command tools,a single handler can be used to manage events from both types of sources.

```
class PyDrawToolBar(wx.ToolBar):
def    init   (self,  parent): super().    init
(parent) self.AddTool(toolId=wx.ID_NEW,
label="New",
bitmap=wx.Bitmap("new.gif"),  shortHelp='Open
drawing',
kind=wx.ITEM_NORMAL)
self.AddTool(toolId=wx.ID_OPEN,  label="Open",
bitmap=wx.Bitmap("load.gif"),  shortHelp='Open
drawing',
kind=wx.ITEM_NORMAL)
self.AddTool(toolId=wx.ID_SAVE,  label="Save",
bitmap=wx.Bitmap("save.gif"),  shortHelp='Save
drawing',
kind=wx.ITEM_NORMAL)
self.Realize()
```

The PyDrawController Class

This class provides the control element of the top level view.

It maintains the current mode and implements a handler that can handle events from menu items and from the tool bar tools.An id is used to identify each individual menu or tool which allows a single handler to be registered with the frame.

```python
class PyDrawController:
def    init     (self,  view):
self.view  =  view
# Set the initial mode
self.mode  =  PyDrawConstants.SQUARE_MODE
def set_circle_mode(self):
self.mode  =  PyDrawConstants.CIRCLE_MODE
def set_line_mode(self):
self.mode  =  PyDrawConstants.LINE_MODE
def set_square_mode(self):
self.mode  =  PyDrawConstants.SQUARE_MODE
def set_text_mode(self):
self.mode  =  PyDrawConstants.TEXT_MODE
def clear_drawing(self):
self.view.drawing_controller.clear()
def get_mode(self):
return self.mode
def command_menu_handler(self,  command_event):
id  =  command_event.GetId()
if id  ==  wx.ID_NEW:
print('Clear the drawing area')
self.clear_drawing()
elif id  ==  wx.ID_OPEN:
print('Open a drawing file')
elif id  ==  wx.ID_SAVE:
print('Save a drawing file')
elif id  ==  wx.ID_EXIT:
print('Quite the application')
self.view.Close()
elif id  ==  PyDrawConstants.LINE_ID: print('set
```

```
drawing mode to line') self.set_line_mode()
elif id == PyDrawConstants.SQUARE_ID:
print('set drawing mode to square')
self.set_square_mode()
elif id == PyDrawConstants.CIRCLE_ID:
print('set drawing mode to circle')
self.set_circle_mode()
elif id == PyDrawConstants.TEXT_ID: print('set
drawing mode to Text') self.set_text_mode()
else:
print('Unknown option', id)
```

The DrawingModel Class

The DrawingModel class has a contents attribute that is
used to hold all the figures in the drawing. It also provides
some convenience methods to reset the contents and to add
a figure to the contents.

```
class DrawingModel:
def init (self):
self.contents = []
def clear_figures(self):
self.contents = []
def add_figure(self, figure):
self.contents.append(figure)
```

The DrawingModel is a relatively simple model which
merely records a set of graphical figures in a List. These
can be any type of object and can be displayed in any way
as long as they implement the on_paint() method. It is the
objects themselves which determine what they look like

when drawn.

The DrawingPanel Class

The DrawingPanel class is a subclass of the wx.Panel class. It provides the view for the drawing data model. This uses the classical MVC architecture and has a model (Drawing-Model), a view (the DrawingPanel) and a controller (the DrawingController).

The DrawingPanel instantiates its own DrawingController to handle mouse events.

It also registers for paint events so that it knows when to refresh the display.

```
class DrawingPanel(wx.Panel):
def  init   (self, parent, get_mode): super().
   init   (parent, -1)
self.SetBackgroundColour(wx.Colour(255, 255,
255)) self.model =  DrawingModel()
self.controller =  DrawingController(self,
self.model, get_mode)
self.Bind(wx.EVT_PAINT, self.on_paint)
self.Bind(wx.EVT_LEFT_DOWN,
self.controller.on_mouse_click)
def on_paint(self, event):
"""set up the device context (DC) for painting"""
dc =  wx.PaintDC(self)
for figure in self.model.contents:
figure.on_paint(dc)
```

The DrawingController Class

The DrawingController class provides the control class for the top level MVC architecture used with the DrawingModel (model) and DrawingPanel (view)classes. In particular it handles the mouse events in the DrawingPanel via the on_mouse_click() method.

It also defines an add method that is used to add a figure to the DrawingModel (the actual figure depends on the current mode of the PyDrawController). A final method,the clear() method, removes all figures from the drawing model and refreshes the display.

```python
class DrawingController:
def    init    (self,  view,  model,  get_mode):
self.view  =  view self.model  =  model
self.get_mode  =  get_mode
def on_mouse_click(self, mouse_event): point  =
mouse_event.GetPosition()
self.add(self.get_mode(),  point)
def add(self,  mode,  point,  size=30):
if mode  ==  PyDrawConstants.SQUARE_MODE:
fig  =  Square(self.view,  point,  wx.Size(size,
size))
elif mode  ==  PyDrawConstants.CIRCLE_MODE:
fig  =  Circle(self.view,  point,  size)
elif mode  ==  PyDrawConstants.TEXT_MODE:
fig  =  Text(self.view,  point,  size)
elif mode  ==  PyDrawConstants.LINE_MODE:
fig  =  Line(self.view,  point,  size)
self.model.add_figure(fig)
def clear(self): self.model.clear_figures()
self.view.Refresh()
```

The Figure Class

The Figure class (an abstract super class of the Figure class hierarchy)captures the elements which are common to graphic objects displayed within a drawing. The point defines the position of the figure, while the size attribute defines the size of the figure. Note that the Figure is a subclass of a wx.Panel and thus the display is constructed from inner panels onto which the various figure shapes are drawn.

The Figure class defines a single abstract method on_paint(dc) that must be implemented by all concrete sub classes. This method should define how the shape is drawn on the drawing panel.

```
class Figure(wx.Panel):
def    init    (self,  parent,  id=wx.ID_ANY,
pos=None, size=None,  style=wx.TAB_TRAVERSAL):
wx.Panel.    init    (self,  parent,  id=id,
pos=pos, size=size,  style=style)
self.point  =  pos self.size  =  size
@abstractmethod
def on_paint(self,  dc):
Pass
```

The Square Class

This is a subclass of Figure that specifies how to draw a square shape in a drawing. It implements the on_paint() method inherited from Figure.

```
class Square(Figure):
def   init   (self,  parent,  pos,  size):
super().   init   (parent=parent,  pos=pos,
size=size)
def on_paint(self,  dc):
dc.DrawRectangle(self.point,  self.size)
```

The Circle Class

This is another sub class of Figure. It implements the on_paint() method by drawing a circle. Note that the shape will be drawn within the panel size defined via the Figure class (using the call to super). It is therefore necessary to see the circle to fit within these bounds. This means that the size attribute must be used to generate an appropriate radius. Also note that the DrawCircle() method of the device context takes a point that is the center of the circle so this must also be calculated.

```
class Circle(Figure):
def   init   (self,  parent,  pos,  size):
super().   init   (parent=parent,
pos=pos,size=wx.Size(size,  size))
self.radius = (size - 10) / 2
self.circle_center = wx.Point(self.point.x +
self.radius,  self.point.y + self.radius)
def on_paint(self,  dc):
dc.DrawCircle(pt=self.circle_center,
radius=self.radius)
```

The Line Class

This is another subclass of Figure. In this very simple example, a default end point for the line is generated. Alternatively the program could look for a mouse released event and pick up the mouse at this location and use this as the end point of the line.

```
class Line(Figure):
def    init    (self,  parent,  pos,  size):
super().    init    (parent=parent,  pos=pos,
size=wx.Size(size,  size))
self.end_point  =  wx.Point(self.point.x  +
size, self.point.y  +  size)
def on_paint(self,  dc):
dc.DrawLine(pt1=self.point,
pt2=self.end_point)25.1.4
```

The Text Class

This is also a subclass of Figure. A default value is used for the text to display; however a dialog could be presented to the user allowing them to input the text they wish to display:

```
class Text(Figure):
def    init    (self,  parent,  pos,  size):
super().    init__(parent=parent,
pos=pos,size=wx.Size(size,  size))
def on_paint(self,  dc):
dc.DrawText(text='Text',  pt=self.point)
```

References

The following provides some background on the Model-View–Controller architecture in user interfaces.

· G.E. Krasner,S.T. Pope, A cookbook for using the model-view controller user interface paradigm in small talk-80. JOOP 1(3), 26−49 (1988).

Try

You could develop the PyDraw application further by adding the following features:

- A delete option You can add a button labeled Delete to the window. It should set the mode to "delete".The drawingPanel must be altered so that the mouseReleased method sends a delete message to the drawing. The drawing must find and remove the appropriate graphic object and send the changed message to itself.
- A resize option This involves identifying which of the shapes has been selected and then either using a dialog to enter the new size or providing some option that allows the size for the shape to be indicated using the mouse.

Introduction to Games Programming

Introduction

Games programming is performed by developers/coders who implement the logic that drives a game.

Historically games developers did everything; they wrote the code, designed the sprites and icons, handled the game play, dealt with sounds and music, generated any animations required etc. However, as the game industry has matured games companies have developed specific roles including Computer Graphics (CG) animators, artists, games developers and games engine and physics engine developers etc.

Those involved with code development may develop a physics engine, a games engine, the games themselves, etc. Such developers focus on different aspects of a game. For examples a game engine developer focuses on creating the framework within which the game will run. In turn a physics engine developer will focus on implementing the mathematics behind the physics of the simulated games world (such as the effect of gravity on characters and components within that world). In many cases there will also be developers working on the AI engine for a game. These developers will focus on providing facilities that allow the game or characters in the game to operate intelligently.

Those developing the actual game play will use these engines and frameworks to create the overall end result. It is they who give life to the game and make it an enjoyable (and playable) experience.

Games Frameworks and Libraries

There are many frameworks and libraries available that allow you to create anything from simple games to large complex role playing games with infinite worlds.

One example is the Unity framework that can be used with the C# programming language. Another such framework is the Unreal engine used with the C++ programming language.

Python has also been used for games development with several well known games titles depending on it in one way or another. For example, Battle field 2 by Digital Illusions CE is a military simulator first person shooter game. Battle field Heroes handles portions of the game logic involving game modes and scoring using Python.

Other games that use Python include Civilization IV (for many of the tasks), Pirates of the Caribbean Online and

Over watch (which makes its choices with Python).

Python is also embedded as a scripting engine within tools such as Autodesk's Maya which is a computer animation toolkit that is often used with games.

Python Games Development

For those wanting to learn more about game development; Python has much to offer. There are many examples available online as well as several game oriented frameworks.

The frameworks/libraries available for games development in Python including:

- Arcade. This is a Python library for creating 2D style video games.
- pyglet is a windowing and multimedia library for Python that can also be used for games development.
- Cocos2d is a framework for building 2D games that is built on top of pyglet.
- pygame is probably the most widely used library for creating games within the Python world.There are also many extensions available for pygame that help to create a wide range of different types of games.

We will focus on pygame in the next two chapters in this book. Other libraries of interest to Python games developers include:

- PyODE. This is an open-source Python binding for

the OpenDynamics Engine which is an open-source physics engine.

- pymunk Pymunk is a easy-to-use 2D physics library that can be used whenever you need 2d rigid body physics with Python. It is very good when you need 2D physics in your game, demo or other application. It is built on top of the 2D physics library Chipmunk.

- pyBox2D pybox2d is a 2D physics library for your games and simple simulations. It's based on the Box2D library written in C++. It supports several shape types (circle,polygon, thin line segments) as well as a number of joint types (revolute, prismatic, wheel, etc.).

- Blender. This is a open-source 3D computer graphics software tool set used for creating animated films, visual effects, art, 3D printed models, interactive 3D applications and video games. Blender's features include 3D modeling, texturing, raster graphics editing, rigging and skinning,etc. Python can be used as a scripting tool for creation,prototyping, game logic and more.

- Quake Army Knife which is an environment for developing 3D maps for games based on the Quake engine. It is written in Delphi and Python.

Using Pygame

In the next two chapters we will explore the core pygame library and how it can be used to develop interactive computer games. The next chapter explores pygame itself and the facilities it provides. The following chapter developers a simple interactive game in which the user moves a star ship around avoiding meteors which scroll vertically down the screen.

Online Resources

For further information games programming and the libraries mentioned in this chapter see:

- https://unity.com/ the C# framework for games development.
- https://www.unrealengine.com for C++ games development.
- http://arcade.academy/ provides details on the Arcade games framework.
- http://www.pyglet.org/ for information on the piglet library.
- http://cocos2d.org/ is the home page for the Cocos2d framework.
- https://www.pygame.org for information on pygame.
- http://pyode.sourceforge.net/ for details of the PyODE bindings to the Open Dynamics Engine.
- http://www.pymunk.org/ provides information on pymunk.
- https://github.com/pybox2d/pybox2d which is a Git hub repository for pyBox2d.
- https://git.blender.org/gitweb/gitweb.cgi/blender.git Git Hub repository for Blender.
- https://sourceforge.net/p/quark/code SourceForge repository for Quake Army Knife.
- https://www.autodesk.co.uk/products/maya/overview for information on Autodesks Maya computer

animation software.

Building Games with pygame

Introduction

pygame is a cross-platform, free and Open Source Python library designed to make building multimedia applications such as games easy. Development of pygame started back in October 2000 with pygame version 1.0 being released six months later. The version of pygame discussed in this chapter is version 1.9.6.If you have a later version check to see what changes have been made to see if they have any impact on the examples presented here.

pygame is built on top of the SDL library. SDL (or Simple Direct media Layer) is a cross platform development library designed to provide access to audio, key- boards, mouse, joystick and graphics hardware via OpenGL and Direct3D. To promote portability, pygame also supports a variety of additional back ends including WinDIB, X11, Linux Frame Buffer etc.

SDL officially supports Windows, Mac OS X, Linux, iOS and Android (although other platforms are unofficially supported). SDL itself is written in C and pygame provides a wrapper around SDL. However, pygame adds functionality not found in SDL to make the creation of graphical or video games easier. These functions include vector maths, collision detection, 2D sprite scene graph management, MIDI support, camera, pixel array manipulation, trans-formations, filtering, advanced free type font support and drawing.

The remainder of this chapter introduces pygame, the key concepts; the key modules, classes and functions and a very simple first pygame application. The next chapter steps through the development of a simple arcade style video game which illustrates how a game can be created using pygame.

The Display Surface

The Display Surface (aka the display)is the most important part of a pygame game. It is the main window display of your game and can be of any size, however you can only have one Display Surface.

In many ways the Display Surface is like a blank piece of paper on which you can draw. The surface itself is made up of pixels which are numbered from 0,0 in the top left hand corner with the pixel locations being indexed in the x axis and the y axis. This is shown below:

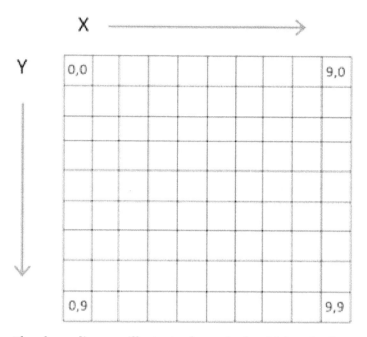

The above diagram illustrates how pixels within a Surface are indexed. Indeed a Surface can be used to draw lines, shapes (such as rectangles, squares, circles and ellipses), display images, manipulate individual pixels etc. Lines are drawn from one pixel location to another (for example from location 0,0 to location 9,0 which would draw a line across the top of the above display surface). Images can be displayed within the display surface given a starting point such as 1, 1.

The Display Surface is created by the pygame.display.set_mode() function. This function takes a tuple that can be used to specify the size of the Display Surface to be returned. For example:

```
display_surface  =  pygame.display.set_mode((400,
 300))
```

This will create a Display Surface (window) of 400 by 300 pixels.

Once you have the Display Surface you can fill it with an appropriate back- ground color (the default is black) however if you want a different background color or want to clear everything that has previously been drawn on the surface, then you can use the surface's fill() method:

```
WHITE  =  (255,  255,  255)
display_surface.fill(WHITE)
```

The fill method takes a tuple that is used to define a color in terms of Red, Green and Blue (or RGB) colors. Although the above examples uses a meaningful name for the tuple representing the RGB values used for white; there is of course no requirement to do this (although it is considered good practice).

To aid in performance any changes you make to the Display Surface actually happen in the background and will not be rendered onto the actual display that the user sees until you call the update() or flip() methods on the surface. For example:

- pygame.display.update()

176

- pygame.display.flip()

The update() method will redraw the display with all changes made to the display in the background. It has an optional parameter that allows you to specify just a region of the display to update (this is defined using a Rect which represents a rectangular area on the screen). The flip() method always refreshes the whole of the display (and as such does exactly the same as the update() method with no parameters).

Another method, which is not specifically a Display Surface method, but which is often used when the display surface is created, provides a caption or title for the top level window. This is the pygame.display.set_caption() function. For example:

```
pygame.display.set_caption('Hello World')
```

This will give the top level window the caption (or title) 'Hello World'.

Events

Just as the Graphical User Interface systems described in earlier chapters have an event loop that allows the programmer to work out what the user is doing (in those cases this is typically selecting a menu item, clicking a button or entering data etc.); pygame has an event loop that allows the game to work out what the player is doing.

For example, the user may press the left or right arrow key. This is represented by an event.

Event Types

Each event that occurs has associated information such as the type of that event. For example:

- Pressing a key will result in a KEYDOWN type of event, while releasing a key will result in a KEYUP event type.
- Selecting the window close button will generate a QUIT event type etc.
- Using the mouse can generate MOUSEMOTION events as well as MOUSEBUTTONDOWN and MOUSEBUT-TONUP event types.
- Using a Joystick can generate several different types of event including JOYAXISMOTION, JOYBALLMO-TION,JOYBUTTONDOWN and JOYBU TTONUP.

These event types tell you what occurred to generate the event. This means that you can choose which types of events you want to deal with and ignore other events.

Event Information

Each type of event object provides information associated with that event. For example a Key oriented event object will provide the actual key pressed while a mouse oriented event object will provide information on the position of the mouse, which button was pressed etc. If you try an access an attribute on an event that does not support that attribute, then an error will be generated.

The following lists some of the attributes available for different event types:

- KEYDOWN and KEYUP, the event has a key attribute and a mod attribute (indicating if any other modifying keys such as Shift are also being pressed).
- MOUSEBUTTONUP and MOUSEBUTTONDOWN has an attribute pos that holds a tuple indicating the mouse location in terms of x and y coordinates on the under-lying surface. It also has a button attribute indicating which mouse was pressed.
- MOUSEMOTION has pos, rel and buttons attributes. The pos is a tuple indicating the x and y location of mouse cursor. The real attribute indicates the amount of mouse movement and buttons indicates the state of the mouse buttons.

As an example if we want to check for a keyboard event type and then check that the key pressed was the space bar, then we can write:

```
if event.type  ==  pygame.KEYDOWN:
# Check to see which key is pressed
if event.key  ==  pygame.K_SPACE:
print('space')
```

This indicates that if it is a key pressed event and that the actual key was the space bar; then print the string 'space'.

There are many keyboard constants that are used to represent the keys on the keyboard and pygame.K_SPACE constant used above is just one of them.

All the keyboard constants are prefixed with 'K_' followed by the key or the name of the key, for example:

- K_TAB, K_SPACE, K_PLUS, K_0, K_1, K_AT, K_a, K_b, K_z, K_DELTE, K_DOWN, K_LEFT, K_RIGHT, K_LEFT etc.

Further keyboard constants are provided for modifier states that can be combined with the above such as KMOD_SHIFT, KMOD_CAPS, KMOD_CTRL and KMOD_ALT.

The Event Queue

Events are supplied to a pygame application via the Event Queue. The Event Queue is used to collect together events as they happen. For example, let us assume that a user clicks on the mouse twice and a key twice before a program has a chance to process them; then there will be four events in the Event Queue as shown below:

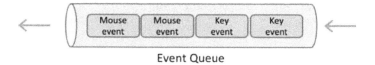

Event Queue

The application can then obtain an iterable from the event

queue and process through the events in turn. While the program is processing these events further events may occur and will be added to the Event Queue. When the program has finished processing the initial collection of events it can obtain the next set of events to process.

One significant advantage of this approach is that no events are ever lost; that is if the user clicks the mouse twice while the program is processing a previous set of events; they will be recorded and added to the event queue. Another advantage is that the events will be presented to the program in the order that they occurred.

The pygame.event.get() function will read all the events currently on the Event Queue (removing them from the event queue). The method returns an Event List which is an iterable list of the events read. Each event can then be processed in turn. For example:

```
for event  in pygame.event.get():
if event.type  ==  pygame.QUIT:
print('Received Quit Event:')
elif event.type  ==  pygame.MOUSEBUTTONDOWN:
print('Received Mouse Event')
elif event.type  ==  pygame.KEYDOWN:
print('Received KeyDown Event')
```

In the above code snippet an EventList is obtained from the Event Queue containing the current set of events. The for loop then processes each event in turn checking the type and printing an appropriate message.

You can use this approach to trigger appropriate behavior such as moving an image around the screen or calculating the players score etc. However, be aware that if this behavior takes too long it can make the game difficult to play(although the examples in this chapter and the next are simple enough that this is not a problem).

A First pygame Application

We are now at the point where we can put together what we have looked at so far and create a simple pygame application.

It is common to create a hello world style program when using a new programming language or using a new application framework etc. The intention is that the core elements of the language or framework are explored in order to generate the most basic form of an application using the language or framework. We will therefore implement the most basic application possible using pygame.

The application we will create will display a pygame window, with a 'Hello World' title. We will then be able to quit the game. Although technically speaking this isn't a game, it does possess the basic architecture of a pygame application.

The simple Hello World game will initialize pygame and the graphical dis- play. It will then have a main game playing loop that will continue until the user selects to quit the application. It will then shut down pygame. The display created by the program is shown below for both Mac and Windows operating systems:

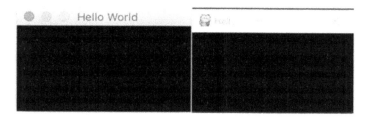

To quit the program click on the exit button for the windowing system you are using.

The simple Hello World game is given below:

```
import pygame
def main():
print('Starting Game')
print('Initialising pygame')
pygame.init()   # Requiredby every pygame
application
print('Initialising HelloWorldGame')
pygame.display.set_mode((200,
100))pygame.display.set_caption('Hello World')
print('Update display')
pygame.display.update()
print('Starting main Game Playing Loop')
running  =  True while running:
for event  in pygame.event.get():
if event.type  ==  pygame.QUIT: print('Received
Quit Event:',  event)running  =  False
print('Game Over')
```

```
pygame.quit()
if_name_=='_main_':
main()
```

There are several key steps highlighted by this example, these steps are:

1. Import pygame. pygame is of course not one of the default modules available within Python. You must first import pygame into you code. The import pygame statement imports the pygame module into your code and makes the functions and classes in pygame available to you (note the capitalization - pygame is not the same module name as PyGame). It is also common to find that programs import from pygame.locals import. This adds several constants and functions into the namespace of your pro- gram. In this very simple example we have not needed to do this.

2. Initialize pygame. Almost every pygame module needs to be initialized in some way and the simplest way to do this is to call pygame.init(). This will do what is required to set the pygame environment up for use. If you forget to call this function you will typically get an error message such as pygame.error: video system not initialized (or something similar). If you get such a method check to see that you have called pygame.init(). Note that you can initialize indi- vidual pygame modules (for example the pygame.font module can be initialized using pygame.font.init())

if required. However pygame.init() is the most commonly used approach to setting up pygame.

3. Setup the display. Once you have initialized the
   pygame framework you can setup the display.In the
   above code example, the display is set up using the
   pygame.display.set_mode() function. This function
   takes a tuple specifying the size of the window to be
   created (in this case 200 pixels wide by 100 pixels
   high). Note that if you try and invoke this function by
   passing in two parameters instead of a tuple, then you
   will get an error. This function returns the drawing
   surface or screen/window that can be used to display
   items within the game such as icons, messages,shapes
   etc. As our example is so simple we do not bother
   saving it into a variable.However, anything more
   complex than this will need to do so. We also set the
   window/frame's caption (or title). This is displayed
   in the title bar of the window.

4. Render the display. We now call the pygame.dis-
   play.update() function. This function causes the current details of the display to be drawn. At the moment
   this is a blank window. However, it is common in
   games to perform a series of updates to the display
   in the background and then when the program is
   ready to update the display to call this function. This
   batches a series of updates and the causes the display
   to be refreshed. In a complex display it is possible to
   indicate which parts of the display need to be redrawn
   rather than redrawing the whole window. This is done
   by passing a parameter into the update() function to
   indicate the rectangle to be redrawn. However, our

example is so simple we are OK with redrawing the whole window and therefore we do not need to pass any parameters to the function.

5. Main game playing loop. It is common to have a main game playing loop that drives the processing of user inputs, modifies the state of the game and updates the display. This is represented above by the while running:loop. The local variable running is initialized to True. This means that the while loop ensures that the game continues until the user selects to quit the game at which point the running variable is set to False which causes the loop to exit. In many cases this loop will call update() to refresh the display. The above example does not do this as nothing is changed in the display. However the example developed later in this chapter will illustrate this idea.

6. Monitor for events that drive the game. As mentioned earlier the event queue is used to allow user inputs to be queued and then processed by the game.In the simple example shown above this is represented by a for loop that receives events using pygame.event.get() and then checking to see if the event is a pygame.QUIT event. If it is, then it sets the running flag to False. Which will cause the main while loop of the game to terminate.

7. Quit pygame once finished. In pygame any module that has an init() function also has an equivalent quit() function that can be used to perform any cleanup operations. As we called init() on the pygame module at the start of our program we will therefore need to call pygame.quit() at the end of the program to ensure

everything is tidied up appropriately.

The output generated from a sample run of this program is given below:

```
pygame 1.9.6
Hello from the pygame community.
https://www.pygame.org/contribute.html Starting
Game
Initialising pygame Initialising HelloWorldGame
Update display
Starting main Game Playing  Loop
Received Quit Event: <Event(12-Quit {})> Game Over
```

Further Concepts

There are very many facilities in pygame that go beyond what we can cover in this book, however a few of the more common are discussed below.

Surfaces are a hierarchy. The top level Display Surface may contain other surfaces that may be used to draw images or text. In turn containers such as Panels may render surfaces to display images or text etc.

Other types of surface. The primary Display Surface is not the only surface in pygame. For example, when an image, such as a PNG or JPEG image is loaded into a game then it is rendered onto a surface. This surface can then be displayed within another surface such as the Display Surface. This means that anything you can do to the Display Surface you can do with any other surface such as draw on it, put text on it, color it, add another icon onto the surface etc.

Fonts. The pygame.font.Font object is used to create a Font that can be used to render text onto a surface. The render method returns a surface with the text rendered on it that can be displayed within another surface such as the Display Surface. Note that you cannot write text onto an existing surface you must always obtain a new surface (using render) and then add that to an existing surface.The text can only be displayed in a single line and the surface holding the text will be of the dimensions required to render the text. For example:

```
text_font =
pygame.font.Font('freesansbold.ttf', 18)
text_surface = text_font.render('Hello World',
 antialias=True, color=BLUE)
```

This creates a new Font object using the specified font with the specified font size (in this case 18). It will then render the string 'Hello World' on to a new surface using the specified font and font size in Blue. Specifying that anti alias is True indicates that we would like to smooth the edges of the text on the screen.

Rectangles (or Rects). The pygame.Rect class is an object used to represent rectangular coordinates. A Rect can be created from a combination of the top left corner co-ordinates plus a width and height. For flexibility many functions that expect a Rect object can also be given a Rect like list; this is a list that contains the data necessary to create a Rect object. Rects are very useful in a pygame Game as they can be used to define the borders of a game object. This means that they can be used within games to detect if two objects have collided.This is made particularly easy because the Rect class provides several collision detection methods:

- pygame.Rect.contains() test if one rectangle is inside another
- pygame.Rect.collide point() test if a point is inside a rectangle
- pygame.Rect.colliderect() test if two rectangles overlap
- pygame.Rect.collidelist() test if one rectangle in a list intersects
- pygame.Rect.collidelistall() test if all rectangles in a list intersect
- pygame.Rect.collidedict() test if one rectangle in a dictionary intersects
- pygame.Rect.collidedictall() test if all rectangles in a dictionary intersect

The class also provides several other utility methods such as move() which moves the rectangle and inflate() which can grow or shrink the rectangles size.

Drawing shapes. The pygame.draw module has numerous functions that can be used to draw lines and shapes onto a surface, for example:

pygame.draw.rect(display_surface, BLUE, [x, y, WIDTH, HEIGHT])

This will draw a filled blue rectangle(the default) onto the display surface. The rectangle will be located at the location indicated by x and y (on the surface).This indicates the top left hand corner of the rectangle. The width and height of the rectangle indicate its size. Note that these dimensions are defined within a list which is a structure referred to as being rect like (see below). If you do not want a filled rectangle (i.e. You just want the outline)then you can use the optional width parameter to indicate the thickness of the outer edge. Other methods available include:

- pygame.draw.polygon() draw a shape with any number of sides
- pygame.draw.circle() draw a circle around a point
- pygame.draw.ellipse() draw a round shape inside a rectangle
- pygame.draw.arc() draw a partial section of an ellipse
- pygame.draw.line() draw a straight line segment
- pygame.draw.lines() draw multiple contiguous line segments
- pygame.draw.aaline() draw fine antialiazed lines
- pygame.draw.aalines() draw a connected sequence of antialiased lines

Images. The pygame.image module contains functions for loading, saving and transforming images.When an image is loaded into pygame, it is represented by a Surface object. This means that it is possible to draw, manipulate and process an image in exactly the same way as any other surface which provides a great deal of flexibility.

At a minimum the module only supports loading uncompressed BMP images but usually also supports JPEG, PNG, GIF (non-animated), BMP, TIFF as well as other formats.

However, it only supports a limited set of formats when saving images; these are BMP, TGA, PNG and JPEG.

An image can be loaded from a file using:

```
image_surface   =
pygame.image.load(filename).convert()
```

This will load the image from the specified file onto a surface. One thing you might wonder at is the use of the convert() method on the object returned from the pygame.image.load() function. This function returns a Surface that is used to display the image contained in the file. We call the method convert() on this Surface, not to convert the image from a particular file format (such as PNG, or JPEG) instead this method is used to convert the pixel format used by the Surface. If the pixel format used by the Surface is not the same as the display format, then it will need to be converted on the fly each time the image is displayed on the screen; this can be a fairly time consuming (and unnecessary) process. We therefore do this once when the image is loaded which means that it should not hinder runtime performance and may improve performance significantly on some systems.

Once you have a surface containing an image it can be rendered onto another surface, such as the display surface using the Surface.blit() method. For example:

```
display_surface.blit(image_surface, (x, y))
```

Note that the position argument is a tuple specifying the x and y coordinates to the image on the display surface. Strictly speaking the blit() method draws one surface (the source surface)

onto another surface at the destination coordinates. Thus the target surface does not need to be the top level display surface.

Clock. A Clock object is an object that can be used to track time. In particular it can be used to define the frame rate for the game. That is the number of frames rendered per second.This is done using the Clock.tick() method. This method should be called once (and only once) per frame. If you pass the optional frame rate argument to the tick() the function, then pygame will ensure that the games refresh rate is slower then the the given ticks per second. This can be used to help limit the runtime speed of a game. By calling clock.tick (30) once per frame, the program will never run at more than 30 frames per second.

A More Interactive pygame Application

The first pygame application we looked at earlier just displayed a window with the caption 'Hello World'. We can now extend this a little by playing with some of the features we have looked at above.

The new application will add some mouse event handling. This will allow us to pickup the location of the mouse when the user clicked on the window and draw a small blue box at that point.

If the user clicks the mouse multiple times we will get multiple blue boxes being drawn. This is shown below.

This is still not much of a game but does make the pygame application more interactive.

The program used to generate this application is presented below:

```python
import pygame
FRAME_REFRESH_RATE = 30
BLUE = (0, 0, 255)
BACKGROUND = (255, 255, 255)  # White
WIDTH = 10
HEIGHT = 10
def main():
print('Initialising PyGame')
pygame.init()   # Required by every PyGame
application
print('Initialising Box Game')
display_surface = pygame.display.set_mode((400,
 300))
pygame.display.set_caption('Box Game')
print('Update display') pygame.display.update()
print('Setup the Clock')
clock = pygame.time.Clock()
# Clear the screen of current contents
display_surface.fill(BACKGROUND)
print('Starting main Game Playing Loop')
running = True while running:
for event in pygame.event.get():
if event.type == pygame.QUIT: print('Received
Quit Event:', event) running = False
elif event.type == pygame.MOUSEBUTTONDOWN:
print('Received Mouse Event', event) x, y =
event.pos pygame.draw.rect(display_surface,
BLUE, [x, y,
WIDTH, HEIGHT])
second
# Update the display
pygame.display.update()
# Defines the frame rate - the number of frames
per
```

```
# Should be called once per frame (but only once)
clock.tick(FRAME_REFRESH_RATE)
print('Game Over')
# Now tidy up and quit Python
pygame.quit()
if_name_=='_main_':
    main()
```

Note that we now need to record the display surface in a local variable so that we can use it to draw the blue rectangles. We also need to call the pygame.dis- play.up- date() function each time round the main while loop so that the new rectangles we have drawn as part of the event processing for loop are displayed to the user.

We also set the frame rate each time round the main while loop. This should happen once per frame (but only once) and uses the clock object initialized at the start of the program.

Alternative Approach to Processing Input Devices

There are actually two ways in which inputs from a device such as a mouse, joystick or the keyboard can be processed. One approach is the Event based model described earlier. The other approach is the State based approach.

Although the Event based approach has many advantages is has two disadvantages:

- Each event represents a single action and continuous

actions are not explicitly represented. Thus if the user presses both the X key and the Z key then this will generate two events and it will be up to the program to determine that they have been pressed at the same time.

· It is also up to the program to determine that the user is still pressing a key (by noting that no KEYUP event has occurred).

· Both of these are possible but can be error prone.

An alternative approach is to use the State based approach. In the state based approach the program can directly check the state of a input device (such as a key or mouse or keyboard). For example, you can use pygame.key.get_pressed() which returns the state of all the keys. This can be used to determine if a specific key is being pressed at this moment in time. For example, pygame.key. get_pressed()[pygame.K_SPACE] can be used to check to see if the space bar is being pressed.

This can be used to determine what action to take. If you keep checking that the key is pressed then you can keep performing the associated action. This can be very useful for continues actions in a game such as moving an object etc.

However, if the user presses a key and then releases it before the program checks the state of the keyboard then that input will be missed.

pygame Modules

There are numerous modules provided as part of pygame as well as associated libraries. Some of the core modules are listed below:

- pygame.display This module is used to control the display window or screen. It provides facilities to initialize and shutdown the display module. It can be used to initialize a window or screen. It can also be used to cause a window or screen to refresh etc.
- pygame.event This module manages events and the event queue. For example pygame.event.get() retrieves events from the event queue, pygame.event.poll() gets a single event from the queue and pygame.event.peek() tests to see if there are any event types on the queue.
- pygame.draw The draw module is used to draw simple shapes onto a Surface. For example, it provides functions for drawing a rectangle (pygame.draw.rect), a polygon, a circle, an ellipse, a line etc.
- pygame.font The font module is used to create and render TrueType fonts into a new Surface object. Most of the features associated with fonts are supported by the pygame.font.Font class. Free standing module functions allow the module to be initialized and shutdown, plus functions to access fonts such as pygame.font.get_fonts() which provides a list of the currently available fonts.
- pygame.image This module allows images to be saved and loaded. Note that images are loaded into a Surface object (there is no Image class unlike many other GUI oriented frameworks).
- pygame.joystick The joystick module provides the Joy-

stick object and several supporting functions. These can be used for interacting with joysticks, game pads and trackballs.

- pygame.key This module provides support for working with inputs from the keyboard. This allows the input keys to be obtained and modifier keys (such as Control and Shift)to be identified. It also allows the approach to repeating keys to be specified.
- pygame.mouse This module provides facilities for working with mouse input such as obtaining the current mouse position, the state of mouse buttons as well as the image to use for the mouse.
- pygame.time This is the pygame module for managing timing within a game. It provides the pygame.time.Clock class that can be used to track time.

StarshipMeteors pygame

Creating a Spaceship Game

In this chapter we will create a game in which you pilot a starship through a field of meteors. The longer you play the game the larger the number of meteors you will encounter. A typical display from the game is shown below for a Apple Mac and a Windows PC:

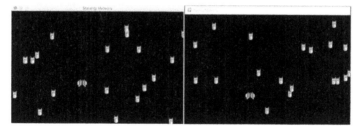

We will implement several classes to represent the entities within the game. Using classes is not a required way to implement a game and it should be noted that many developers avoid the use of classes. However, using a class allows data associated with an object within the game to be maintained in one place; it also simplifies the creation of multiple instances of the same object(such as the meteors) within the game.

The classes and their relationships are shown below:

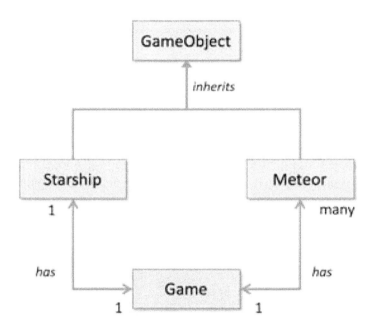

This diagram shows that the Starship and Meteor classes will extend a class called GameObject. In turn it also shows that the Game has a 1:1 relationship with the Starship class. That is the Game holds a reference to one Starship and in turn the Starship holds a single reference back to the Game.

In contrast the Game has a 1 to many relationship with the Meteor class. That is the Game object holds references to many Meteors and each Meteor holds a reference back to the single Game object.

The Main Game Class

The first class we will look at will be the Game class itself. TheGame class will hold the list of meteors and the starship as well as the main game playing loop. It will also initialize the main window display (for example by setting the size and the caption of the window).

In this case we will store the display surface returned by the pygame.display.set_mode() function in an attribute of the Game object called display_surface. This is because we will need to use it later on to display the starship and the meteors. We will also hold onto an instance of the pygame.time.Clock() class that we will use to set the frame rate each time round the main game playing while loop.

The basic framework of our game is shown below; this listing provides the basic Game class and the main method that will launch the game. The game also defines three global constants that will be used to define the frame refresh rate and the size of the display.

```
import pygame
# Set up Global'constants'
FRAME_REFRESH_RATE  =  30
DISPLAY_WIDTH  =  600
DISPLAY_HEIGHT  =  400
class Game:
```

```
""" Represents the game itself and game playing
loop """
def   init   (self): print('Initialising
PyGame') pygame.init()
# Set up the display
self.display_surface  =
pygame.display.set_mode((DISPLAY_WIDTH,
DISPLAY_HEIGHT))
pygame.display.set_caption('Starship Meteors')
# Used for timingwithin the program.
self.clock  =  pygame.time.Clock()
def play(self):
is_running  =  True
# Main game playing Loop
while is_running:
# Work out what the user wants to do
for event  in pygame.event.get():
if event.type  ==  pygame.QUIT:
is_running  =  False
elif event.type  ==  pygame.KEYDOWN:
if event.key  ==  pygame.K_q:
is_running  =  False
# Update the display
pygame.display.update()
# Definesthe frame rate
self.clock.tick(FRAME_REFRESH_RATE)
# Let pygame shutdown gracefully
pygame.quit()
def main():
print('Starting Game') game  =  Game() game.play()
print('Game Over')
if_name_=='_main_':
main()
```

The main play() method of the Game class has a loop that
will continue until the user selects to quit the game. They

can do this in one of two ways, either by pressing the 'q' key (represented by the event.key K_q) or by clicking on the window close button. In either case these events are picked up in the main event processing for loop within the main while loop method.

If the user does not want to quit the game then the display is updated (refreshed) and then the clock.tick() (or frame) rate is set. When the user selects to quit the game then the main while loop is terminated (the is_running flag is set to False) and the pygame.quit() method is called to shut down pygame.

At the moment this not a very interactive game as it does not do anything except allow the user to quit. In the next section we will add in behavior that will allow us to display the space ship within the display.

TheGameObject Class

The GameObject class defines three methods:

The load_image() method can be used to load an image to be used to visually represent the specific type of game object. The method then uses the width and height of the image to define the width and height of the game object.

The rect() method returns a rectangle representing the current area used by the game object on the underlying drawing surface. This differs from the images own rect() which is not related to the location of the game object on the underlying surface. Rects are very useful for comparing the location of one object with another (for example when determining if a collision has occurred).

The draw() method draws the GameObjects' image onto the display_ - surface held by the game using the GameObjects current x and y coordinates. It can be overridden by sub classes if they wish to be drawn in a different way.

The code for the GameObject class is presented below:

```
class GameObject:
def load_image(self,  filename):
self.image  =
pygame.image.load(filename).convert()
self.width  =  self.image.get_width()
self.height  =  self.image.get_height()
def rect(self):
""" Generates a rectanglerepresenting the objects
location
and dimensions"""
return pygame.Rect(self.x,  self.y,  self.width,
self.height)
def draw(self):
""" draw the game object at the current x, y
coordinates """
self.game.display_surface.blit(self.image,
(self.x,
self.y))
```

The GameObject class is directly extended by the Starship class and the Meteor class.

Currently there are only two types of game elements, the starship and the meteors; but this could be extended in future to planets, comets,shooting stars etc.

Displaying the Starship

The human player of this game will control a starship that can be moved around the display. The Starship will be represented by an instance of the class Starship. This class will extend the GameObject class that holds common behaviors for any type of element that is represented within the game.

The Starship class defines its own _init_()method that takes a reference to the game that the starship is part of. This initialization method sets the initial starting location of the Starship as half the width of the display for the x coordinate and the display height minus 40 for the y coordinate (this gives a bit of a buffer before the end of the screen). It then uses the load_image() method from the GameObject parent class to load the image to be used to represent the Starship. This is held in a file called starship.png. For the moment we will leave the Starship class as it is (however we will return to this class so that we can make it into a movable object in the next section).

The current version of the Starship class is given below:

```
class Starship(GameObject):
    """ Represents a starship"""
```

```
def    init     (self,  game):
self.game  =  game
self.x  =  DISPLAY_WIDTH  /  2 self.y  =
DISPLAY_HEIGHT  -  40
self.load_image('starship.png')
```

In the Game class we will now add a line to the init ()method to initialize the Starship object. This line is:

```
# Set up  the starship
self.starship = Starship(self)
```

We will also add a line to the main while loop within the play() method just before we refresh the display.This line will call the draw() method on the starship object:

```
# Draw the starship self.starship.draw()
```

This will have the effect of drawing the starship onto the windows drawing surface in the background before the display is refreshed. When we now run this version of the StarshipMeteor game we now see the Starship in the display:

Of course at the moment the starship does not move; but we will address that in the next section.

Moving the Spaceship

We want to be able to move the Starship about within the bounds of the display screen. To do this we need to change the starships x and y coordinates in response to the user pressing various keys.

We will use the arrow keys to move up and down the screen or to the left or right of the screen. To do this we will define four methods within the Starship class; these methods will move the starship up, down, left and right etc.

The updated Starship class is shown below:

```
class Starship(GameObject):
    """ Represents a starship"""

    def __init__(self, game):
        self.game = game
        self.x = DISPLAY_WIDTH / 2
        self.y = DISPLAY_HEIGHT - 40
        self.load_image('starship.png')

    def move_right(self):
        """ moves the starship right across the     """
        self.x = self.x + STARSHIP_SPEED            screen
        if self.x + self.width > DISPLAY_WIDTH:
            self.x = DISPLAY_WIDTH - self.width

    def move_left(self):
        """ Move the starship left across the screen  """
        self.x = self.x - STARSHIP_SPEED
        if self.x < 0:
            self.x = 0

    def move_up(self):
        """ Move the starship up the screen """
        self.y = self.y - STARSHIP_SPEED
        if self.y < 0:
            self.y = 0

    def move_down(self):
        """ Move the starship down the screen """
        self.y = self.y + STARSHIP_SPEED
        if self.y + self.height > DISPLAY_HEIGHT:
            self.y = DISPLAY_HEIGHT - self.height

    def __str__(self):
        return 'Starship(' + str(self.x) + ', ' + str(self.y)
    ')'
```

This version of the Starship class defines the various move
methods. These methods use a new global value STAR-
SHIP_SPEED to determine how far and how fast the Starship moves. If you want to change the speed that the
Starship moves then you can change this global value.

Depending upon the direction intended we will need to
modify either the x or y coordinate of the Starship.

- If the starship moves to the left then the x coordinate
  is reduced by STARSHIP_SPEED,
- if it moves to the right then the x coordinate is increased

by STARSHIP_SPEED,

- in turn if the Starship moves up the screen then the y coordinate is decremented by STARSHIP_SPEED,
- but if it moves down the screen then the y coordinate is increased by STARSHIP_SPEED.

Of course we do not want our Starship to fly off the edge of the screen and so a test must be made to see if it has reached the boundaries of the screen. Thus tests are made to see if the x or y values have gone below Zero or above the DISPLAY_WIDTH or DISPLAY_HEIGHT values. If any of these conditions are met then the x or y values are reset to an appropriate default.

We can now use these methods with player input. This player input will indicate the direction that the player wants to move the Starship. As we are using the left, right, up and down arrow keys for this we can extend the event processing loop that we have already defined for the main game playing loop. As with the letter q, the event keys are prefixed by the letter K and an under bar, but this time the keys are named K_LEFT, K_RIGHT, K_UP and K_DOWN.

When one of these keys is pressed then we will call the appropriate move method on the starship object already held by the Game object.

The main event processing for loop is now:

```
# Work out what the user wants to do
for event in pygame.event.get():
if event.type ==  pygame.QUIT:
is_running = False
elif event.type ==  pygame.KEYDOWN:
# Check to see which key is pressed
if event.key ==  pygame.K_RIGHT:
# Right arrow key has been pressed
# move the player right
self.starship.move_right()
elif event.key ==  pygame.K_LEFT:
# Left arrow has been pressed
# move the playerleft
self.starship.move_left()
elif event.key ==  pygame.K_UP:
self.starship.move_up()
elif event.key ==  pygame.K_DOWN:
self.starship.move_down()
elif event.key ==  pygame.K_q:
is_running =  False
```

However, we are not quite finished. If we try and run this version of the program we will get a trail of Starships drawn across the screen; for example:

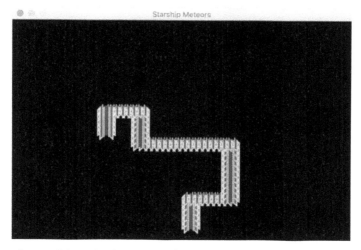

The problem is that we are redrawing the starship at a different position; but the previous image is still present.

We now have two choices one is to merely fill the whole screen with black; effectively hiding anything that has been drawn so far; or alternatively we could just draw over the area used by the previous image position. Which approach is adopted depends on the particular scenario represented by your game. As we will have a lot of meteors on the screen once we have added them; the easiest option is to over- write everything on the screen before redrawing the starship. We will therefore add the following line:

```
    # Clear the screen of current contents
self.display_surfacefi.ll(BACKGROUND)
```

This line is added just before we draw the Starship within the main game playing while loop. Now when we move the Starship the old image is removed before we draw the new image:

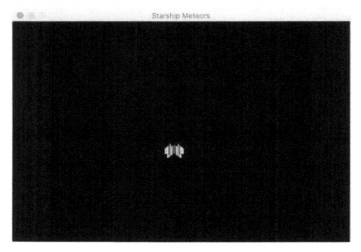

One point to note is that we have also defined another global value BACKGROUND used to hold the background color of the game playing surface. This is set to black as shown below:

```
# fiDene default RGB colours
BACKGROUND = (0, 0, 0)
```

If you want to use a different background color then change this global value.

Adding a Meteor Class

The Meteor class will also be a subclass of the GameObject class. However, it will only provide a move_down() method rather than the variety of move methods of the Starship.

It will also need to have a random startingx coordinate so that when a meteor is added to the game its starting position will vary. This random position can be generated using the random.randint() function using a value between 0 and the width of the drawing surface. The meteor will also start at the top of the screen so will have a different initial coordinate to the Starship. Finally, we also want our meteors to have different speeds; this can be another random number between 1 and some specified maximum meteor speed. To support these we need to add random to the modules being imported and define several new global values, for example:

```
import pygame, random
INITIAL_METEOR_Y_LOCATION = 10
MAX_METEOR_SPEED = 5
We can finowdenethe Meteor class:
class Meteor(GameObject):
"""represents a meteor in the game """
def init    (self, game):
self.game = game
self.x = random.randint(0, DISPLAY_WIDTH)
self.y = INITIAL_METEOR_Y_LOCATION
self.speed = random.randint(1,
MAX_METEOR_SPEED)
self.load_image('meteor.png')
def move_down(self):
"""Move the meteor down the screen """
self.y = self.y + self.speed
```

```
if self.y >  DISPLAY_HEIGHT:
self.y =  5
')'
def   str    (self):
return 'Meteor('+  str(self.x)  +  ', ' +
str(self.y)  +
```

The init () method for the Meteor class has the same steps
as the Starship; the difference is that the x coordinate and
the speed are randomly generated. The image used for the
Meteor is also different as it is 'meteor.png'. We have also
implemented amove_ down() method. This is essentially
the same as the Starships move_down().

Note that at this point we could create a subclass of
GameObject called MoveableGameObject (which extends
GameObject) and push the move operations up into that
class and have the Meteor and Starship classes extend that
class. However we don't really want to allow meteors to
move just anywhere on the screen.

We can now add the meteors to the Game class.We will add
a new global value to indicate the number of initial meteors
in the game:

```
INITIAL_NUMBER_OF_METEORS  =  8
```

Next we will initialize a new attribute for the Game class
that will hold a list of Meteors. We will use a list here as

we want to increase the number of meteors as the game progresses. To make this process easy we will use a list comprehension which allows a for loop to run with the results of an expression captured by the list:

```
# Set up meteors
self.meteors = [Meteor(self) for _ in range(0,
```

INITIAL_NUMBER_OF_METEORS)] We now have a list of meteors that need to be displayed. We thus need to update the while loop of the play() method to draw not only the starship but also all the meteors:

```
# Draw the meteorsand the starship
self.starship.draw()
for meteor  in self.meteors:
meteor.draw()
```

The end result is that a set of meteor objects are created at random starting locations across the top of the screen:

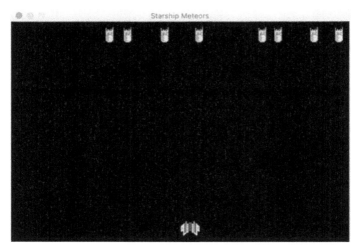

Moving the Meteors

We now want to be able to move the meteors down the screen so that the Starship has some objects to avoid. We can do this very easily as we have already implemented a move_down() method in the Meteor class. We therefore only need to add a for loop to the main game playing while loop that will move all the meteors.For example:

```
# Move the Meteors
for meteor  in self.meteors:
meteor.move_down()
```

This can be added after the event processing for loop and before the screen is refreshed/redrawn or updated. Now when we run the game the meteors move and the player can navigate the Starship between the falling meteors.

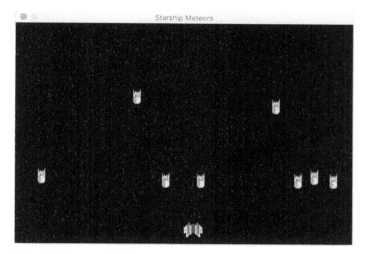

Identifying a Collision

At the moment the game will play for ever as there is no end state and no attempt to identify if a Starship has collided with a meteor. We can add Meteor/Starship collision detection using PyGame Rects. As mentioned in the last chapter a Rect is a PyGame class used to represent rectangular coordinates. It is particularly useful as the pygame.Rect class provides several collision detection methods that can be used to test if one rectangle (or point) is inside another rectangle. We can therefore use one of the methods to test if the rectangle around the Starship intersects with any of the rectangles around the Meteors.

The GameObject class already provides a method rect() that

will return a Rect object representing the objects' current rectangle with respect to the drawing surface (essentially the box around the object representing its location on the screen).

Thus we can write a collision detection method for the Game class using the GameObject generated rects and the Rect class colliderect() method:

```
def _check_for_collision(self):
""" Checks to see if any of the meteors have
collided with the starship"""
result = False
for meteor  in self.meteors:
if
self.starship.rect().colliderect(meteor.rect()):
result = True break
return result
```

Note that we have followed the convention here of preceding the method name with an under bar indicating that this method should be considered private to the class. It should therefore never be called by anything outside of the Game class. This convention is defined in PEP 8 (Python Enhancement Proposal) but is not enforced by the language.

We can now use this method in the main while loop of the game to check for a collision:

```
# Check to see if a meteor has hit the ship
if self._check_for_collision():
```

```
starship_collided = True
```

This code snippet also introduces a new local variable starship_collided. We will initially set this to False and is another condition under which the main game playing while loop will terminate:

```
is_running = True
starship_collided = False

# Main game playing Loop
```

while is_running **and not** starship_collided:

Thus the game playing loop will terminate if the user selects to quit or if the starship collides with a meteor.

Identifying a Win

We currently have a way to loose the game but we don't have a way to win the game! However, we want the player to be able to win the game by surviving for a specified period of time.We could represent this with a timer of some sort. However, in our case we will represent it as a specific number of cycles of the main game playing loop. If the player survives for this number of cycles then they have won. For example:

```
# See if the player has won
if cycle_count == MAX_NUMBER_OF_CYCLES:
```

```
print('WINNER!')
break
```

In this case a message is printed out stating that the player won and then the main game playing loop is terminated (using the break statement). The MAX_NUMBER_OF_CY-CLES global value can be set as appropriate, for example:

```
MAX_NUMBER_OF_CYCLES  =  1000
```

Increasing the Number of Meteors

We could leave the game as it is at this point, as it is now possible to win or loose the game. However, there are a few things that can be easily added that will enhance the game playing experience. One of these is to increase the number of Meteors on the screen making it harder as the game progresses. We can do this using a

```
NEW_METEOR_CYCLE_INTERVAL.
NEW_METEOR_CYCLE_INTERVAL  =  40
```

When this interval is reached we can add a new Meteor to the list of current Meteors; it will then be automatically drawn by the Game class. For example:

```
# Determineif new meteors should be added
if cycle_count  %  NEW_METEOR_CYCLE_INTERVAL  ==
0:
self.meteors.append(Meteor(self))
```

Now every NEW_METEOR_CYCLE_INTERVAL another meteor will be added at a random x coordinate to the game.

Pausing the Game

Another feature that many games have is the ability to pause the game. This can be easily added by monitoring for a pause key (this could be the letter p represented by the event_key pygame.K_p). When this is pressed the game could be paused until the key is pressed again.

The pause operation can be implemented as a method _pause() that will consume all events until the appropriate key is pressed. For example:

```
def _pause(self):
paused  =  True while paused:
for event  in pygame.event.get():
if event.type  ==  pygame.KEYDOWN:
if event.key  ==  pygame.K_p:
paused  =  False break
```

In this method the outer while loop will loop until the paused local variable is set too False. This only happens when the 'p' key is pressed. The break after the statement setting paused to False ensures that the inner for loop is terminated allowing the outer while loop to check the value of paused and terminate.

The_pause() method can be invoked during the game playing cycle by monitoring for the 'p' key within the event for loop and calling the _pause() method from there:

```
elif event.key  ==  pygame.K_p:
self._pause()
```

Note that again we have indicated that we don't expect the _pause() method to be called from outside the game by prefixing the method name with an under bar ('_').

Displaying the Game Over Message

PyGame does not come with an easy way of creating a popup dialog box to display messages such as 'You Won'; or 'You Lost' which is why we have used print statements so far. However, we could use a GUI framework such as wxPython to do this or we could display a message on the display surface to indicate whether the player has won or lost.

We can display a message on the display surface using the pygame.font. Font class. This can be used to create a Font object that can be rendered onto a surface that can be displayed onto the main display surface.

We can therefore add a method _display_message() to the Game class that can be used to display appropriate messages:

```
def _display_message(self,  message):
"""Displays a message to the user on the screen
"""
print(message)
```

```
text_font =
pygame.font.Font('freesansbold.ttf', 48)
text_surface = text_font.render(message, True,
 BLUE, WHITE) text_rectangle =
text_surface.get_rect() text_rectangle.center =
(DISPLAY_WIDTH / 2,
DISPLAY_HEIGHT / 2)
self.display_surface.fill(WHITE)
self.display_surface.blit(text_surface,
text_rectangle)
```

Again the leading under bar in the method name indicates that it should not be called from outside the Game class.

We can now modify the main loop such that appropriate messages are displayed to the user, for example:

```
# Check to see if a meteor has hit the ship
if self._check_for_collision(): starship_collided
 = True self._display_message('Collision: Game
Over')
```

The result of the above code being run when a collision occurs is shown below:

The StarshipMeteors Game

The complete listing for the final version of the Starship-Meteors game is given below:

```
import pygame, random, time
FRAME_REFRESH_RATE = 30
DISPLAY_WIDTH = 600
DISPLAY_HEIGHT = 400
WHITE = (255, 255, 255) BACKGROUND = (0,
0, 0)
INITIAL_METEOR_Y_LOCATION = 10
INITIAL_NUMBER_OF_METEORS = 8
MAX_METEOR_SPEED = 5
STARSHIP_SPEED = 10
MAX_NUMBER_OF_CYCLES = 1000
NEW_METEOR_CYCLE_INTERVAL = 40
class GameObject:
def load_image(self, filename):
```

```python
self.image =
pygame.image.load(filename).convert()
self.width = self.image.get_width()
self.height = self.image.get_height()
def rect(self):
""" Generates a rectangle representing the
objects location
and dimensions """
return pygame.Rect(self.x, self.y, self.width,
self.height)
def draw(self):
""" draw the game object at the current x, y
coordinates """
self.game.display_surface.blit(self.image,
(self.x,
self.y))
class Starship(GameObject):
""" Represents a starship"""
def init    (self, game):
self.game = game
self.x = DISPLAY_WIDTH / 2 self.y =
DISPLAY_HEIGHT - 40
self.load_image('starship.png')
def move_right(self):
""" moves the starship right across the screen """
self.x = self.x + STARSHIP_SPEED
if self.x + self.width > DISPLAY_WIDTH:
self.x = DISPLAY_WIDTH - self.width
def move_left(self):
""" Move the starship left across the screen """
self.x = self.x - STARSHIP_SPEED
if self.x < 0:
self.x = 0
def move_up(self):
""" Move the starship up the screen """
self.y = self.y - STARSHIP_SPEED
if self.y < 0:
```

```python
self.y = 0
def move_down(self):
""" Move the starship down the screen """
self.y = self.y + STARSHIP_SPEED
if self.y + self.height > DISPLAY_HEIGHT:
self.y = DISPLAY_HEIGHT - self.height
')'
def str (self):
return 'Starship(' + str(self.x) + ', ' +
str(self.y) +
class Meteor(GameObject):
""" represents a meteor in the game """
def init (self, game):
self.game = game
self.x = random.randint(0, DISPLAY_WIDTH)
self.y = INITIAL_METEOR_Y_LOCATION
self.speed = random.randint(1,
MAX_METEOR_SPEED)
self.load_image('meteor.png')
def move_down(self):
""" Move the meteor down the screen """
self.y = self.y + self.speed
if self.y > DISPLAY_HEIGHT:
self.y = 5
')'
def str (self):
return 'Meteor(' + str(self.x) + ', ' +
str(self.y) +
class Game:
""" Represents the game itself, holds the main
game playing loop """
def init (self):
pygame.init()
# Set up the display
self.display_surface =
pygame.display.set_mode((DISPLAY_WIDTH,
DISPLAY_HEIGHT))
```

```python
pygame.display.set_caption('Starship Meteors')
# Used for timing within the program.
self.clock = pygame.time.Clock()
# Set up the starship
self.starship = Starship(self)
# Set up meteors
self.meteors = [Meteor(self) for _ in
range(0, INITIAL_NUMBER_OF_METEORS)]
def _check_for_collision(self):
""" Checks to see if any of the meteors have
collided with the starship """
result = False
for meteor in self.meteors:
if
self.starship.rect().colliderect(meteor.rect()):
result = True
break return result
def _display_message(self, message):
""" Displays a message to the user on the screen
""" text_font =
pygame.font.Font('freesansbold.ttf', 48)
text_surface = text_font.render(message, True,
 BLUE,
WHITE)
text_rectangle = text_surface.get_rect()
text_rectangle.center = (DISPLAY_WIDTH / 2,
DISPLAY_HEIGHT / 2)
self.display_surface.fill(WHITE)
self.display_surface.blit(text_surface,
text_rectangle)
def _pause(self): paused = True while paused:
for event in pygame.event.get():
if event.type == pygame.KEYDOWN:
if event.key == pygame.K_p:
paused = False break
def play(self): is_running = True
starship_collided = False cycle_count = 0
```

```python
# Main game playing Loop
while is_running  and not starship_collided:
# Indicates how many times the main game loop has
been run
cycle_count  +=  1
# See if the player has won
if cycle_count  ==  MAX_NUMBER_OF_CYCLES:
self._display_message('WINNER!') break
# Work out what the user wants to do
for event  in pygame.event.get():
if event.type  ==  pygame.QUIT:
is_running  =  False
elif event.type  ==  pygame.KEYDOWN:
# Check to see which key is pressed
if event.key  ==  pygame.K_RIGHT:
# Right arrow key has been pressed
# move the player right
self.starship.move_right()
elif event.key  ==  pygame.K_LEFT:
# Left arrow has been pressed
# move the player left
self.starship.move_left()
elif event.key  ==  pygame.K_UP:
self.starship.move_up()
elif event.key  ==  pygame.K_DOWN:
self.starship.move_down()
elif event.key  ==  pygame.K_p:
self._pause()
elif event.key  ==  pygame.K_q:
is_running  =  False
# Move the Meteors
for meteor  in self.meteors:
meteor.move_down()
# Clear the screen of current contents
self.display_surface.fill(BACKGROUND)
# Draw the meteors and the starship
self.starship.draw()
```

```
for meteor  in self.meteors:
meteor.draw()
# Check to see if a meteor has hit the ship
if self._check_for_collision(): starship_collided
 =  True self._display_message('Collision: Game
Over')
# Determine if new mateors should be added
if cycle_count  %  NEW_METEOR_CYCLE_INTERVAL  ==
 0:
self.meteors.append(Meteor(self))
# Update the display
pygame.display.update()
frames per once)
# Defines the frame rate. The number is number of
# second. Should be called once per frame (but
only
self.clock.tick(FRAME_REFRESH_RATE)
time.sleep(1)
# Let pygame shutdown gracefully
pygame.quit()
def main():
print('Starting Game') game  =  Game() game.play()
print('Game Over')
if_name_== '_main_':
main()
```

Try

Using the example presented in this chapter add the following:

- Provide a score counter. This could be based on the
  number of cycles the player survives or the number of
  meteors that restart from the top of the screen etc.

- Add another type of GameObject, this could be a shooting star that moves across the screen horizontally; perhaps using an random starting y coordinate.
- Allow the game difficulty to be specified at the start. This could affect the number of initial meteors, the maximum speed of a meteor, the number of shooting stars etc.

Introduction to Testing

Introduction to Testing

This chapter considers the different types of tests that you might want to perform with the systems you develop in Python. It also introduces Test Driven Development.

Types of Testing

There are at least two ways of thinking about testing:

1. It is the process of executing a program with the intent of finding errors/bugs (see Glenford Myers, The Art of Software Testing).
2. It is a process used to establish that software components fulfill the requirements identified for them, that is that they do what they are supposed to do.

These two aspects of testing tend to have been emphasized at different points in the software life cycle. Error Testing is an intrinsic part of the development process, and an increasing emphasis is being placed on making testing a central part of software development (see Test Driven Development).

It should be noted that it is extremely difficult—and in many cases impossible— to prove that software works and is completely error free. The fact that a set of tests finds no defects does not prove that the software is error-free. 'Absence of evidence is not evidence of absence!'. This was discussed in the late 1960s and early 1970s by Dijkstra and can be summarized as:

Testing shows the presence, not the absence of bugs

Testing to establish that software components fulfill their contract involves checking operations against their requirements. Although this does happen at development time, it forms a major part of Quality Assurance (QA) and User Acceptance testing. It should be noted that with the advent of Test-Driven Development,the emphasis on testing against requirements during development has become significantly higher.

There are of course many other aspects to testing, for example, Performance Testing which identifies how a system will perform as various factors that affect that system change. For example, as the number of concurrent requests increase, as the number of processors used by the underlying hardware changes, as the size of the database grows etc.

However you view testing, the more testing applied to a

system the higher the level of confidence that the system will work as required.

What Should Be Tested?

An interesting question is 'What aspects of your software system should be subject to testing?'. In general, anything that is repeatable should be subject to formal (and ideally automated) testing. This includes(but is not limited to):

- The build process for all technologies involved.
- The deployment process to all platforms under consideration.
- The installation process for all runtime environments.
- The upgrade process for all supported versions (if appropriate).
- The performance of the system/servers as loads increase.
- The stability for systems that must run for any period of time (e.g. 24 7 systems).
- The backup processes.
- The security of the system.
- The recovery ability of the system on failure.
- The functionality of the system.
- The integrity of the system.

Notice that only the last two of the above list might be what is commonly considered areas that would be subject to testing. However, to ensure the quality of the system under consideration, all of the above are relevant. In fact, testing should cover all aspects of the software development life cycle and not just the QA phase. During requirements gathering testing is the process of looking for missing or ambiguous requirements.

During this phase consideration should also be made with regard to how the overall requirements will be tested, in the final software system.

Test planning should also look at all aspects of the software under test for functionality, usability, legal compliance, conformance to regulatory constraints, security, performance, availability, resilience, etc. Testing should be driven by the need to identify and reduce risk.

Testing Software Systems

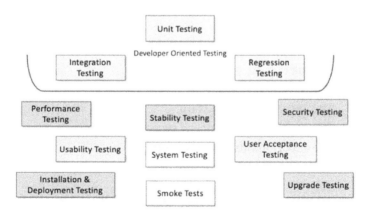

As indicated above there are a number of different types of testing that are commonly used within industry. These types are:

- Unit Testing, which is used to verify the behavior of individual components.
- Integration Testing that tests that when individual components are combined together to provide higher-level functional units, that the combination of the units operates appropriately.
- Regression Testing. When new components are added to a system, or existing components are changed, it is necessary to verify that the new functionality does not break any existing functionality. Such testing is known as Regression Testing.
- Performance Testing is used to ensure that the systems' performance is as required and, within the design parameters, and is able to scale as utilization increases.
- Stability Testing represents a style of testing which attempts to simulate system operation over an extended period of time. For example, for a online shopping application that is expected to be up and running 24 7 a stability test might ensure that with an average load that the system can indeed run 24 hours a day for 7 days a week.
- Security Testing ensures that access to the system is controlled appropriately given the requirements. For example, for an online shopping system there may be different security requirements depending upon whether you are browsing the store, purchasing some products or maintaining the product catalogue.
- Usability Testing which may be performed by a specialist usability group and may involved filming users while they use the system.
- System Testing validates that the system as a whole

actually meets the user requirements and conforms to required application integrity.

- User Acceptance Testing is a form of user oriented testing where users confirm that the system does and behaves in the way they expect.
- Installation, Deployment and Upgrade Testing. These three types of testing validate that a system can be installed and deployed appropriate including any upgrade processes that may be required.
- Smoke Tests used to check that the core elements of a large system operate correctly. They can typically be run quickly and in a faction of the time taken to run the full system tests.

Key testing approaches are discussed in the remainder of this section.

Unit Testing

A unit can be as small as a single function or as large as a subsystem but typically is a class, object,self-contained library (API) or web page. By looking at a small self-contained component an extensive set of tests can be developed to exercise the defined requirements and functionality of the unit.

Unit testing typically follows a white box approach, (also called Glass Box or Structural testing), where the testing utilizes knowledge and understanding of the code and its structure, rather than just its interface (which is known as the black box approach).

In white box testing,test coverage is measured by the number of code paths that have been tested. The goal in unit testing is to provide 100% coverage: to exercise every instruction, all sides of each logical branch,all called objects, handling of all data structures, normal and abnormal termination of all loops etc. Of course this may not always be possible but it is a goal that should be aimed for. Many auto- mated test tools will include a code coverage measure so that you are aware of how much of your code has been exercised by any given set of tests.

Unit Testing is almost always automated—there are many tools to help with this, perhaps the best-known being the xUnit family of test frameworks such as JUnit for Java and PyUnit for Python. The framework allows developers to:

- focus on testing the unit,
- simulate data or results from calling another unit (representative good and bad results)
- create data driven tests for maximum flexibility and repeatability,
- rely on mock objects that represent elements outside the unit that it must interact with.

Having the tests automated means that they can be run frequently, at the very least after initial development and after each change that affects the unit.

Once confidence is established in the correct functioning of one unit, developers can then use it to help test other units with which it interfaces, forming larger units that can also be unit tested or, as the scale gets larger, put through Integration Testing.

Integration Testing

Integration testing is where several units (or modules) are brought together to be tested as an entity in their own right. Typically, integration testing aims to ensure that modules interact correctly and the individual unit developers have interpreted the requirements in a consistent manner.

An integrated set of modules can be treated as a unit and unit tested in much the same way as the constituent modules, but usually working at a "higher" level of functionality. Integration testing is the intermediate stage between unit testing and full system testing.

Therefore, integration testing focuses on the interaction between two or more units to make sure that those units work together successfully and appropriately. Such testing is typically conducted from the bottom up but may also be conducted top down using mocks or stubs to represented called or calling functions. An important point to note is that you should not aim to test everything together at once (so called Big Bang testing) as it is more difficult to isolate bugs in order that they can be rectified. This is why it is more common to find that integration testing has been performed in a bottom up style.

System Testing

System Testing aims to validate that the combination of all the modules, units, data, installation, configuration etc. operates appropriately and meets the requirements specified for the whole system. Testing the system has a whole typically involves testing the top most function-ality or behaviors of the system. Such Behavior Based testing often involves end users and other stake holders who are less technical. To support such tests a range of technologies have evolved that allow a more English style for test descriptions. This style of testing can be used as part of the requirements gathering process and can lead to a Behavior Driven Development (BDD) process. The Python module pytest-bdd provides a BDD style extension to the core pytest framework.

Installation/Upgrade Testing

Installation testing is the testing of full, partial or upgrade install processes. It also validates that the installation and transition software needed to move to the new release for the product is functioning properly. Typically, it

- verifies that the software may be completely unin-stalled through its back-out process.
- determines what files are added, changed or deleted on the hardware on which the program was installed.
- determines whether any other programs on the hard-ware are affected by the new software that has been installed.
- determines whether the software installs and operates properly on all hardware platforms and operating sys-

tems that it is supposed to work on.

Smoke Tests

A smoke test is a test or suite of tests designed to verify that the fundamentals of the system work. Smoke tests may be run against a new deployment or a patched deployment in order to verify that the installation performs well enough to justify further testing. Failure to pass a smoke test would halt any further testing until the smoke tests pass. The name derives from the early days of electronics: If a device began to smoke after it was powered on, testers knew that there was no point in testing it further. For software technologies, the advantages of performing smoke tests include:

- Smoke tests are often automated and standardized from one build to another.
- Because smoke tests validate things that are expected to work, when they fail it is usually an indication that something fundamental has gone wrong (the wrong version of a library has been used) or that a new build has introduced a bug into core aspects of the system.
- If a system is built daily, it should be smoke tested daily.
- It will be necessary to periodically add to the smoke tests as new functionality is added to the system.

Automating Testing

The actual way in which tests are written and executed needs careful consideration. In general, we wish to automate as much of the testing process as is possible as this makes it easy to run the tests and also ensures not only that all tests are run but that they are run in the same way each time. In addition,once an automated test is set up it will typically be quicker to re-run that automated test than to manually repeat a series of tests. However, not all of the features of a system can be easily tested via an automated test tool and in some cases the physical environment may make it hard to automate tests.

Typically, most unit testing is automated and most acceptance testing is manual. You will also need to decide which forms of testing must take place. Most software projects should have unit testing,integration testing, system testing and acceptance testing as a necessary requirement. Not all projects will implement performance or stability testing, but you should be careful about omitting any stage of testing and be sure it is not applicable.

Test Driven Development

Test Driven Development (or TDD) is a development technique whereby developers write test cases before they write any implementation code. The tests thus drive or dictate the code that is developed. The implementation only provides as much functionality as is required to pass the test and thus the tests act as a specification of what the code does (and some argue that the tests are thus part of that specification and provide documentation of what the system is capable of).

TDD has the benefit that as tests must be written first, there are always a set of tests available to perform unit, integration, regression testing etc. This is good as developers can find that writing tests and maintaining tests is boring and of less interest than the actual code itself and thus put less emphasis into the testing regime than might be desirable. TDD encourages, and indeed requires,that developers maintain an exhaustive set of repeatable tests and that those tests are developed to the same quality and standards as the main body of code.

There are three rules of TDD as defined by Robert Martin, these are:

1. You are not allowed to write any production code unless it is to make a failing unit test pass
2. You are not allowed to write any more of a unit test than is sufficient to fail; and compilation failures are failures
3. You are not allowed to write any more production code than is sufficient to pass the one failing unit test.

This leads to the TDD cycle described in the next section.

The TDD Cycle

There is a cycle to development when working in a TDD manner. The shortest form of this cycle is the TDD mantra:

Red /Green /Refactor

Which relates to the unit testing suite of tools where it is possible to write a unit test. Within tools such as PyCharm, when you run a pyunit or pytest test a Test View is shown with Red indicating that a test failed or Green indicating that the test passed. Hence Red/Green, in other words write the test and let it fail, then implement the code to ensure it passes. The last part of this mantra is Refactor which indicates once you have it working make the code cleaner, better, fitter by Refactoring it. Refactoring is the process by which the behavior of the system is not changed but the implementation is altered to improve it.

The full TDD cycle is shown by the following diagram which highlights the test first approach of TDD:

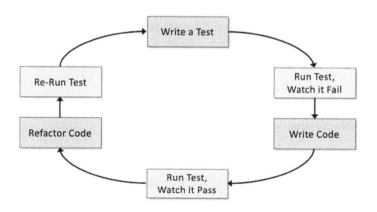

The TDD mantra can be seen in the TDD cycle that is shown

above and described in more detail below:

1. Write a single test.
2. Run the test and see it fail.
3. Implement just enough code to get the test to pass.
4. Run the test and see it pass.
5. Refactor for clarity and deal with any issue of reuse etc.
6. Repeat for next test.

Test Complexity

The aim is to strive for simplicity in all that you do within TDD. Thus, you write a test that fails, then do just enough to make that test pass (but no more). Then you refactor the implementation code (that is change the internals of the unit under test) to improve the code base. You continue to do this until all the functionality for a unit has been completed. In terms of each test, you should again strive for simplicity with each test only testing one thing with only a single assertion per test (although this is the subject of a lot of debate within the TDD world).

Refactoring

The emphasis on refactoring within TDD makes it more than just testing or Test First Development. This focus on refactoring is really a focus on (re)design and incremental improvement. The tests provide the specification of what is needed as well as the verification that existing behavior is maintained, but refactoring leads to better design software.

Thus, without refactoring TDD is not TDD!

Design for Testability

Testability has a number of facets

- Configurability. Set up the object under test to an appropriate configuration for the test
- Controllability.Control the input (and internal state)
- Observability.Observe its output
- Verifiability. That we can verify that output in an appropriate manner.

Testability Rules of Thumb

1. If you cannot test code then change it so that you can!
2. If your code is difficult to validate then change it so that it isn't!
3. Only one concrete class should be tested per Unit test and then Mock the Rest!
4. If you code is hard to reconfigure to work with Mocks then make it so that you code can use Mocks!
5. Design your code for testability!

Book Resources

The Art of Software Testing, G.J. Myers, C. Sandlerand T. Badgett, John Wiley & Sons, 3rd Edition (Dec 2011), 1118031962.

PyTestTesting Framework

Introduction

There are several testing frameworks available for Python, although only one, unit test comes as part of the typical Python installation. Typical libraries include Unit test, (which is available within the Python distribution by default) and PyTest.

In this chapter we will look at PyTest and how it can be used to write unit tests in Python for both functions and classes.

What Is PyTest?

PyTest is a testing library for Python; it is currently one of the most popular Python testing libraries (others include unit test and doc test). PyTest can be used for various levels of testing, although its most common application is as a unit testing framework. It is also often used as a testing framework within a TDD based development project. In fact, it is used by Mozilla and Dropbox as their Python testing framework.

PyTest offers a large number of features and great flexibility in how tests are written and in how set up behavior is defined. It automatically finds test based on naming conventions and can be easily integrated into a range of editors and IDEs including PyCharm.

Setting Up PyTest

You will probably need to set up PyTest so that you can use it from within your environment. If you are using the PyCharm editor, then you will need to add the PyTest module to the current PyCharm project and tell PyCharm that you want to use PyTest to run all tests for you.

A Simple PyTest Example

Something to Test

To be able to explore PyTest we first need something to test; we will therefore define a simple Calculator class. The calculator keeps a running total of the operations performed; it allows a new value to be set and then this value can be added to, or subtracted from, that accumulated total.

```
class Calculator:
def   init (self): self.current = 0 self.total = 0
def set(self, value):
self.current = value
def add(self):
self.total += self.current
```

```
def sub(self):
    self.total -= self.current
def total(self):
    return self.total
```

Save this class into a file called calculator.py.

Writing a Test

We will now create a very simple PyTest unit test for our Calculator class. This test will be defined in a class called test_calculator.py. You will need to import the calculator class we wrote above into your test_calculator.py file (remember each file is a module in Python).

The exact import statement will depend on where you placed the calculator file relative to the test class. In this case the two files are both in the same directory and so we can write:

from calculator **import** Calculator

We will now define a test,the test should be pre-fixed with test_ for PyTest to find them. In fact PyTest uses several conventions to find tests, which are:

- Search for test_*.py or*_test.py files.
- From those files, collect test items:

– test_ prefixed test functions,
  – test_ prefixed test methods inside Test prefixed test classes (without an_init_method).

Note that we keep test files and the files containing the code to be tested separate; indeed in many cases they are kept in different directory structures. This means that there is not chance of developers accidentally using tests in production code etc.

Now we will add to the file a function that defines a test. We will call the function test_add_one; it needs to start with test_ due to the above convention. However, we have tried to make the rest of the function name descriptive, so that its clear what it is testing. The function definition is given below:

```
from calculator import Calculator
def test_add_one():
calc = Calculator() calc.set(1) calc.add()
assert calc.total == 1
```

The test function creates a new instance of the Calculator class and then calls several methods on it; to set up the value to add, then the call to the add() method itself etc.

The final part of the test is the assertion. The assert verifies that the behavior of the calculator is as expected. The PyTest assert statement works out what is being tested and what it should do with the result—including adding information to be added to a test run report. It avoids the need to have to learn a load of assert Something type methods (unlike some other testing frameworks).

Note that a test without an assertion is not a test; i.e. it does not test anything. Many IDEs provide direct support for testing frameworks including PyCharm. For example, PyCharm will now detect that you have written a function with an assert statement in it and add a Run Test icon to the grey area to the left of the editor. This can be seen in the following picture where a green arrow has been added at line 4; this is the 'Run Test' button:

```
calculator.py        test_calculator.py
1        from pythonintro.calculator import Calculator
2
3
4  ▶    def test_add_one():
5            calc = Calculator()
6            calc.set(1)
7            calc.add()
8            assert calc.total == 1
9
```

The developer can click on the green arrow to run the test. They will then be presented with the Run menu that is preconfigured to use PyTest for you:

```
4
5   ▶  Run 'pytest for test_calc...'        ^ ⬆ R
6   ⚙  Debug 'pytest for test_calc...'      ^ ⬆ D
7
```

If the developer now selects the Run option; this will use the PyTest runner to execute the test and collect information about what happened and present it in a PyTest output view at the bottom of the IDE:

Here you can see a tree in the left-hand panel that currently holds the one test defined in the test_calculator.py file. This tree shows whether tests have passed or failed. In this case we have a green tick showing that the test passed.

To the right of this tree is the main output panel which shows the results of running the tests. In this case it shows that PyTest ran only one test and that this was the test_add_one test which was defined in test_calculator.py and that 1 test passed.

If you now change the assertion in the test to check to see that the result is 0 the test will fail. When run, the IDE display will update accordingly.

The tree in the left-hand pane now shows the test as failed while the right-hand pane provides detailed information about the test that failed including where in the test the failed assertion was defined. This is very helpful when trying to debug test failures.

Working with PyTest

Testing Functions

We can test standalone functions as well as classes using
PyTest. For example, given the function increment below
(which merely adds one to any number passed into it):

```
def increment(x):
return x + 1
We can write a PyTest test for this as follows:
def test_increment_integer_3():
assert increment(3) == 4
```

The only real difference is that we have not had to make an instance of a class:

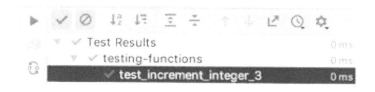

Organizing Tests

Tests can be grouped together into one or more files; PyTest will search for all files following the naming convention (file names that either start or end with 'test') in specified locations:

- If no arguments are specified when PyTest is run then the search for suitably named test files starts from the test paths environment variable (if configured) or the current directory. Alternatively, command line arguments can be used in any combination of directories or filenames etc.
- PyTest will recursively search down into sub directories, unless they match no recurs dirs environment variable.
- In those directories, it will search for files that match the naming conventions test_*.py or*_test.py files.

Tests can also be arranged within test files into Test

classes.Using test classes can be helpful in grouping tests together and managing the setup and tear down behaviors of separate groups of tests. However, the same effect can be achieved by separating the tests relating to different functions or classes into different files.

Test Fixtures

It is not uncommon to need to run some behavior before or after each test or indeed before or after a group of tests. Such behaviors are defined within what is commonly known as test fixtures.

We can add specific code to run:

- at the beginning and end of a test class module of test code (setup_module/teardown_module)
- at the beginning and end of a test class (setup_class/teardown_class) or using the alternate style of the class level fixtures (setup/teardown)
- before and after a test function call (setup_function/teardown_function)
- before and after a test method call (setup_method/teardown_method)

To illustrate why we might use a fixture, let us expand our Calculator test:

```
def test_initial_value(): calc = Calculator()
assert calc.total== 0
def test_add_one():
calc = Calculator() calc.set(1) calc.add()
assert calc.total == 1
def test_subtract_one(): calc = Calculator()
calc.set(1) calc.sub()
assert calc.total == -1
def test_add_one_and_one(): calc = Calculator()
calc.set(1)
calc.add() calc.set(1) calc.add()
assert calc.total == 2
```

We now have four tests to run (we could go further but this is enough for now). One of the issues with this set of tests is that we have repeated the creation of the Calculator object at the start of each test. While this is not a problem in itself it does result in duplicated code and the possibility of future issues in terms of maintenance if we want to change the way a calculator is created. It may also not be as efficient as reusing the Calculator object for each test.

We can however, define a fixture that can be run before each individual test function is executed. To do this we will write a new function and use the pytest.fixture decorator on that function. This marks the function as being special and that it can be used as a fixture on an individual function.

Functions that require the fixture should accept a reference to the fixture as an argument to the individual test function. For example, for a test to accept a fixture called calculator; it should have an argument with the fixture name, i.e.

calculator. This name can then be used to access the object returned. This is illustrated below:

```
import pytest
from calculator import Calculator
@pytest.fixture defcalculator():
"""Returns a Calculatorinstance"""
return Calculator()
def test_initial_value(calculator):
assert calculator.total == 0
def test_add_one(calculator): calculator.set(1)
calculator.add()
assert calculator.total == 1
def test_subtract_one(calculator):
calculator.set(1) calculator.sub()
assert calculator.total == -1
def test_add_one_and_one(calculator):
calculator.set(1) calculator.add()
calculator.set(1) calculator.add()
assert calculator.total == 2
```

In the above code, each of the test functions accepts the calculator fixture that is used to instantiate the Calculator object. We have therefore de-duplicated our code; there is now only one piece of code that defines how a calculator object should be created for our tests. Note each test is supplied with a completely new instance of the Calculator object; there is therefore no chance of one test impacting on another test.

It is also considered good practice to add a doc string to your fixtures as we have done above. This is because PyTest can produce a list of all fixtures available along with their doc strings. From the command line this is done using:

> pytest fixtures

The PyTest fixtures can be applied to functions (as above), classes, modules, packages or sessions. The scope of a fixture can be indicated via the (optional) scope parameter to the fixture decorator. The default is "function" which is why we did not need to specify anything above. The scope determines at what point a fixture should be run. For example, a fixture with 'session' scope will be run once for the test session, a fixture with module scope will be run once for the module (that is the fixture and anything it generates will be shared across all tests in the current module), a fixture with class scope indicates a fixture that is run for each new instance of a test class created etc.

Another parameter to the fixture decorator is auto use which if set to True will activate the fixture for all tests that can see it. If it is set to False (which is the default)then an explicit reference in a test function(or method etc.) is required to activate the fixture.

If we add some additional fixtures to our tests we can see when they are run:

```
import pytest
from calculator import Calculator
@pytest.fixture(scope='session', autouse=True)
def session_scope_fixture():
print('session_scope_fixture')
```

```python
@pytest.fixture(scope='module', autouse=True)
def module_scope_fixture():
print('module_scope_fixture')
@pytest.fixture(scope='class', autouse=True)
def class_scope_fixture():
print('class_scope_fixture')
@pytest.fixture def calculator():
"""Returns a Calculator instance"""
print('calculator fixture')
return Calculator()
def test_initial_value(calculator):
assert calculator.total == 0
def test_add_one(calculator): calculator.set(1)
calculator.add()
assert calculator.total == 1
def test_subtract_one(calculator):
calculator.set(1) calculator.sub()
assert calculator.total == -1
def test_add_one_and_one(calculator):
calculator.set(1) calculator.add()
calculator.set(1) calculator.add()
assert calculator.total == 2
```

If we run this version of the tests, then the output shows when the variousfi

xtures are run:

```
session_scope_fixture module_scope_fixture
class_scope_fixture calculator fixture
.class_scope_fixture calculator fixture
.class_scope_fixture calculator fixture
.class_scope_fixture calculator fixture
```

Parameterized Tests

One common requirement of a test to run the same tests multiple times with several different input values. This can greatly reduce the number of tests that must be defined. Such tests are referred to as parameterized tests; with the parameter values for the test specified using the @pytest .mark.parametrize decorator.

```
@pytest.mark.parametrize decorator.

@pytest.mark.parametrize('input1,input2,expected',
[ (3, 1, 4),
(3, 2, 5),
])
def test_calculator_add_operation(calculator,
input1, input2,expected):
calculator.set(input1)
calculator.add() calculator.set(input2)
calculator.add()
assert calculator.total == expected
```

This illustrates setting up a parameterized test for the Calculator in which two input values are added together and compared with the expected result. Note that the parameters are named in the decorator and then a list of tuples is used to define the values to be used for the parameters. In this case the test_ calculator_add_operation will be run two passing in 3, 1 and 4 and then passing in 3, 2 and 5 for the parameters input1, input2 and expected respectively.

Testing for Exceptions

You can write tests that verify that an exception was raised. This is useful as testing negative behavior is as important as testing positive behavior. For example, we might want to verify that a particular exception is raised when we attempt to withdraw money from a bank account which will take us over our overdraft limit.

To verify the presence of an exception in PyTest use the with statement and pytest.raises. This is a context manager that will verify on exit that the specified exception was raised. It is used as follows:

```
with pytest.raises(accounts.BalanceError):
current_account.withdraw(200.0)
```

Ignoring Tests

In some cases it is useful to write a test for functionality that has not yet been implemented; this may be to ensure that the test is not forgotten or because it helps to document what the item under test should do. However, if the test is run then the test suite as a whole will fail because the test is running against behavior that has yet to be written.

One way to address this problem is to decorate a test with the @pytest.- mark.skip decorator:

```
@pytest.mark.skip(reason='not implemented yet')
def test_calculator_multiply(calculator):
calculator.multiply(2, 3)
assert calculator.total == 6
```

This indicates that PyTest should record the presence of the test but should not try to execute it. PyTest will then note that the test was skipped, for example in PyCharm this is shown using a circle with a line through it.

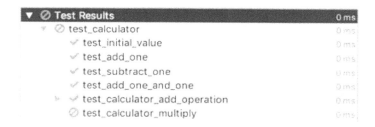

It is generally considered best practice to provide a reason why the test has been skipped so that it is easier to track. This information is also available when PyTest skips the test:

⊘ Tests passed: 6, ignored: 1 of 7 tests – 0 ms

```
s
Skipped: not implemented yet
```

Try

Create a simple Calculator class that can be used for testing purposes. This simple calculator can be used to add, subtract, multiple and divide numbers.

This will be a purely command driven application that will allow the user to specify

- the operation to perform and
- the two numbers to use with that operation.

The Calculator object will then return a result.The same object can be used to repeat this sequence of steps. This general behavior of the Calculator is illustrated below in flow chart form:

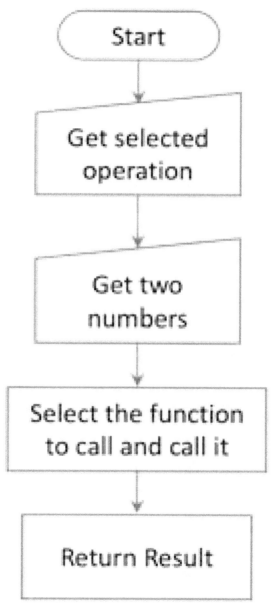

You should also provide a memory function that allows the current result to be added to or subtracted from current memory total. It should also be possible to retrieve the value in memory and clear the memory. Next write a PyTest set of tests for the Calculator class.

Think about what tests you need to write; remember you can't write tests for every value that might be used for an operation; but consider the boundaries, 0, -1, 1, -10, +10 etc.

Of course you also need to consider the cumulative effect of the behavior of the memory feature of the calculator; that is multiple memory adds or memory subtractions and combinations of these.

As you identify tests you may find that you have to update your implementation of the Calculator class. Have you taken into account all input options, for example dividing by zero—what should happen in these situations.

Mocking for Testing

Introduction

Testing software systems is not an easy thing to do; the functions, objects,methods etc. That are involved in any program can be complex things in their own right. In many cases they depend on and interact with other functions, methods and objects; very few functions and methods operate in isolation. Thus the success of failure of a function or method or the overall state of an object is dependent on other program elements.

However, in general it is a lot easier to test a single unit in isolation rather than to test it as part of a larger more complex system. For example, let us take a Python class as a single unit to be tested. If we can test this class on its own we only have to take into account the state of the classes object and the behavior defined for the class when writing our test and determining appropriate outcomes.

However, if that class interacts with external systems such as external services, databases, third party software, data sources etc. Then the testing process becomes more complex:

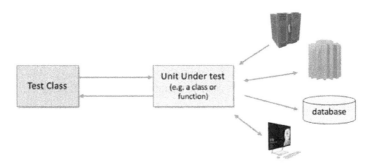

It may now be necessary to verify data updates made to the database,or information sent to a remote service etc. to confirm that the operation of a class's object is correct. This makes not only the software being tested more complex but it also makes the tests themselves more complex. This means that there is greater chance that the test will fail, that the tests will contain bugs or issues themselves and that the test will be harder for someone to understand and maintain. Thus a common objective when writing unit tests or subsystem tests is to be able to test elements/ units in isolation.

The question is how to do this when a function or method relies on other elements?

The key to decoupling functions, methods and objects from other program or system elements is to use mocks. These mocks can be used to decouple one object rom another, one function from another and one system from another; thereby simplifying the testing environment. These mocks are only intended to be used for testing purposes, for example the above scenario could be simplified by mocking out each of the external systems as shown below:

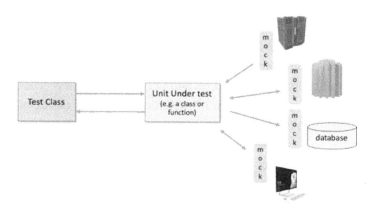

Mocking is not a Python specific concept and there are many mocking libraries available for may different languages. However, in this chapter we will be focusing on the unites.mock library which has been part of the standard Python distribution since Python 3.3.

Why Mock?

A useful first question to consider with regard to mocking, in software testing, is 'Why mock?'. That is, why bother with the concept of a mock in the first place;

why not test with the real thing?

There are several answers to this, some of which are discussed below:

Testing in isolation is easier. As mentioned in the introduction, testing a unit (whether that is a class, a function, a module etc.) is easier in isolation then when dependent on external classes, functions, modules etc.

The real thing is not available. In many cases it is necessary to mock out part of a system or an interface to another system because the real thing is just not available. This could be for several reasons including that it has not been developed yet.In the natural course of software development some parts of a system are likely to be developed and ready for testing before other parts. If one part relies on another part for some element of its operation then the system that is not yet available can be mocked out. In other situations the development team or test team may not have access to the real thing. This may because it is only available within a production context. For example, if a software development house is developing one subsystem it may not have access to another subsystem as it is proprietary and only accessible once the software has been deployed within the client organization.

Real elements can be time consuming. We want our tests to run as quickly as possible and certainly within a Continuous Integration (CI) environment we want them to run fast enough that we can repeatedly test a system throughout the day. In some situations the real thing may take a significant amount of time to process the test scenario. As we want to test our own code we may not be worried about whether a system outside of our control operates correctly or not (at least at this level of testing; it may still be a concern for integration and system testing). We can therefore improve the response times of our tests if we mock out the real system and replace it with a mock that provides much faster response times (possibly because it use scanned responses).

The real thing takes time to set up. In a Continuous Integration (CI) environment, new builds of a system are regularly and repeatedly tested (for example whenever a change is made to their code base). In such situations it may be necessary to configure and deploy the final system to a suitable environment to perform appropriate tests. If an external system is time consuming to configure, deploy and initialize it may be more effective to mock that system out.

Difficult to emulate certain situations. It can be difficult within a test scenario to emulate specific situations. These situations are often related to error or exceptional circum-stances that should never happen within a correctly func-tioning environment. However, it may well be necessary to validate that if such a situation does occur, then the software can deal with that scenario. If these scanners are related to how external (the unit under test) system fail or operate incorrectly then it may be necessary to mock out these systems to be able to generate the scenarios.

We want repeatable tests. By their very nature when you run a test you either want it to pass or fail each time it is run with the same inputs. You certainly do not want tests that pass sometimes and fail other times. This mean that there is no confidence in the tests and people often start ignoring failed tests. This situation can happen if the data provided by systems that a test depends on do not supply repeatable data. This can happen for several different reason but a common cause is because they return real data. Such real data may be subject to change, for example consider a system that uses a data feed for the current exchange rate between funds and dollars. If the associated test confirms that a trade when priced in dollars is correctly converted to funds using the current exchange rate then that test is likely to generate a different result every time it is run. In this situation it would lie better to mock out the current exchange rate service so that a fixed/known exchange rate is used.

The Real System is not reliable enough. In some cases the real system may not be reliable enough itself to allow for repeatable tests. The Real System may not allow tests to be repeated. Finally, the real system may not allow tests to be easily repeated. For example, a test which involves lodging a trade for a certain number of IBM shares with an Trade Order management system may not allow that trade, with those shares, for that customer to be run several times (as it would then appear to be multiple trades). However, for the purposes of testing we may want to test submitting such a trade in multiple different scenarios, multiple times.It may therefore be necessary to mock out the real Order Management System so that such tests can be written.

What Is Mocking?

The previous section gave several reasons to use mocks; the next thing to consider then is what is a mock?

Mocks, including mock functions,methods and mock objects are things that:

- Possess the same interface as the real thing, whether they are mock functions, methods or whole objects. They thus take the same range and types of parameters and return similar information using similar types.
- Define behavior that in some way represents/mimics real exemplar behavior but typically in very controlled ways. This behavior may be hard coed, may really on a set of rules or simplified behavior; may be very simplistic or quiet sophisticated in its own right.

They thus emulate the real system and from outside of the mock may actually appear to be the real system.

In many cases the term mock is used to cover a range of different ways in which the real thing can be emulated; each type of mock has its own characteristics. It is therefore useful to distinguish the different types of mocks as this can help deter- mine the style of mock to be adopted in a particular test situation.

The are different types of Mock including:

- Test Stubs. A test stub is typically a hand coded func-tion, method or object used for testing purposes. The behavior implemented by a test stub may rep- resent a limited sub set of the functionality of the real thing.
- Fakes.Fakes typically provide addition functionality compared with a Test Stub. Fakes may be considered to be a test specific version of the real thing, such as an in memory database used for testing rather than the real database. Such Fakes typically still have some limitations on their functionality, for example when the tests are terminated all data is purged from the in memory database rather than stored permanently on disk.
- Auto generated Test Mocks. These are typically gener-ated automatically using a supporting framework. As part of the set up of the test the expectations associated with the test mock. These expectations may specify the results to return for specific inputs as well as whether the test mock was called etc.
- Test Mock Spy. If we are testing a particular unit and it returns the correct result

we might decided that we do not need to consider the internal behavior of the unit. However, it is common to want to confirm that the test mock was invoked in the way we expected. This helps verify the internal behavior of the unit under test. This can be done using a test mock spy. Such a test mock records how many times it was called and what the parameters used where (as well as other information). The test can then interrogate the test mock to validate that it was invoked as expected/as many times as expected/with the correct parameters etc.

Common Mocking Framework Concepts

As has been mentioned there are several mocking frame-works around for not only Python but other languages such as Java, C# and Scala etc. All of these frameworks have a common core behavior. This behavior allows a mock function, method or object to be created based on the interface presented by the real thing. Of course unlike languages such as C# and Java Python does not have a formal interface concept; however this does not stop the mocking framework from still using the same idea.

In general once a mock has been created it is possible to define how that mock should appear to behave; in general this involves specifying the return result to use fora function or method. It is also possible to verify that the mock has been invoked as expected with the parameters expected.

The actual mock can be added to a test or a set of tests either programmatically or via some form of decorator. In either case for the duration of the test the mock will be used instead of the real thing.

Assertions can then be used to verify the results returned by the unit under test while mock specific methods are typically used to verify (spy on) the methods defined on the mock.

Mocking Frameworks for Python

Due to Python's dynamic nature it is well suited to the construction of mock functions, methods and objects.In fact there are several widely used mocking frameworks available for Python including:

- unittest.mock The unittest.mock (included in the Python distribution from Python 3.3 on wards). This is the default mocking library provided with Python for creating mock objects in Python tests.
- pymox This is a widely used making framework. It is an open source frame- work and has a more complete set of facilities for enforcing the interface of a mocked class.
- Mocktest This is another popular mocking framework. It has its own DSL (Domain Specific Language) to support mocking and a wide set of expectation matching behavior for mock objects.

In the remainder of this chapter we will focus on the unittest.mock library as it is provided as part of the standard Python distribution.

The unittest.mock Library

The standard Python mocking library is the unittest.mock library. It has been included in the standard Python distribution since Python3.3 and provides a simple way to define mocks for unit tests.

The key to the unittest.mock library is the Mock class and its subclass MagicMock. Mock and MagicMock objects can be used to mock functions, methods and even whole classes. These mock objects can have canned responses defined so that when they are involved by the unit under test they will respond appropriately. Existing objects can also have attributes or individual methods mocked allowing an object to be tested with a known state and specified behavior.

To make it easy to work with mock objects, the library provides the
   @unittest.mock.patch() decorator. This decorator can be used to replace real functions and objects with mock instances. The function behind the decorator can also be used as a context manager allowing it to be used in with-as statements providing for fine grained control over the scope of the mock if required.

Mock and Magic Mock Classes

The unittest.mock library provides the Mock class and the MagicMock class. The Mock class is the base class for mock objects. The MagicMock class is a subclass of the Mock class. It is called the MagicMock class as it provides default implementations for several magic method such as ._len_(),
.

str (), and . iter ().

As a simple example consider the following class to be tested:

```
class SomeClass():
def _hidden_method(self):
return 0
def public_method(self, x):
return self.hidden_method() + x
```

This class defines two methods; one is intended as part of the public interface of the class (the public_method()) and one it intended only for internal or private use (the _hidden_method()). Notice that the hidden method uses the convention of preceding its name by an underbar ('_').

Let us assume that we wish to test the behavior of the public_method() and want to mock out the _hidden_method().

We can do this by writing a test that will create a mock object and use this in place of the real _hidden_method(). We could probably use either the Mock class or the MagicMock class for this; however due to the additional functionality provided by the MagicMock class it is common practice to use that class. We will therefore do the same.

The test to be created will be defined within a method within

a test class. The names of the test method and the test class
are by convention descriptive and thus will describe what
is being tested, for example:

```
from unittest.mock  import *
from unittest  import TestCase
from unittest  import main
class test_SomeClass_public_interface(TestCase):
def test_public_method(self):
test_object  =  SomeClass()
# Set up canned response on mock method
test_object._hidden_method  =  MagicMock(name  =
'hidden_method')
test_object._hidden_method.return_value  =  10
# Test the object
result  =  test_object.public_method(5)
self.assertEqual(15,  result,  'return value from
public_method incorrect')
```

In this case note that the class being tested is instantiated
first. The MagicMock is then instantiated and assigned
to the name of the method to be mocked. This in effect
replaces that method for the test_object. TheMagicMock.
The MagicMock object is given a name as this helps with
treating any issues in the report generated by the unites
framework. Following this the canned response from the
mock version of the _hidden_method() is defined; it will
always return the value 10.

At this point we have set up the mock to be used for the test
and are now ready to run the test. This is done in the next
line where the public_method() is called on the test_object

with the parameter 5. The result is then stored.

The test then validates the result to ensure that it is correct; i.e. that the returned value is 15.

Although this is a very simple example it illustrates how a method can be mocked out using the MagicMock class.

The Patchers

The unittest.mock.patch(), unittest.mock.patch.object() and unittest.patch.dict() decorators can be used to simplify the creation of mock objects.

· The patch decorator takes a target for the patch and returns a MagicMock object in its place. It can be used as a TastCase method or class decorator. As a class decorator it decorates each test method in the class automatically.It can also be used as a context manager via the with and with-as statements.
· The patch.object decorator can be provided with either two or three arguments. When given three arguments it will replace the object to be patched, with a mock for the given attribute/method name. When given two arguments the object to be patched is given a default MagicMock object for the specified attribute/function.
· The patch.dict decorator patches a dictionary or dictionary like object.

For example, we can rewrite the example presented in the previous section using the @patch.object decorator to provides the mock object for the _hid- den_method() (it returns a MagicMock linked to SomeClass):

```
class test_SomeClass_public_interface(TestCase):
@patch.object(SomeClass, '_hidden_method')
def test_public_method(self, mock_method):
# Set up cannedresponse
mock_method.return_value =  10
# Createobject to be tested
test_object =  SomeClass()
result =  test_object.public_method(5)
self.assertEqual(15, result, 'return value from
public_methodincorrect')
```

In the above code the _hidden_method() is replaced with a mock version for SomeClass within the test_public_method() method. Note that the mock version of the method is passed in as a parameter to the test method so that the canned response can be specified. You can also use the @patch() decorator to mock a function from a module.

For example, given some external module with a function api_call, we can mock that function out using the @patch() decorator:

```
@patch('external_module.api_call')
def test_some_func(self, mock_api_call):
```

This uses patch() as a decorator and passed the target object's path. The target path was 'external_module.api_call' which consists of the module name and the function to mock.

Mocking Returned Objects

In the examples looked at so far the results returned from the mock functions or methods have been simple integers. However, in some cases the returned values must themselves be mocked as the real system would return a complex object with multiple attributes and methods.

The following example uses a MagicMock object to represent an object returned from a mocked function. This object has two attributes, one is a response code and the other is a JSON string.JSON stands for the JavaScript Object Notation and is a commonly used format in web services.

```python
import external_module
from unittest.mock import *
from unittest import TestCase from unittest
import main import json
def some_func():
# Calls out to external API - which we want to
mock
response = external_module.api_call()
return responseclass
test_some_func_calling_api(TestCase):
class test_some_func_calling_api(TestCase):
@patch('external_module.api_call')
def test_some_func(self, mock_api_call):
# Sets up mock version of api_call
mock_api_call.return_value =
MagicMock(status_code=200,
response=json.dumps({'key':'value'}))
```

```
# Calls some_func() that calls the (mock)
api_call()
function
result  =  some_func()
# Check that the result returned from some_func()
is what was expected
self.assertEqual(result.status_code,  200,
"returned status code is not 200")
self.assertEqual(result.response,  '{"key":
"value"}',
"response JSON incorrect")
```

In this example the function being tested is some_func() but some_func() calls out to the mocked function external_module.api_call(). This mocked function returns a MagicMock object with a pre-specified status_code and response. The assertions then validate that the object returned by some_func() contains the correct status code and response.

Validating Mocks Have Been Called

Using unittest.mock it is possible to validate that a mocked function or method was called appropriately using assert_called(), assert_ - called_with() or assert_called_once_with() depending on whether the function takes parameters or not.

The following version of the test_some_func_with_params() test method verifies that the mock api_call() function was called with the correct parameter.

```
@patch('external_module.api_call_with_param')
def test_some_func_with_param(self,
mock_api_call):
# Sets up mock version of api_call
mock_api_call.return_value  =
MagicMock(status_code=200,
response=json.dumps({'age':  '23'}))
result  =  some_func_with_param('Phoebe')
# Check result returned from some_func() is what
was expected
self.assertEqual(result.response,  '{age":
"23"}',  'JSON
result incorrect')
# Verify that the mock_api_call was called with
the correct params
mock_api_call.api_call_with_param.assert_called_with('Phoebe'
```

If we wished to validate that it had only been called once
we could use the assert_called_once_with() method.

Mock and Magic Mock Usage

Naming Your Mocks

It can be useful to give your mocks a name. The name is
used when the mock appears in test failure messages. The
name is also propagated to attributes or methods of the
mock:

```
mock  =  MagicMock(name='foo')
```

Mock Classes

As well as mocking an individual method on a class it is possible to mock a whole class. This is done by providing the patch() decorator with the name of the class to patch (with no named attribute/method). In this case the while class is replaced by a MagicMock object. You must then specify how that class should behave.

```
import people
from unittest.mock import * from unittest  import
TestCase from unittest  import main
class MyTest(TestCase):
@patch('people.Person')
def test_one(self, MockPerson):
self.assertIs(people.Person,  MockPerson)
instance  =  MockPerson.return_value
instance.calculate_pay.return_value  =  250.0
payroll  =  people.Payroll()
result  =  payroll.generate_payslip(instance)
self.assertEqual('You earned 250.0',  result,
'payslip incorrect')
```

In this example the people.Person class has been mocked out. This class has a method calculate_pay() which is being mocked here. The Payroll class has a method generate_payslip() that expects to be given a Person object. It then uses the information provided by the person objects calculate_pay() method to generate the string returned by the generate_payslip() method.

Attributes on Mock Classes

Attributes on a mock object can be easily defined, for

example if we want to set an attribute on a mock object then we can just assign a value to the attribute:

```python
import people
from unittest.mock  import *
from unittest  import TestCase
class MyTest(TestCase):
@patch('people.Person')
def test_one(self, MockPerson):
self.assertIs(people.Person,  MockPerson)
instance  =  MockPerson.return_value
instance.age=  24
instance.name  =  'Adam'
self.assertEqual(24,  instance.age,  'age
incorrect')
self.assertEqual('Adam',  instance.name,  'name
incorrect')
```

In this case the attribute age and name have been added to the mock instance of the people.Person class.

If the attribute itself needs to be a mock object then all that is required is to assign a MagicMock (or Mock) object to that attribute:

```python
instance.address  =  MagicMock(name='Address')
```

Mocking Constants

It is very easy to mock out a constant; this can be done using the @patch() decorator and proving the name of the constant and the new value to use. This value can be a literal value such as 42 or 'Hello' or it can be a mock object itself (such as a MagicMock object). For example:

```
@patch('mymodule.MAX_COUNT', 10)
def test_something(self):
# Test  can  now  use  mymodule.MAX_COUNT
```

Mocking Properties

It is also possible to mock Python properties. This is done again using the @patch decorator but using the unittest.mock.PropertyMock class and the new_callable parameter. For example:

```
@patch('mymoule.Car.wheels',
new_callable=mock.PropertyMock)
def test_some_property(self,  mock_wheels):
mock_wheels.return_value  =  6
# Rest  of  test  method
```

Raising Exceptions with Mocks

A very useful attribute that can be specified when a mock object is created is the side_effect. If you set this to an exception class or instance then the exception will be raised when the mock is called, for example:

```
mock = Mock(side_effect=Exception('Boom!'))
mock()
```

This will result in the Exception being raised when the mock() is invoked.

Applying Patch to Every Test Method

If you want to mock out something for every test in a test class then you can decorate the whole class rather than each individual method. The effect of decorating the class is that the patch will be automatically applied to all test methods in the class (i.e. To all methods starting with the word 'test'). For example:

```
import people
from unittest.mock import *
from unittest import TestCase
from unittest import main
@patch('people.Person')
class MyTest(TestCase):
def test_one(self, MockPerson):
self.assertIs(people.Person, MockPerson)
def test_two(self, MockSomeClass):
self.assertIs(people.Person, MockSomeClass)
def do_something(self):
return 'something'
```

In the above test class, the tests test_one and test_two are supplied with the mock version of the Person class. However the do_something() method is not affected.

Using Patch as a Context Manager

The patch function can be used as a context manager. This gives fine grained control over the scope of the mock object.

In the following example the the test_one() method contains a with-as statement that we used to patch (mock) the person class as MockPerson. This mock class is only available within the with-as statement.

```
import people
from unittest.mock import * from unittest  import
TestCase from unittest  import main
class MyTest(TestCase):
def test_one(self):
with patch('people.Person')  as MockPerson:
self.assertIs(people.Person,  MockPerson)
instance  =  MockPerson.return_value
instance.calculate_pay.return_value  =  250.0
payroll  =  people.Payroll()
result  =  payroll.generate_payslip(instance)
self.assertEqual('You earned 250.0',  result,
'payslip incorrect')
```

Mock Where You Use It

The most common error made by people using the unittest.mock library is mocking in the wrong place. The rule is that you must mock out where you are going to use it; or to put it another way you must always mock the real thing where it is imported into, not where it's imported from.

Patch Order Issues

It is possible to have multiple patch decorators on a test method. However, the order in which you define the patch decorators is significant. The key to understanding what the order should be is to work backwards so that when the mocks are passed into the test method they are presented to the right parameters. For example:

```
@patch('mymodule.sys')
@patch('mymodule.os')
@patch('mymodule.os.path')
def test_something(self, mock_os_path, mock_os,
mock_sys):
# The rest of the test method
```

Notice that the last patch's mock is passed into the second parameter passed to the test_something() method (self is the first parameter to all methods). In turn the first patch's mock is passed into the last parameter. Thus the mocks are passed into the test method in the reverse order to that which they are defined in.

How Many Mocks?

An interesting question to consider is how many mocks should you use per test?

This is the subject or a lot of debate within the software testing community. The general rules of thumb around this topic are given below, however it should be borne in mind that these are guidelines rather than hard and fast rules.

- Avoid more than 2 or 3 mocks per test. You should avoid more than 2–3 mocks as the mocks themselves the get harder to manage. Many also consider that if you need more then 2–3 mocks per test then there are probably some underlying design issues that need to be considered. For example, if you are testing a Python class then that class may have too many dependencies. Alternatively the class may have too many responsibilities and should be broken down into several independent classes; each with a distinct re-sponsibility. Another cause might be that the class's behavior may not be encapsulated enough and that you are allowing other elements to interact with the class in more informal ways (i.e. The interface between the class and other elements is not clean/exploit enough). The result is that it may be necessary to refactor your class before progressing with your development and testing.
- Only Mock you Nearest Neighbor. You should only ever mock your nearest neighbor whether that is a function,method or object. You should try to avoid mocking dependencies of dependencies. If you find yourself doing this then it will become harder to con-figure, maintain, understand and develop. It is also increasingly likely that you are testing the mocks rather than your own function, method or class.

Mocking Considerations

The following provide some rules of thumb to consider when using mocks with your tests:

- Don't over mock—if you do then you can end up just testing the mocks themselves.
- Decide what to mock, typical examples of what to mock include those elements that are not yet available, those elements that are not by default repeatable (such as live data feeds) or those elements of the system that are time consuming or complex.
- Decide where to mock such as the interfaces for the unit under test. You want to test the unit so any interface it has with another system, function, class might be a candidate for a mock.
- Decide when to mock so that you can determine the boundaries for the test.
- Decide how you will implement your mocks. For example you need to consider which mocking framework(s) you will use or how to mock larger components such as a database

Try

One of the reasons for mocking is to ensure that tests are repeatable. In this exercise we will mock out the use of a random number generate to ensure that our tests can bee easily repeated.

The following program generates a deck of cards and randomly picks a card from the deck:

```
import random
def create_suite(suite):
return [ (i, suite) for i in range(1, 14)]
def pick_a_card(deck):
print('You picked')
position = random.randint(0, 52)
print(deck[position][0], "of",
deck[position][1]) return (deck[position])
# Set up the data
hearts = create_suite('hearts') spades =
create_suite('spades') diamonds =
create_suite('diamonds') clubs =
create_suite('clubs')
# Make the deck of cards
deck = hearts + spades + diamonds + clubs
# Randomlypick from the deck of cards
card = pick_a_card(deck)
Each time the program is run a different card is
picked, for example in two con- secutive runs the
followingoutput is obtained:
You picked
13 of clubs
You picked
1 of hearts
```

We now want to write a test for the pick_a_card() function. You should mock out the random.randint() function to do this.

Introduction to Files, Paths and IO

Introduction

The operating system is a critical part of any computer systems. It is comprised of elements that manage the processes that run on the CPU, how memory is utilized and managed, how peripheral devices are used (such as printers and scanners), it allows the computer system to communicate with other systems and it also provide support for the file system used.

The File System allows programs to permanently store data. This data can then be retrieved by applications at a later date; potentially after the whole computer has been shut down and restarted.

The File Management System is responsible for managing the creation, access and modification of the long term storage of data in files. This data may be stored locally or remotely on disks, tapes, DVD drives, USB drives etc.

Although this was not always the case; most modern operating systems organize files into a hierarchical structure, usually in the form of an inverted tree. For example in the following diagram the root of the directory structure is shown as '/'. This root directory holds six sub directories. In turn the Users sub directory holds 3 further directories and so on:

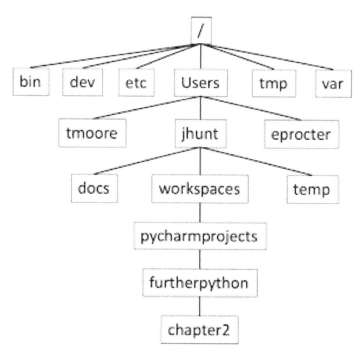

Each file is contained within a directory (also known as a folder on some operating systems such as Windows). A directory can hold zero or more files and zero or more directories.

For any give directory there are relationships with other directories as shown below for the directory jhunt:

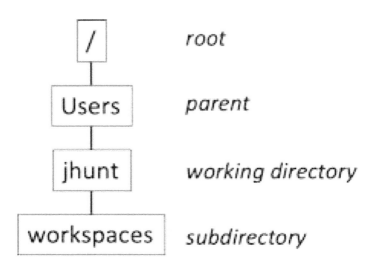

The root directory is the starting point for the hierarchical directory tree structure. A child directory of a given directory is known as a sub directory. The directory that holds the given directory is known as the parent directory. At any one time, the directory within which the program or user is currently working, is known as the current working directory.

A user or a program can move around this directory structure as required. To do this the user can typically either issue a series of commands at a terminal or command

window. Such as cd to change directory or pwd to print the
working directory. Alternatively Graphical User Interfaces
(GUIs) to operating systems usually include some form of
file manager application that allows a user to view the file
structure in terms of a tree. The Finder program for the
Mac is shown below with a tree structure displayed for a
pycharm projects directory. A similar view is also presented
for the Windows Explorer program.

File Attributes

A file will have a set of attributes associated with it such
as the date that it was created, the date it was last updat-
ed/modified, how large the file is etc. It will also typically

have an attribute indicating who the owner of the file is. This may be the creator of the file; however the ownership of a file can be changed either from the command line or through the GUI interface. For example, on Linux and Mac OS X the command chown can be used to change the file ownership.

It can also have other attributes which indicate who can read, write or execute the file. In Unix style systems (such as Linux and Mac OS X) these access rights can be specified for the file owner, for the group that the file is associated with and for all other users.

The file owner can have rights specified for reading, writing and executing a file. These are usually represented by the symbols 'r', 'w' and 'x' respectively. For example the following uses the symbolic notation associated with Unix files and indicates that the file owner is allowed to read, write and execute a file:

```
-RWX-----
```

Here the first dash is left blank as it is to do with special files (or directories), then the next set of three characters represent the permissions for the owner, the following set of three the permissions for all other users. As this example has *rwx* in

the first group of three characters this indicates that the user can read 'r', write 'w' and execute 'x' the file. However the next six characters are all dashes indicating that the group and all other users cannot access the file at all. The group that a file belongs to is a group that can have any number of users as members. A member of the group will have the access rights as indicated by the group settings on the file. As for the owner of a file these can be to read, write or execute the file. For example, if group members are allowed to read and execute a file, then this would be shown using the symbolic notation as:

```
---r-x--
```

Now this example indicates that only members of the group can read and execute the file; note that group members cannot write the file (they therefore cannot modify the file).

If a user is not the owner of a file, nor a member of the group that the file is part of, then their access rights are in the 'everyone else' category. Again this category can have read, write or execute permissions. For example, using the symbolic notation, if all users can read the file but are not able to do anything else, then this would be shown as:

```
----r-
```

Of course a file can mix the above permissions together, so that an owner may be allowed to read, write and execute a file, the group may be able to read and execute the file but all other users can only read the file. This would be shown as:

```
-rwx-xr--
```

In addition to the symbolic notation there is also a numeric notation that is used with Unix style systems. The numeric notation uses three digits to represent the permissions. Each of the three rightmost digits represents a different component of the permissions: owner, group, and others.

Each of these digits is the sum of its component bits in the binary numeral system. As a result, specific bits add to the sum as it is represented by a numeral:

- The read bit adds 4 to its total (in binary 100),
- The write bit adds 2 to its total (in binary 010), and
- The execute bit adds 1 to its total (in binary 001).
- This the following symbolic notations can be represented by an equivalent numeric notation:

Symbolic notation	Numeric notation	Meaning
rwx———	0700	Read, write, and execute only for owner
-rwxrwx—	0770	Read, write, and execute for owner and group
-rwxrwxrwx	0777	Read, write, and execute for owner, group and others

A path is a particular combination of directories that can lead to a specific sub directory or file.

This concept is important as Unix/Linux/Max OS X and Windows file systems represent an inverted tree of directories and files., It is thus important to be able to uniquely reference locations with the tree.

For example, in the following diagram the path/Users/jhunt/work-spaces/pycharmprojects/furtherpython/chapter2   is highlighted:

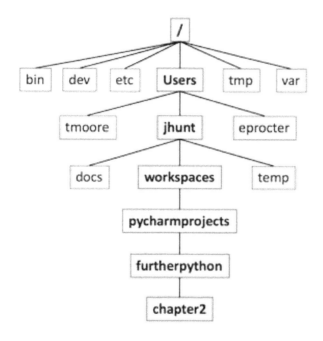

Path: /Users/jhunt/workspaces/pycharmprojects/furtherpython/chapter2

A path may be absolute or relative. An absolute path is one which provides a complete sequence of directories from the root of the file system to a specific sub directory or file.

A relative path provides a sequence from the current working directory to a particular sub directory or file.

The absolute path will work wherever a program or user is currently located within the directory tree. However, a relative path may only be relevant in a specific location.

For example, in the following diagram, the relative path py-charmprojects/furtherpython/chapter2 is only meaningful relative to the directory workspace:

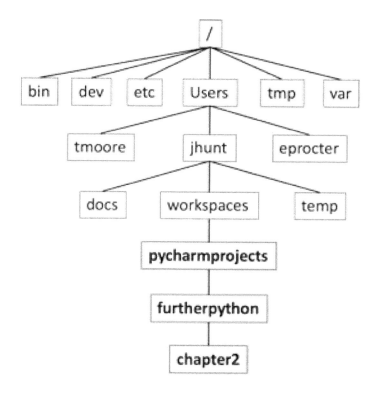

Relative path: pycharmprojects/furtherpython/chapter2

Note that an absolute path starts from the root directory (represented by '/') where as a relative path starts from a particular sub directory (such as pycham projects).

File Input/Output

File Input/Output (often just referred to as File I/O) involves reading and writing data to and from files. The data being written can be in different formats.

For example a common format used in Unix/Linux and Windows systems is the ASCII text format. The ASCII format (or American Standard Code for Information Interchange) is a set of codes that represent various characters that is widely used by operating systems. The following table illustrates some of the ASCII character codes and what they represent:

Decimal code	Character	Meaning
42	*	Asterisk
43	+	Plus
48	0	Zero
49	1	One
50	2	Two
51	3	Three
65	A	Uppercase A
66	B	Uppercase B
67	C	Uppercase C
68	D	Uppercase D

(continued)

(continued)

Decimal code	Character	Meaning
97	a	Lowercase a
98	b	Lowercase b
99	c	Lowercase c
100	d	Lowercase d

ASCII is a very useful format to use for text files as they can be read by a wide range of editors and browsers. These editors and browsers make it very easy to create human readable files. However, programming languages such as Python often use a different set of character encoding such as a Unicode character encoding (such as UTF-8). Unicode is another standard for representing characters using various codes. Unicode encoding systems offer a wider range of possible character encoding than ASCII, for example the latest version of Unicode in May 2019, Unicode 12.1, contains a repertoire of 137,994 characters covering 150 modern and historic scripts, as well as multiple symbol sets and emojis.

However, this means that it can be necessary to translate ASCII into Unicode (e.g. UTF-8) and vice versa when reading and writing ASCII files in Python.

Another option is to use a binary format for data in a file. The advantage of using binary data is that there is little or no translation required from the internal representation of the data used in the Python program into the format stored in the file. It is also often more concise than an equivalent ASCII format and it is quicker for a program to read and write and takes up less disk space etc. However, the down side of a binary format is that it is not in an easily human readable format. It may also be difficult for other programs, particularly those written in other programming languages such as Java or C#, to read the data in the files.

Sequential Access Versus Random Access

Data can be read from (or indeed written to) a file either sequentially or via a random access approach.

Sequential access to data in a file means that the program reads (or writes) data to a file sequentially, starting at the beginning of a file and processing the data an item at a time until the end of the file is reached.The read process only ever moves forward and only to the next item of data to read.

Random Access to a data file means that the program can read (or write) data anywhere into the file at any time. That is the program can position itself at a particular point in the file (or rather a pointer can be positioned within the file) and it can then start to read (or write) at that point. If it is reading then it will read the next data item relative to the pointer rather than the start of the file. If it is writing data then it will write data from that point rather than at the end of the file. If there is already data at that point in the file then it will be over written. This type of access is also known as Direct Access as the computer program needs to know where the data is stored within the file and thus goes directly to that location for the data. In some cases the location of the data is recorded in an index and thus is also known as indexed access.

Sequential file access has advantages when a program needs to access information in the same order each time the data is read. It is also is faster to read or write all the data sequentially than via direct access as there is no need to move the file pointer around.

Random access files however are more flexible as data does not need to be written or read in the order in which it is obtained. It is also possible to jump to just the location of the data required and read that data (rather than needing to sequentially read through all the data to find the data items of interest).

Files and I/O in Python

In the remainder of this section of the book we will explore the basic facilities provided for reading and writing files in Python.We will also look at the underlying streams model for file I/O. After this we will explore the widely used CSV and Excel file formats and libraries available to support those. This section concludes by exploring the Regular Expression facilities in Python. While this last topic is not strictly part of file I/O it is often used to parse data read from files to screen out unwanted information.

Reading and Writing Files

Introduction

Reading data from and writing data to a file is very common within many programs. Python provides a large amount of support for working with files of various types. This chapter introduces you to the core file IO functionality in Python.

Obtaining References to Files

Reading from, and writing to, text files in Python is relatively straightforward.The built in open() function creates a file object for you that you can use to read and/ or write data from and/ or to a file.

The function requires as a minimum the name of the file you want to work with. Optionally you can specify the access mode (e.g. read, write, append etc.). If you do not specify a mode then the file is open in read-only mode. You can also specify whether you want the interactions with the file to be buffered which can improve performance by grouping data reads together.

The syntax for the open() function is

```
file_object = open(file_name, access_mode,
buffering)
```

Where

- file_name indicates the file to be accessed.
- access_mode The access_mode determines the mode in which the file is to be opened, i.e. read, write, append, etc. A complete list of possible values is given below in the table.This is an optional parameter and the default file access mode is read (r).
- buffering If the buffering value is set to 0, no buffering takes place. If the buffering value is 1, line buffering is performed while accessing a file.

The access_mode values are given in the following table.

Mode	Description
r	Opens a file for reading only. The file pointer is placed at the beginning of the file. This is the default mode
rb	Opens a file for reading only in binary format. The file pointer is placed at the beginning of the file. This is the default mode
r+	Opens a file for both reading and writing. The file pointer placed at the beginning of the file
rb+	Opens a file for both reading and writing in binary format. The file pointer placed at the beginning of the file
w	Opens a file for writing only. Overwrites the file if the file exists. If the file does not exist, creates a new file for writing
wb	Opens a file for writing only in binary format. Overwrites the file if the file exists. If the file does not exist, creates a new file for writing
w+	Opens a file for both writing and reading. Overwrites the existing file if the file exists. If the file does not exist, creates a new file for reading and writing
wb+	Opens a file for both writing and reading in binary format. Overwrites the existing file if the file exists. If the file does not exist, creates a new file for reading and writing
a	Opens a file for appending. The file pointer is at the end of the file if the file exists. That is, the file is in the append mode. If the file does not exist, it creates a new file for writing
ab	Opens a file for appending in binary format. The file pointer is at the end of the file if the file exists. That is, the file is in the append mode. If the file does not exist, it creates a new file for writing
a+	Opens a file for both appending and reading. The file pointer is at the end of the file if the file exists. The file opens in the append mode. If the file does not exist, it creates a new file for reading and writing
ab+	Opens a file for both appending and reading in binary format. The file pointer is at the end of the file if the file exists. The file opens in the append mode. If the file does not exist, it creates a new file for reading and writing

The file object itself has several useful attributes such as

- file.closed returns True if the file has been closed (can no longer be accessed because the close() method has been called on it).
- file.mode returns the access mode with which the file was opened.
- file.name The name of the file.

The file.close() method is used to close the file once you have finished with it.This will flush any unwritten information to the file (this may occur because of buffering) and will close the reference from the file object to the actual underlying operating system file. This is important to do as leaving a reference to a file open can cause problems in larger applications as typically there are only a certain number of file references possible at one time and over a long period of time these may all be used up resulting in future errors being thrown as files can no longer be opened.

The following short code snippet illustrates the above ideas:

```
file = open('myfile.txt', 'r+')
print('file.name:', file.name)
print('file.closed:', file.closed)
print('file.mode:', file.mode) file.close()
print('file.closed now:', file.closed)
```

The output from this is:
  file.name: myfile.txt
  file.closed: False
  file.mode: r+
  file.closed now: True

Reading Files

Of course, having set up a file object we want to be able to either access the contents of the file or write data to that file (or do both). Reading data from a text file is supported by the read(), readline() and readlines() methods:

· The read() method This method will return the entire contents of the file as a single string.

- The readline() method reads the next line of text from a file. It returns all the text on one line up to and including the newline character. It can be used to read a file a line at a time.
- The readlines() method returns a list of all the lines in a file, where each item of the list represents a single line.

Note that once you have read some text from a file using one of the above operations then that line is not read again. Thus using readlines() would result in a further readlines() returning an empty list whatever the contents of the file.

The following illustrates using the readlines() method to read all the text in a text file into a program and then print each line out in turn:

```
file  =  open('myfile.txt',  'r')
lines = file.readlines()
for line  in lines:
print(line,  end='')
file.close()
```

Notice that within the for loop we have indicated to the print function that we want the end character to be ' ' rather than a newline; this is because the line string already possesses the newline character read from the file.

File Contents Iteration

As suggested by the previous example; it is very common to want to process the contents of a file one line at a time. In fact Python makes this extremely easy by making the file object support iteration. File iteration accesses each line in the file and makes that line available to the for loop. We can therefore write:

```
file = open('myfile.txt', 'r')
for line in file:
print(line, end='')
file.close()
```

It is also possible to use the list comprehension to provide a very concise way to load and process lines in a file into a list. It is similar to the effect of readlines() but we are now able to preprocess the data before creating the list:

```
file = open('myfile.txt', 'r')
lines = [line.upper() for line in file]
file.close()
print(lines)
```

Writing Data to Files

Writing a string to a file is supported by the write() method. Of course, the file object we create must have an access mode that allows writing (such as 'w'). Note that the write method does not add a newline character (represented as '\n') to the end of the string—you must do this manually.

An example short program to write a text file is given below:

```
print('Writing file')
f = open('my-new-file.txt', 'w') f.write('Hello
from Python!!\n')f.write('Working with files is
easy...\n') f.write('It is cool ...\n')
f.close()
```

This creates a new file called my-new-file.txt. It then writes three strings to the file each with a newline character on the end; it then closes the file.

The effect of this is to create a new file called myfile.txt with three lines in it:

Using Files and with Statements

Like several other types where it is important to shut down resources; the file object class implements the Context Manager Protocol and thus can be used with the with statement. It is therefore common to write code that will open a file using the with as structure thus ensuring that the file will be closed when the block of code is finished with, for example:

```
with open('my-new-file.txt','r') as f:
lines  =  file.readlines()
for line in lines:
print(line,  end='')
```

The File input Module

In some situations, you may need to read the input from several files in one go. You could do this by opening each file independently and then reading the contents and appending that contents to a list etc. However, this is a common enough requirement that the file input module provides a function file input.input() that can take a list of files and treat all the files as a single input significantly simplifying this process, for example:

```
with fileinput.input(files=('spam.txt',
'eggs.txt')) as f:
for line in f:
process(line)
```

Features provided by the file input module include

- Return the name of the file currently being read.
- Return the integer "file descriptor" for the current file.
- Return the cumulative line number of the line that has just been read.
- Return the line number in the current file. Before the first line has been read this returns o.
- A boolean function that indicates if the current line just read is the first line of its file

Some of these are illustrated below:

```
with fileinput.input(files=('textfile1.txt',
'textfile2.txt')) as f:
line  =  f.readline()
print('f.filename():',  f.filename())
print('f.isfirstline():',  f.isfirstline())
print('f.lineno():',
f.lineno())print('f.filelineno():',
f.filelineno()) for line in f:
print(line,  end='')
```

Renaming Files

A file can be renamed using the os.rename() function. This function takes two arguments, the current filename and the new filename. It is part of the Python os module which provides methods that can be used to perform a range of file-processing operations (such as renaming a file). To use the module, you will first need to import it. An example of using the rename function is given below:

```
import os
os.rename('myfileoriginalname.txt','
myfilenewname.txt')
```

Deleting Files

A file can be deleted using the os.remove() method. This method deletes the file specified by the file name passed to it. Again, it is part of the os module and therefore this must be imported first:

```
import os
os.remove('somefilename.txt')
```

Random Access Files

All the examples presented so far suggest that files are accessed sequentially, with the first line read before the second and so on. Although this is (probably) the most common approach it is not the only approach supported by Python; it is also possible to use a random-access approach to the contents within a file.

To understand the idea of random file access it is useful to understand that we can maintain a pointer into a file to indicate where we are in that file in terms of reading or writing data. Before anything is read from a file the pointer is before the beginning of the file and reading the first line of text would for example, advance the point to the start of the second line in the file etc. This idea is illustrated below:

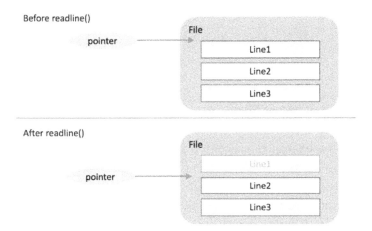

When randomly accessing the contents of a file the pro-grammer manually moves the pointer to the location re-quired and reads or writes text relative to that pointer. This means that they can move around in the file reading and writing data.

The random-access aspect of a file is provided by the seek method of the file object:

- file.seek (offset, whence) this method determines where the next read or write operation (depending on the mode used in the open() call) takes place.

In the above the offset parameter indicates the position of the read/write pointer within the file. The move can also be forwards or backwards (represented by a negative offset). The optional whence parameter indicates where the offset is relative to. The values used for whence are:

- 0 indicates that the offset is relative to start of file (the default).
- 1 means that the offset is relative to the current pointer position.
- 2 indicates the offset is relative to end of file.

Thus, we can move the pointer to a position relative to the start of the file, to the end of the file, or to the current position.

For example, in the following sample code we create a new text file and write a set of characters into that file. At this point the pointer is positioned after the 'z' in the file. However, we then use seek() to move the point to the 10th character in the file and now write 'Hello', next we reposition the pointer to the 6th character in the file and write out 'BOO'. We then close the file. Finally,we read all the lines from the file using a with as statement and the open() function and from this we will see that the text is the file is now abcdefBOOjHELLOpqrstuvwxyz:

```
f = open('text.txt',
'w')f.write('abcdefghijklmnopqrstuvwxyz\n')
f.seek(10,0)
f.write('HELLO') f.seek(6, 0) f.write ('BOO')
f.close()
with open('text.txt', 'r') as f:
for line in f:
```

```
print(line,  end='')
```

Directories

Both Unix like systems and Windows operating systems are hierarchical structures comprising directories and files. The os module has several functions that can help with creating, removing and altering directories. These include:

- mkdir() This function is used to create a directory, it takes the name of the directory to create as a parameter. If the directory already exists FileExistsError is raised.
- chdir() This function can be used to change the current working directory. This is the directory that the application will read from/ write to by default.
- getcwd() This function returns a string representing the name of the current working directory.
- rmdir() This function is used to remove/ delete a directory. It takes the name of the directory to delete as a parameter.
- listdir() This function returns a list containing the names of the entries in the directory specified as a parameter to the function (if no name is given the current directory is used).

A simple example illustrates the use of some of these functions is given below:

```
import os
print('os.getcwd(:', os.getcwd()) print('List
contentsof directory')print(os.listdir())
print('Create mydir')
os.mkdir('mydir')
print('List the updated contents of directory')
print(os.listdir())
print('Change into mydir directory')
os.chdir('mydir')print('os.getcwd(:',
os.getcwd())
print('Change back to parent directory')
os.chdir('..')print('os.getcwd(:', os.getcwd())
print('Remove mydir directory') os.rmdir('mydir')
print('List the resultingcontents of directory')
print(os.listdir())
```

Note that '..' is a short hand for the parent directory of the current directory and

 '.' is short hand for the current directory.

An example of the type of output generated by this program for a specific set up on a Mac is given below:

```
os.getcwd(:
/Users/Shared/workspaces/pycharm/pythonintro/textfiles
List contents of directory
['my-new-file.txt', 'myfile.txt',
'textfile1.txt',
'textfile2.txt']
Create mydir
List the updated contents of directory
['my-new-file.txt', 'myfile.txt',
'textfile1.txt',
'textfile2.txt', 'mydir']
```

```
Change into mydir directory
os.getcwd(:
/Users/Shared/workspaces/pycharm/pythonintro/textfiles/mydir
Change back to parent directory os.getcwd(:
/Users/Shared/workspaces/pycharm/pythonintro/textfiles
Remove mydir directory
List the resulting contents of directory
['my-new-file.txt', 'myfile.txt',
'textfile1.txt',
'textfile2.txt']
```

Temporary Files

During the execution of many applications it may be necessary to create a temporary file that will be created at one
point and deleted before the application finishes. It is of
course possible to manage such temporary files yourself
however, the tempfile module provides a range of facilities
to simplify the creation and management of these temporary files.

Within the tempfile module TemporaryFile, NamedTempo-
raryFile, TemporaryDirectory, and SpooledTemporaryFile
are high-level file objects which provide automatic cleanup
of temporary files and directories. These objects implement
the Context Manager Protocol.

The tempfile module also provides the lower-level function
mkstemp() and mkdtemp() that can be used to create
temporary files that require the developer to management

them and delete them at an appropriate time.

The high-level feature for the tempfile module are:

- TemporaryFile(mode='w+b') Return an anonymous gfile-like object that can be used as a temporary storage area. On completion of the managed context (via a with statement) or destruction of the file object, the temporary file will be removed from the file system. Note that by default all data is written to the temporary file in binary format which is generally more efficient.
- NamedTemporaryFile(mode='w+b') This function operates exactly as TemporaryFile() does, except that the file has s visible name in the file system.
- SpooledTemporaryFile(max_size=0, mode='w+b') This function operates exactly as TemporaryFile() does, except that data is spooled in memory until the file size exceeds max_size, or until the file's fileno() method is called, at which point the contents are written to disk and operation proceeds as with TemporaryFile().
- TemporaryDirectory(suffix=None, prefix=None, dir=None)

This function creates a temporary directory. On completion of the context or destruction of the temporary directory object the newly created temporary directory and all its contents are removed from the file system.

The lower level functions include:

- mkstemp() Creates a temporary file that is only read-

able or writable by the user who created it.
- mkdtemp() Creates a temporary directory. The directory is readable, writable, and searchable only by the creating user ID.
- gettempdir() Return the name of the directory used for temporary files.

This defines the default value for the default temporary directory to be used with the other functions in this module.

An example of using the TemporaryFile function is given below. This code imports the tempfile module then prints out the default directory used for temporary files. It then creates a TemporaryFile object and prints its name and mode (the default mode is binary but for this example we have overwritten this so that plain text is used). We have then written a line to the file. Using seek we are repositioning ourselves at the start of the file and then reading the line we have just written.

```
import tempfile
print('tempfile.gettempdir():',
tempfile.gettempdir())
temp =
tempfile.TemporaryFile('w+')print('temp.name:',
temp.name)print('temp.mode:',
temp.mode)temp.write('Hello world!')temp.seek(0)
line = temp.readline()
print('line:', line)
The output from this when run on an Apple Mac is:
tempfile.gettempdir():
/var/folders/6n/8nrnt9f93pn66ypg9s5dq8y80000gn/T
```

```
temp.name:  4 temp.mode:  w+
line:  Hello  world!
```

Note that the file name is '4' and that the temporary directory is not a meaningful name!

Working with Paths

The path lib module provides a set of classes representing file system paths; that is paths through the hierarchy of directories and files within an operating systems file structure. It was introduced in Python 3.4. The core class in this module is the Path class.

A Path object is useful because it provides operations that allow you to manipulate and manage the path to a file or directory. The Path class also replicates some of the operations available from the os module (such as mkdir, rename and rmdir) which means that it is not necessary to work directly with the OS module.

A path object is created using the Path constructor function; this function actually returns a specific type of Path depending on the type of operating system being used such as a WindowsPath or a PosixPath (for Unix style systems).

The Path() constructor takes the path to create for example 'D:/mydir' (on Windows) or '/Users/user1/mydir' on a Mac or '/var/temp' on Linux etc.

You can then use several different methods on the Path object to obtain information about the path such as:

- exists() returns True of False depending on whether the path points to an existing file or directory.
- is_dir() returns True if the path points to a directory. False if it references a file. False is also returned if the path does not exist.
- is_file() returns True of the path points to a file, it returns False if the path does not exist or the path references a directory.
- absolute() A Path object is considered absolute if it has both a root and (if appropriate) a drive.
- is_absolute() returns a Boolean value indicating whether the Path is absolute or not.

An example of using some of these methods is given below:

```
from pathlib  import Path
print('Create Path object for current directory')
p  =  Path('.') print('p:',  p)
print('p.exists():',  p.exists())
print('p.is_dir():',  p.is_dir())
print('p.is_file():',  p.is_file())
print('p.absolute():',  p.absolute())
```

Sample output produced by this code snippet is:

```
Create  Path  object  for  current  directory p:
.
p.exists():  True
p.is_dir():  Truep.is_file():  Falsep.absolute():
```

324

```
/Users/Shared/workspaces/pycharm/pythonintro/textfiles
```

There are also several methods on the Path class that can be used to create and remove directories and files such as:

- mkdir() is used to create a directory path if it does not exist. If the path already exists, then a FileExistsError is raised.
- rmdir() remove this directory; the directory must be empty otherwise an error will be raised.
- rename(target) rename this file or directory to the given target.
- unlink() removes the file referenced by the path object.
- joinpath(*other) appends elements to the path object e.g. path.joinpath('/temp').
- with_name(new_name)return a new path object with the name changed.
- The '/' operator can also be used to create new path objects from existing paths for example path/ 'test'/ 'output' which would append the directories test and out to the path object.

Two Path class methods can be used to obtain path objects representing key directories such as the current working directory (the directory the program is logically in at that point) and the home directory of the user running the program:

- Path.cwd() return a new path object representing the current directory.

- Path.home() return a new path object representing the user's home directory.

An example using several of the above features is given below. This example obtains a path object representing the current working directory and then appends 'text' to this. The result path object is then checked to see if the path exists (on the computer running the program), assuming that the path does not exist it is created and the exists() method is rerun.

```
p = Path.cwd()
print('Set up new directory')
newdir = p / 'test'
print('Check to see if newdir exists')
print('newdir.exists():', newdir.exists())
print('Create new dir')
newdir.mkdir()
print('newdir.exists():', newdir.exists())
```

The effect of creating the directory can be seen in the output:

```
Set up new directory
Check to see if newdir exists
newdir.exists(): False
Create new dir newdir.exists(): True
```

A very useful method in the Path object is the glob(pattern) method. This method returns all elements within the path that meet the pattern specified.

For example path.glob('*.py') will return all the files ending .py within the current path.

Note that '**/*.py' would indicate the current directory and any sub directory. For example, the following code will return all files where the file name ends with '.txt' for a given path:

```
print('-' * 10)
for file in path.glob('*.txt'):
print('file:', file)
print('-' * 10)
```

An example of the output generated by this code is:

— — — — —

   file: my-new-file.txt
   file: myfile.txt
   file: textfile1.txt
   file: textfile2.txt

— — — — —

Paths that reference a file can also be used to read and write data to that file. For example the open() method can be used to open a file that by default allows a file to be read:

- open(mode='r') this can be used to open the file referenced by the path object.

This is used below to read the contents of a file a line at a

327

time (note that with as statement is used here to ensure that the file represented by the Path is closed):

```
p = Path('mytext.txt')
with p.open() as f:
print(f.readline())
```

However, there are also some high-level methods available that allow you to easily write data to a file or read data from a file. These include the Path methods write_text and read_text methods:

- write_text(data) opens the file pointed to in text mode and writes the data to it and then closes the file.
- read_text() opens the file in read mode, reads the text and closes the file; it then returns the contents of the file as a string.

These are used below

```
dir = Path('./test') print('Create new file')
newfile = dir / 'text.txt'
print('Write some text to
file')newfile.write_text('Hello Python World!')
print('Read the text back again')
print(newfile.read_text())
print('Remove the file')
newfile.unlink()
```

Which generates the following output:

Create new file
  Write some text to file
  Read the text back again
  Hello Python World!
  Remove the file

Try

The aim of this exercise is to explore the creation of, and access to, the contents of a file.

You should write two programs,these programs are out-lined below:

1. Create a program that will write today's date into a file – the name of the file can be hard coded or supplied by the user. You can use the datetime.today() function to obtain the current date and time. You can use the str() function to convert this date time object into a string so that it can be written out to a file.

2. Create a second program to reload the date from the file and convert the string into a date object. You can use the datetime.strptime() function to convert a string into a date time object (see https://docs.python.org/3/library/datetime.html#datetime.datetime.strptime for documentation on this function).

This function stakes a string containing a date and time in it and a second string which defines the format expected.

If you use the approach outlined in step 1 above to write the string out to a file then you should find that the following defines an appropriate format to parse the date_str so that a date time object can be created:

```
datetime_object = datetime.strptime(date_str,
'%Y-%m-%d
%H:%M:%S.%f')
```

StreamIO

Introduction

In this chapter we will explore the Stream I/O model that under pins the way in which data is read from and written to data sources and sinks. One example of a data source or sink is a file but another might be a byte array.

This model is actually what sits underneath the file access mechanisms discussed in the previous chapter.

It is not actually necessary to understand this model to be able to read and write data to and from a file, however in some situations it is useful to have an under- standing of this model so that you can modify the default behavior when necessary.

The remainder of this chapter first introduces the Stream model, discusses Python streams in general and then presents the classes provided by Python. It then considers what is the actual effect of using the open() function presented in the last chapter.

What is a Stream?

Streams are objects which serve as sources or sinks of data. At first this concept can seem a bit strange. The easiest way to think of a stream is as a conduit of data flowing from or into a pool. Some streams read data straight from the "source of the data" and some streams read data from other streams. These latter streams then do some "useful" processing of the data such as converting the raw data into a specific format. The following figure illustrates this idea.

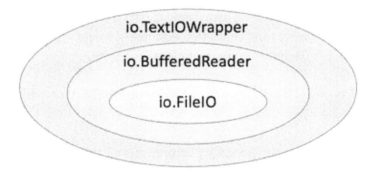

In the above figure the initial FileIO stream reads raw data from the actual data source (in this case a file). The BufferedReader then buffers the data reading process for efficiency. Finally the TextIOW rapper handles string encoding; that is it converts strings from the typical ASCII representation used in a file into the internal representation used by Python (which uses Unicode).

You might ask at this point why have a streams model at all;

after all we read and wrote data to files without needing to know about streams in the last chapter? The answer is that a stream can read or write data to or from a source of data rather than just from a file. Of course a file can be a source of data but so can a socket, a pipe,a string, a web service etc. It is therefore a more flexible data I/O model.

Python Streams

The Python io module provides Python's main facilities for dealing with data input and output. There are three main types of input/output these are text I/O, binary I/O and raw I/.O. These categories can be used with various types of data source/sinks.

Whatever the category, each concrete stream can have a number of properties such as being read-only, write-only or read-write. It can also support sequential access or random access depending on the nature of the underlying data sink. For example, reading data from a socket or pipe is inherently sequential where as reading data from a file can be performed sequentially or via a random access approach.

Whichever stream is used however, they are aware of the type of data they can process. For example, attempting to supply a string to a binary write-only stream will raise a TypeError. As indeed will presenting binary data to a text stream etc.

As suggested by this there are a number of different types of stream provided by the Python io module and some of these are presented below:

The abstract IOBase class is at the root of the stream IO class hierarchy. Below this class are stream classes for unbuffered and buffered IO and for text orientedIO.

IOBase

This is the abstract base class for all I/O stream classes.The class provides many abstract methods that sub classes will need to implement.

The IOBase class (and its sub classes) all support the iterator protocol.This means that an IOBase object (or an object of a subclass) can iterate over the input data from the underling stream.

IOBase also implements the Context Manager Protocol and therefore it can be used with the with and with-as statements.

The IOBase class defines a core set of methods and attributes including:

- close() flush and close the stream.
- closed an attribute indicating whether the stream is closed.
- flush() flush the write buffer of the stream if applicable.
- readable() returns True if the stream can be read from.
- readline(size=-1) return a line from the stream. If size is specified at most size bytes will be read.
- readline(hint=-1) read a list of lines. If hint is specified then it is used to control the number of lines read.
- seek(offset[, whence]) This method moves the current the stream position/pointer to the given offset. The meaning of the offset depends on the whence parameter. The default value for whence is SEEK_SET.
- SEEK_SET or 0: seek from the start of the stream (the default);offset must either be a number returned by TextIOBase.tell(), or zero. Any other offset value produces undefined behavior.
- SEEK_CUR or 1: "seek" to the current position; offset must be zero, which is a no-operation (all other values are unsupported).
- SEEK_END or 2: seek to the end of the stream; offset must be zero (all other values
- seekable() does the stream support seek().
- tell() return the current stream position/pointer.
- writeable() returns true if data can be written to the stream.
- writelines(lines) write a list of lines to the stream.

Raw IO/UnBuffered IO Classes

Raw IO or unbuffered IO is provided by the RawIOBase and FileIO classes. RawIOBase This class is a subclass of IOBase and is the base class for raw binary (aka unbuffered) I/O. Raw binary I/O typically provides low-level access to an underlying OS device or API, and does not try to encapsulate it in high-level primitives (this is the responsibility of the Buffered I/O and Text I/O classes that can wrap a raw I/O stream). The class adds methods such as:

- read(size=-1) This method reads up to size bytes from the stream and returns them. If size is unspecified or-1 then all available bytes are read.
- readall() This method reads and returns all available bytes within the stream.
- readint(b) This method reads the bytes in the stream into a per-allocated, writable bytes-like object b (e.g. into a byte array). It returns the number of bytes read.
- write(b) This method writes the data provided by b (a bytes -like object such as a byte array) into the underlying raw stream.

FileIO The FileIO class represents a raw unbuffered binary IO stream linked to an operating system level file. When the FileIO class is instantiated it can be given a file name and the mode (such as 'r' or 'w' etc.). It can also be given a flag to indicate whether the file descriptor associated with the underlying OS level file should be closed or not.

This class is used for the low-level reading of binary data and is at the heart of all file oriented data access (although it is often wrapped by another stream such as a buffered reader or writer).

Binary IO/Buffered IO Classes

Binary IO aka Buffered IO is a filter stream that wraps a lower level RawIOBase stream(such as a FileIO stream). The classes implementing buffered IO all extend the BufferedIOBase class and are:

BufferedReader When reading data from this object, a larger amount of data may be requested from the underlying raw stream, and kept in an internal buffer. The buffered data can then be returned directly on subsequent reads.

BufferedWriter When writing to this object, data is normally placed into an internal buffer. The buffer will be written out to the underlying RawIOBase object under various conditions, including:

- when the buffer gets too small for all pending data;
- when flush() is called;
- when the BufferedWriter object is closed or destroyed.

BufferedRandom A buffered interface to random access streams. It supports seek() and tell() functionality.

BufferedRWPair A buffered I/O object combining two uni-directional RawIOBase objects – one readable, the other writable—into a single bidirectional endpoint.

Each of the above classes wrap a lower level byte oriented stream class such as the io.FileIO class, for example:

```
f = io.FileIO('data.dat')
br = io.BufferedReader(f)
print(br.read())
```

This allows data in the form of bytes to be read from the file 'data.dat'. You can of course also read data from a different source, such as an in memory BytesIO object:

```
binary_stream_from_file =
io.BufferedReader(io.BytesIO(b'starship.png'))
bytes = binary_stream_from_file.read(4)
print(bytes)
```

In this example the data is read from the BytesIO object by the BufferedReader. The read() method is then used to read the first 4 bytes, the output is:

b'star'

Note the 'b' in front of both the string 'starship.png' and the result 'star'. This indicates that the string literal should become a bytes literal in Python 3. Bytes literals are always prefixed with 'b' or 'B'; they produce an instance of the bytes type instead of the str type. They may only contain ASCII characters.

The operations supported by buffered streams include, for reading:

- peek(n) return up to n bytes of data without advancing the stream pointer. The number of bytes returned may be less or more than requested depending on the amount of data available.
- read(n) return n bytes of data as bytes, if n is not supplied (or is negative) the read all available data.
- readl(n) read up to n bytes of data using a single call on the raw data stream

The operations supported by buffered writers include:

- write(bytes) writes the bytes-like data and returns the number of bytes written.
- flush() This method forces the bytes held in the buffer into the raw stream.

Text Stream Classes

The text stream classes are the TextIOBase class and its two sub classes TextIOWrapper and StringIO.

TextIOBase This is the root class for all Text Stream classes. It provides a character and line based interface to Stream I/O. This class provides several additional methods to that defined in its parent class:

- read(size=-1) This method will return at most size

characters from the stream as a single string. If size is negative or None, it will read all remaining data.

· readline(size=-1) This method will return a string representing the current line (up to a newline or the end of the data whichever comes first). If the stream is already at EOF, an empty string is returned. If size is specified, at most size characters will be read.

· seek(offset, [, whence]) change the stream position/-pointer by the specified offset. The optional whence parameter indicates where the seek should start from:

– SEEK_SET or 0: (the default) seek from the start of the stream.

– SEEK_CUR or 1: seek to the current position; offset must be zero, which is a no operation.

– SEEK_END or 2: seek to the end of the stream; offset must be zero.

· tell() Returns the current stream position/pointer as an opaque number. The number does not usually represent a number of bytes in the underlying binary storage.

· write(s) This method will write the string s to the stream and return the number of characters written.

TextIOWrapper. This is a buffered text stream that wraps a buffered binary stream and is a direct subclass of TextIOBase. When a TextIOWrapper is created there are a range of options available to control its behavior:

```
io.TextIOWrapper(buffer, encoding=None,
errors=None, newline=No ne, line_buffering=False,
write_through=False)
```

Where

- buffer is the buffered binary stream.
- encoding represents the text encoding used such as UTF-8.
- errors defines the error handling policy such as strict or ignore.
- newline controls how line endings are handled for example should they be ignored (None) or represented as a linefeed, carriage return or a newline/carriage return etc.
- line_buffering if True then flush() is implied when a call to write contains a new line character or a carriage return.
- write_through if True then a call to write is guaranteed not to be buffered.

The TextIOWrapper is wrapped around a lower level binary buffered I/O stream, for example:

```
f = io.FileIO('data.txt')
br = io.BufferedReader(f)
text_stream = io.TextIOWrapper(br, 'utf-8')
```

StringIO This is an in memory stream for text I/O. The

initial value of the buffer held by the StringIO object can be provided when the instance is created, for example:

```
in_memory_text_stream = io.StringIO('to be or not
to be that is the question')
print('in_memory_text_stream',
in_memory_text_stream)
print(in_memory_text_stream.getvalue())
in_memory_text_stream.close()
```

This generates:

in_memory_text_stream <_io.StringIOobject at 0x10fd-faee8>

To be or not to be that is the question

Note that the underlying buffer (represented by the string passed into the StringIO instance) is discarded when the close() method is called. The getvalue() method returns a string containing the entire contents of the buffer. If it is called after the stream was closed then an error is generated.

Stream Properties

It is possible to query a stream to determine what types of operations it supports. This can be done using the readable(), seekable() and writeable() methods. For example:

```
f = io.FileIO('myfile.txt')
br = io.BufferedReader(f)
text_stream =
io.TextIOWrapper(br,encoding='utf-8')
print('text_stream', text_stream)
print('text_stream.readable():',
text_stream.readable())
print('text_stream.seekable()',
text_stream.seekable())
print('text_stream.writeable()',
text_stream.writable())
text_stream.close()
```

The output from this code snippet is:

text_stream <_io.TextIOWrapper name='myfile.txt' encoding='utf-8'>text_stream.readable(): True
  text_stream.seekable() True
  text_stream.writeable() False

Closing Streams

All opened streams must be closed. However, you can close the top level stream and this will automatically close lower level streams, for example:

```
f = io.FileIO('data.txt')
br = io.BufferedReader(f)
text_stream = io.TextIOWrapper(br, 'utf-8')
print(text_stream.read()) text_stream.close()
```

Returning to the open() Function

If streams are so good then why don't you use them all the time? Well actually in Python 3 you do! The core open function (and indeed the io.open() function) both return a stream object. The actual type of object returned depends on the file mode specified, whether buffering is being used etc. For example:

```
import io
# Text stream
f1 = open('myfile.txt', mode='r',
encoding='utf-8')
print(f1)
# Binary IO aka Buffered IO
f2 = open('myfile.dat', mode='rb')
print(f2)
f3 = open('myfile.dat', mode='wb')
print(f3)
# Raw IO aka Unbufferedf IO
f4 = open('starship.png', mode='rb', buffering=0)
print(f4)
```

When this short example is run the output is:

<_io.TextIOWrapper name='myfile.txt' mode='r' encoding='utf-8'>

   <_io.BufferedReader name='myfile.dat'>

   <_io.BufferedWriter name='myfile.dat'>

   <_io.FileIO name='starship.png' mode='rb' closefd=True>

As you can see from the output,four different types of object have been returned from the open() function. The first is a TextIOWrapper, the second a BufferedReader, the third a BufferedWriter and the final one is a FileIO object. This reflects the differences in the parameters passed into the open (0 function. For example, f1 references a io.TextIOWrapper because it must encode (convert) the input text into Unicode using the UTF-8 encoding scheme. While f2 holds a io.BufferedReader because the mode indicates that we want to read binary data while f3 holds a io.BufferedWriter because the mode used indicates we want to write binary data. The final call to open returns a FileIO because we have indicated that we do not want to buffer the data and thus we can use the lowest level of stream object.

In general the following rules are applied to determine the type of object returned based on the modes and encoding specified:

Class	mode	Buffering
FileIO	binary	no
BufferedReader	'rb'	yes
BufferedWriter	'wb'	yes
BufferedRandom	'rb+' 'wb+' 'ab+'	yes
TextIOWrapper	Any text	yes

Note that not all mode combinations make sense and thus some combinations will generate an error.

In general you don't therefore need to worry about which stream you are using or what that stream does; not least because all the streams extend the IOBase class and thus have a common set of methods and attributes.

However, it is useful to understand the implications of what you are doing so that you can make better informed choices. For example, binary streams (that do less processing) are faster than Unicode oriented streams that must convert from ASCII into Unicode.

Also understanding the role of streams in Input and Output can also allow you to change the source and destination of data without needing to rewrite the whole of your application. You can thus use a file or stdin for testing and a socket for reading data in production.

Try

Use the underlying streams model to create an application that will write binary data to a file. You can use the 'b' prefix to create a binary literal to be written, for example b 'Hello World'.

Next create another application to reload the binary data from the file and print it out.

Working with CSV Files

Introduction

This chapter introduces a module that supports the generation of CSV (or Comma Separated Values) files.

CSVFiles

The CSV (Comma Separated Values)format is the most common import and export format for spreadsheets and databases. However, CSV is not a precise standard with multiple different applications having different conventions and specific standards.

The Python csv module implements classes to read and write tabular data in CSV format. As part of this it supports the concept of a dialect which is a CSV format used by a specific application or suite of programs, for example,it supports an Excel dialect.

This allows programmers to say, "write this data in the format preferred by Excel," or "read data from this file which was generated by Excel," without knowing the precise details of the CSV format used by Excel.

Programmers can also describe the CSV dialects understood by other applications or define their own special-purpose CSV dialects.

The csv module provides a range of functions including:

- csv.reader (csvfile, dialect='excel', **fmtparams) Returns a reader object which will iterate over lines in the given csvfile. An optional dialect parameter can be given. This may be an instance of a subclass of the Dialect class or one of the strings returned by the list_dialects() function. The other optional fmtparams keyword arguments can be given to override individual formatting parameters in the current dialect.
- csv.writer (csvfile, dialect='excel', **fmtparams) Returns a writer object responsible for converting the user's data into delimited strings on the given csvfile. An optional dialect parameter provided. The fmtparams keyword arguments can be given to override individual formatting parameters in the current dialect.
- csv.list_dialects() Return the names of all registered dialects. For example on a Mac OS X the default list of dialects is ['excel', 'excel-tab', 'unix'].

The CSV Writer Class

A CSV Writer is obtained from the csv.writer()function. The csv writer supports two methods used to write data to the

CSV file:

- csvwriter.writerow(row) Write the row parameter to the writer's file object, formatted according to the current dialect.
- csvwriter.writerows(rows) Write all elements in rows (an iterable of row objects as described above) to the writer's file object, formatted according to the current dialect.
- Writer objects also have the following public attribute:
- csvwriter.dialect A read-only description of the dialect in use by the writer.

The following program illustrates a simple use of the csv module which creates a file called sample.csv.

As we have not specified a dialect, the default 'excel' dialect will be used. The writerow() method is used to write each comma separate list of strings to the CSV file.

```
print('Crearting  CSV  file')
with open('sample.csv',  'w',  newline='')  as
csvfile: writer = csv.writer(csvfile)
writer.writerow(['She  Loves  You',  'Sept
1963'])
writer.writerow(['I  Want  to  Hold  Your  Hand',
 'Dec  1963']) writer.writerow(['Cant  Buy  Me
Love',  'Apr  1964']) writer.writerow(['A  Hard
Days  Night',  'July  1964'])
```

The resulting file can be viewed as shown below:

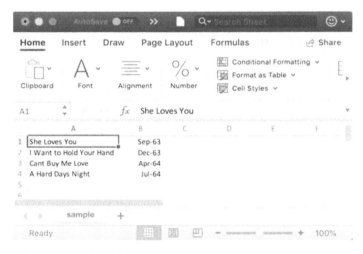

```
sample.csv
1      She Loves You,Sept 1963
2      I Want to Hold Your Hand,Dec 1963
3      Cant Buy Me Love,Apr 1964
4      A Hard Days Night,July 1964
```

However, as it is a CSV file, we can also open it in Excel:

The CSV Reader Class

A CSV Reader object is obtained from the csv.reader() function. It implements the iteration protocol.

If a csv reader object is used with a for loop then each time round the loop it supplies the next row from the CSV file as a list, parsed according to the current CSV dialect.

Reader objects also have the following public attributes:

- csvreader.dialect A read-only description of the dialect in use by the parser.
- csvreader.line_num The number of lines read from the source iterator.

This is not the same as the number of records returned, as records can span multiple lines.

The following provides a very simple example of reading a CSV file using a csv reader object:

```
print('Starting  to  read  csv  file')
with open('sample.csv',  newline='')  as csvfile:
reader = csv.reader(csvfile)
for row  in reader:
print(*row,  sep=',  ')
print('Done  Reading')
```

The output from this program, based on the sample.csv file created earlier is:

Starting to read csv file

    She Loves You, Sept 1963

    I Want to Hold Your Hand, Dec 1963

    Cant Buy Me Love, Apr 1964

    A Hard Days Night, July 1964

    Done Reading

The CSV DictWriter Class

In many cases the first row of a CSV file contains a set of names (or keys) that define the fields within the rest of the CSV. That is the first row gives meaning to the columns and the data held in the rest of the CSV file. It is therefor every useful to capture this information and to structure the data written to a CSV file or loaded from a CSV file based on the keys in the first row.

The csv.DictWriter returns an object that can be used to write values into the CSV file based on the use of such named columns. The file to be used with the DictWriter is provided when the class is instantiated.

```python
import csv
with open('names.csv', 'w', newline='') as
csvfile: fieldnames = ['first_name',
'last_name', 'result'] writer =
csv.DictWriter(csvfile, fieldnames=fieldnames)
writer.writeheader()
writer.writerow({'first_name': 'John',
'last_name': 'Smith',
'result' : 54})
writer.writerow({'first_name': 'Jane',
'last_name': 'Lewis',
'result': 63})
writer.writerow({'first_name': 'Chris',
'last_name': 'Davies',
'result' : 72})
```

Note that when the DictWriter is created a list of the keys must be provided that are used for the columns in the CSV file.

The method writeheader()is then used to write the header row out to the CSV file.

The method writerow() takes a dictionary object that has keys based on the keys defined for the DictWriter. These are then used to write data out to the CSV (note the order of the keys in the dictionary is not important).

In the above example code the result of this is that a new file called names.csv is created which can be opened in Excel:

Of course, as this is a CSV file it can also be opened in a plain text editor as well.

F5			fx	
	A	B	C	D
1	first_name	last_name	result	
2	John	Smith	54	
3	Jane	Lewis	63	
4	Chris	Davies	72	
5				

The CSV DictReader Class

As well as the csv.DictWriter there is a csv.DictReader. The file to be used with the DictReader is provided when the class is instantiated. As with the DictReader the DictWriter class takes a list of keys used to define the columns in the CSV file. If the headings to be used for the first row can be provided although this is optional (if a set of keys are not provided, then the values in the first row of the CSV file will be used as the field names).

The DictReader class provides several useful features including the field names property that contains a list of the keys/headings for the CSV file as defined by the first row of the file.

The DictReader class also implements the iteration protocol and thus it can be used in a for loop in which each row (after the first row) is returned in turn as a dictionary. The dictionary object representing each row can then be used to access each column value based on the keys defined in the first row.

An example is shown below for the CSV file created earlier:

```
import csv
print('Starting to read dict CSV example')
with open('names.csv', newline='') as csvfile:
reader = csv.DictReader(csvfile)
for heading in reader.fieldnames:
print(heading, end=' ')
print('\n-----------------------------')
for row in reader:
print(row['first_name'], row['last_name'],
row['result'])
```

```
print('Done')
```

This generates the following output:

Starting to read dict CSV example first_name last_name result

— — — — — — — — — — — — — —

John Smith 54

Jane Lewis 63

Chris Davies 72

Done

Try

In this exercise you will create a CSV file based on a set of transactions stored in a current account.

1. To do this first define a new Account class to represent a type of bank account.
2. When the class is instantiated you should provide the account number, the name of the account holder, an opening balance and the type of account (which can be a string representing 'current', 'deposit' or 'investment' etc.). This means that there must be an init_method and you will need to store the data within the object.
3. Provide three instance methods for the Account; deposit(amount), withdraw(amount) and get_balance(). The behavior of these methods should be as expected, deposit will increase the balance, withdraw will de-

crease the balance and get_balance() returns the current balance.

Your Account class should also keep a history of the transactions it is involved in.

A Transaction is a record of a deposit or withdrawal along with an amount. Note that the initial amount in an account can be treated as an initial deposit.

The history could be implemented as a list containing an ordered sequence to transactions. A Transaction itself could be defined by a class with an action (deposit or withdrawal) and an amount. Each time a withdrawal or a deposit is made a new transaction record should be added to a transaction history list. Next provide a function(which could be called something like write_account_transactions_to_csv()) that can take an account and then write each of the transactions it holds out to a CSV file, with each transaction type and the transaction amount separated by a comma.

The following sample application illustrates how this function might be used:

accounts.csv

```
1    transaction_type,amount
2    deposit,10.05
3    deposit,23.45
4    withdraw,12.33
```

Working with Excel Files

Introduction

This chapter introduces the open pyxl module that can be used when working with Excel files. Excel is a software application developed by Microsoft that allows users to work with spreadsheets. It is a very widely used tool and files using the Excel file format are commonly encountered within many organizations. It is in effect the industry standard for spreadsheets and as such is a very useful tool to have in the developers toolbox.

Excel Files

Although CSV files are a convenient and simple way to handle data;it is very common to need to be able to read or write Excel files directly. To this end there are several libraries available in Python for this purpose. One widely used library is the OpenPyXL library. This library was originally written to support access to Excel 2010 files. It is an open source project and is well documented.

The OpenPyXL library provides facilities for

- reading and writing Excel workbooks,
- creating/accessing Excel worksheets,
- creating Excel formulas,
- creating graphs (with support from additional modules).

As OpenPyXL is not part of the standard Python distribution you will need to install the library yourself using a tool such as Anaconda or pip (e.g. pip install open pyxl). Alternatively, if you are using PyCharm you will be able to add the Open PyXL library to your project.

The key element in the Open PyXL library is the Workbook class. This can be imported from the module:

from ope npyxl **import** Workbook

A new instance of the (in memory) Workbook can be created using the Workbook class (note at this point it is purely a structure within the Python program and must be saved before an actual Excel file is created).

```
wb = Workbook()
```

The Openpyxl. Work Sheet Objects

A workbook is always created with at least one worksheet. You can get hold of the currently active worksheet using the Workbook.active property:

```
ws = wb.active
```

You can create additional worksheets using the workbooks' create_sheet

```
() method:
ws = wb.create_sheet('Mysheet')
You can access or update the title of the
worksheet using the title property:
ws.title = 'New Title'
```

The background color of the tab holding this title is white by default. You can change this providing an RRGGBB color code to the worksheet. sheet_properties.tab Color attribute, for example:

```
ws.sheet_properties.tabColor = "1072BA"
```

Working with Cells

It is possible to access the cells within a worksheet. A cell can be accessed directly as keys on the worksheet, for example:

```
ws['A1'] = 42
```

or

```
cell = ws['A1']
```

This returns a cell object; you can obtain the value of the cell using the value property, for example

```
print(cell.value)
```

There is also the Worksheet.cell() method. This provides access to cells using row and column notation:

```
d = ws.cell(row=4, column=2, value=10)
```

A row of values can also be added at the current position within the Excel file using append:

```
ws.append([1, 2, 3])
```

This will add a row to the Excel file containing 1, 2, and 3. Ranges of cells can be accessed using slicing:

```
cell_range = ws['A1':'C2']
```

Ranges of rows or columns can also be obtained:

```
col = ws['C'] col_range = ws['C:D'] row10 =
ws[10] row_range = ws[5:10]
```

The value of a cell can also be an Excel formula such as

```
ws['A3'] = '=SUM(A1, A2)'
```

A workbook is actually only a structure in memory; it must

be saved to a file for permanent storage. These workbooks can be saved using the save() method. This method takes a file name and writes the Workbook out in Excel format.

```
workbook = Workbook()
... workbook.save('balances.xlsx')
```

Sample Excel File Creation Application

The following simple application creates a Workbook with two worksheets.It also contains a simple Excel formula that sums the values held in to other cells:

```
from openpyxl import Workbook
def main():
print('Starting Write Excel Example with
openPyXL')
workbook = Workbook()
# Get the currentactive worksheet
ws = workbook.active ws.title = 'my worksheet'
ws.sheet_properties.tabColor= '1072BA'
ws['A1'] = 42 ws['A2'] = 12
ws['A3'] = '=SUM(A1, A2)'
ws2 = workbook.create_sheet(title='my other
sheet')
ws2['A1'] = 3.42 ws2.append([1, 2, 3])
ws2.cell(column=2,row=1, value=15)
workbook.save('sample.xlsx')
print('Done Write Excel Example')
if _name  == '_main_':
main()
```

The Excel file generated from this can be viewed in Excel as shown below:

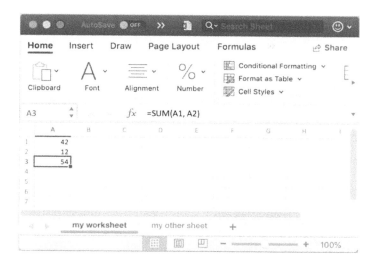

Loading a Workbook from an Excel File

Of course, in many cases it is necessary not just to create Excel files for data export but also to import data from an existing Excel file. This can be done using the OpenPyXL load_workbook() function. This function opens the specified Excel file (in read only mode by default)and returns a Workbook object.

```
from openpyxl import load_workbook
workbook = load_workbook(filename='sample.xlsx')
```

You can now access a list of sheets, their names, obtain the currently active sheet etc. using properties provided by the workbook object:

- workbook.active returns the active worksheet object.
- workbook.sheet names returns the names (strings) of the worksheets in this workbook.
- workbook.worksheets returns a list of worksheet objects.

The following sample application reads the Excel file created earlier in this chapter:

```
from openpyxl import load_workbook
def main():
print('Starting reading Excel file using
openPyXL')
workbook = load_workbook(filename='sample.xlsx')
print(workbook.active) print(workbook.sheetnames)
print(workbook.worksheets)
print('-' * 10)
ws = workbook['my worksheet'] print(ws['A1'])
print(ws['A1'].value) print(ws['A2'].value)
print(ws['A3'].value)
print('-' * 10)
for sheet in workbook:
print(sheet.title)
print('-' * 10)
cell_range = ws['A1':'A3']
for cell in cell_range:
print(cell[0].value)
print('-' * 10)
print('Finished reading Excel file using
openPyXL')
```

```
if_name_=='_main_':
main()
```

The output from this application is illustrated below:

```
Starting readingExcel file using openPyXL
<Worksheet "my worksheet">
['my worksheet', 'my other sheet']
[<Worksheet "my worksheet">, <Worksheet "my other
sheet">]
----------
<Cell 'my worksheet'.A1>
42
12
=SUM(A1, A2)
----------
my worksheet
my other sheet
----------
42
12
=SUM(A1, A2)
----------
Finished reading Excel file using openPyXL
```

Try

Using the Account class that you created in the last chapter; write the account transaction information to an Excel file instead of a CSV file.

To do this create a function called write_account_transaction_to_excel() that takes the name of the Excel file and the account to store. The function should then write the data to the file using the excel format.

The following sample application illustrates how this function might be used:

```
print('Starting')
acc = accounts.CurrentAccount('123', 'John',
10.05, 100.0)
acc.deposit(23.45)
acc.withdraw(12.33)
print('Writing AccountTransactions')
write_account_transaction_to_excel('accounts.xlsx',
acc)
print('Done')
```

The contents of the Excel file would then be:

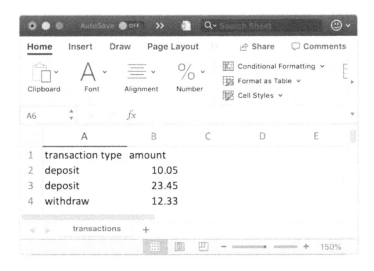

Regular Expressions in Python

Introduction

Regular Expression are a very powerful way of processing text while looking for recurring patterns; they are often used with data held in plain text files (such as log files), CSV files as well as Excel files. This chapter introduces regular expressions, discusses the syntax used to define a regular expression pattern and presents the Python re module and its use.

What Are Regular Expressions?

A Regular Expression (also known as a regex or even just re) is a sequence of characters (letters, numbers and special characters) that form a pattern that can be used to search text to see if that text contains sequences of characters that match the pattern.

For example, you might have a pattern defined as three characters followed by three numbers. This pattern could be used to look for such a pattern in other strings. Thus, the following strings either match (or contain) this pattern or they do not:

Abc123	Matches the pattern
A123A	Does not match the pattern
123AAA	Does not match the pattern

Regular Expression are very widely used for finding information in files, for example

- finding all lines in a log file associated with a specific user or a specific operation,
- for validating input such as checking that a string is a valid email address or postcode/ZIP code etc.

Support for Regular Expressions is wide spread within programming languages such as Java, C#, PHP and particularly Perl. Python is no exception and has the built-in module re (as well as additional third-party modules) that support Regular Expressions.

Regular Expression Patterns

You can define a regular expression pattern using any ASCII character or number. Thus, the string 'John' can be used to define a regex pattern that can be used to match any other string that contains the characters 'J', 'o', 'h', 'n'. Thus each of the following strings will match this pattern:
- 'John Hunt'
- 'John Jones'
- 'Andrew John Smith'
- 'Mary Helen John'

- 'John John John'
- 'I am going to visit the John'
- 'I once saw a film by John Wayne'

But the following strings would not match the pattern:

- 'Jon Davies' in this case because the spelling of John is different.
- 'john Williams' in this case because the capital J does not match the lowercase j.
- 'David James' in this case because the string does not contain the string John!

Regular expressions (regexs) use special characters to allow more complex patterns to be described. For example, we can use the special characters '[]' to define a set of characters that can match. For example, if we want to indicate that the J may be a capital or a lower-case letter then we can write '[Jj]'—this indicates that either 'J' or 'j' can match the first.

- [Jj]ohn—this states that the pattern starts with either a capital J or a lowercase j followed by 'ohn'.

Now both 'john Williams' and 'John Williams' will match this regex pattern

Pattern Meta characters

There are several special characters (often referred to as meta characters) that have a specific meaning within a regex pattern,these are listed in the following table:

Character	Description	Example
[]	A set of characters	[a-d] characters in the sequence 'a' to 'd'
\	Indicates a special sequence (can also be used to escape special characters)	'\d' indicates the character should be an integer
.	Any character with the exception of the newline character	'J.hn' indicates that there can be any character after the 'J' and before the 'h'
^	Indicates a string must start with the following pattern	"^hello" indicates the string must start with 'hello'
$	Indicates a string must end with the preceding pattern	"world$" indicates the string must end with 'world'
*	Zero or more occurrences of the preceding pattern	"Python*" indicates we are looking for zero or more times Python is in a string
+	One or more occurrences of preceding pattern	"info+" indicates that we must find info in the string at least once
?	Indicates zero or 1 occurrences of the preceding pattern	"John?" indicates zero or one instances of the 'John'
{}	Exactly the specified number of occurrences	"John{3}" this indicates we expect to see the 'John' in the string three times. "X{1,2}" indicates that there can be one or two Xs next to each other in the string
|	Either or	"True|OK" indicates we are looking for either True or OK
()	Groups together a regular expression: you can then apply another operator to the whole group	"(abcxyz){2}" indicates that we are looking for the string abc or xyz repeated twice

Special Sequences

A special sequence is a combination of a '\' (backslash) followed by a character combination which then has a special meaning. The following table lists the common special sequences used in Regular Expressions:

Sequence	Description	Example
A	Returns a match if the following characters are at the beginning of the string	"\AThe" must start with 'The'
b	Returns a match where the specified characters are at the beginning or at the end of a word	"\bon" or "on\b" indicates a string must start or end with 'on'
B	Indicates that the following characters must be present in a string but not at the start (or at the end) of a word	r"\Bon" or r"on\B" must not start or end with 'on'
d	Returns a match where the string contains digits (numbers from 0–9)	"\d"
D	Returns a match where the string DOES NOT contain digits	"\D"
s	Returns a match where the string contains a white space character	"\s"
S	Returns a match where the string DOES NOT contain a white space character	"\S"
w	Returns a match where the string contains any word characters (characters from a to Z, digits from 0–9, and the underscore _ character)	"\w"
W	Returns a match where the string DOES NOT contain any word characters	"\W"
Z	Returns a match if the following characters are present at the end of the string	"Hunt\Z"

Sets

A set is a sequence of characters inside a pair of square brackets which have specific meanings. The following table provides some examples.

Set	Description
[jeh]	Returns a match where one of the specified characters (j, e or h) are present
[a-x]	Returns a match for any lower-case character, alphabetically between a and x
[^zxc]	Returns a match for any character EXCEPT z, x and c
[0123]	Returns a match where any of the specified digits (0, 1, 2, or 3) are present
[0-9]	Returns a match for any digit between 0 and 9
[0-9][0-9]	Returns a match for any two-digit numbers from 00 and 99
[a-zA-Z]	Returns a match for any character alphabetically between a and z or A and Z

The Python re Module

The Python re module is the built-in module provided by

371

Python for working with regular Expressions.

You might also like to examine the third party regex module (see https://pypi. org/project/regex) which is backwards compatible with the default re module but provides additional functionality.

Working withPython Regular Expressions

Using Raw Strings

An important point to note about many of the strings used to define the regular expression patterns is that they are preceded by an 'r' for example r'/bin/sh$'.

The 'r' before the string indicates that the string should be treated as a raw string.

A raw string is a Python string in which all characters are treated as exactly that; individual characters. It means that backslash ('\') is treated as a literal character rather than as a special character that is used to escape the next character.

For example, in a standard string '\n' is treated as a special character representing a newline, thus if we wrote the following:

```
s = 'Hello \n world' print(s)
We will get as output:
Hello
World
```

However, if we prefix the string with an 'r' then we are telling Python to treat it as a raw string. For example:

```
s = r'Hello \n world'
print(s)
```

The output is now

Hello \n world

This is important for regular expression as characters such as backslash('\') are used within patterns to have a special regular expression meaning and thus we do not want Python to process them in the normal way.

Simple Example

The following simple Python program illustrates the basic use of the re module. It is necessary to import the re module before you can use it.

```
import re
text1 = 'john williams' pattern = '[Jj]ohn'
print('looking in', text1, 'for the pattern',
pattern)
if re.search(pattern, text1):
print('Match has been found')
```

When this program is run, we get the following output:

looking in john williams for the pattern [Jj]ohn Match has been

373

found

If we look at the code, we can see that the string that we are examining contains 'john williams' and that the pattern used with this string indicates that we are looking for a sequence of 'J' or 'j' followed by 'ohn'. To perform this test we use the re. search() function passing the regex pattern, and the text to test, as parameters. This function returns either None (which is taken as meaning False by the If statement) or a Match Object (which always has a Boolean value of True). As of course 'john' at the start of text1 does match the pattern, the re.search() function returns a match object and we see the 'Match has been found' message is printed out.

Both the Match object and search() method will be described in more detail below; however, this short program illustrates the basic operation of a Regular Expression.

The Match Object

Match objects are returned by the search() and match() functions. They always have a boolean value of True. The functions match() and search() return None when there is no match and a Match object when a match is found. It is therefore possible to use a match object with an if statement:

```
import re
match = re.search(pattern, string)
```

```
if match:
process(match)
```

Match objects support a range of methods and attributes including:

- match.re The regular expression object whose match() or search()method produced this match instance.
- match.string The string passed to match() or search().
- match.start([group])/ match.end([group]) Return the indices of the start and end of the sub string matched by group.
- match.group() returns the part of the string where there was a match.

The search() Function

The search() function searches the string for a match, and returns a Match object if there is a match. The signature of the function is:

```
re.search(pattern, string, flags=0)
```

The meaning of the parameters are:

- pattern this is the regular expression pattern to be used in the matching process.
- string this is the string to be searched.
- flags these (optional) flags can be used to modify the operation of the search.

The re module defines a set of flags (or indicators)that can be used to indicate any optional behaviors associated with the pattern.These flags include:

Flag	Description
re.IGNORECASE	Performs case-insensitive matching
re.LOCALE	Interprets words according to the current locale. This interpretation affects the alphabetic group (\w and \W), as well as word boundary behavior(\b and \B)
re.MULTILINE	Makes $ match the end of a line (not just the end of the string) and makes ^ match the start of any line (not just the start of the string)
re.DOTALL	Makes a period (dot) match any character. including a newline
re.UNICODE	Interprets letters according to the Unicode character set. This flag affects the behavior of \w, \W, \b, \B
re.VERBOSE	Ignores whitespace within the pattern (except inside a set [] or when escaped by a backslash) and treats unescaped # as a comment marker

If there is more than one match, only the first occurrence of the match will be returned:

```
import re
line1 = 'The price is 23.55' containsIntegers =
r'\d+'
if re.search(containsIntegers, line1):
print('Line 1 contains an integer')
else:
print('Line 1 does not contain an integer')
```

In this case the output is

Line 1 contains an integer

Another example of using the search() function is given below. In this case the pattern to look for defines three alternative strings (that is the string must contain either Beatles, Adele or Gorillaz):

```
import re
# Alternative words
music = r'Beatles|Adele|Gorillaz' request = 'Play
some Adele'
if re.search(music, request):
print('Set Fire to the Rain')
else:
print('No Adele Available')
```

In this case we generate the output:

Set Fire to the Rain

The match( ) Function

This function attempts to match a regular expression pattern at the beginning of a string. The signature of this function is given below:

```
re.match(pattern, string, flags=0)
```

pattern this is the regular expression to be matched.

- · string this is the string to be searched.
- · flags modifier flags that can be used.

The re.match( ) function returns a Match object on success, None on failure.

377

The Difference Between Matching and Searching

Python offers two different primitive operations based on regular expressions:

- match() checks for a match only at the beginning of the string,
- search() checks for a match anywhere in the string.

The findall() Function

The findall() function returns a list containing all matches. The signature of this function is:

```
re.findall(pattern, string, flags=0)
```

This function returns all non-overlapping matches of pattern in string, as a list of strings.

The string is scanned left-to-right, and matches are returned in the order found. If one or more groups are present in the pattern, then a list of groups is returned; this will be a list of tuples if the pattern has more than one group. If no matches are found, an empty list is returned.

An example of using the findall() function is given below. This example looks for a sub string starting with two letters

378

and followed by 'ai' and a single character. It is applied to a sentence and returns only the sub string 'Spain' and 'plain'.

```
import re
str = 'The rain in Spain stays mainly on the
plain' results = re.findall('[a-zA-Z]{2}ai.',
str) print(results)
for s in results:
print(s)
```

The output from this program is

['Spain', 'plain']

   Spain

   plain

The finditer( ) Function

This function returns an iterator yielding matched objects for the regular expression pattern in the string supplied. The signature for this function is:

```
re.finditer(pattern, string, flags=0)
```

The string is scanned left-to-right,and matches are re-turned in the order found. Empty matches are included in the result. Flags can be used to modify the matches.

The split( ) Function

The split() function returns a list where the string has been split at each match. The syntax of the split() function is

```
re.split(pattern, string, maxsplit=0, flags=0)
```

The result is to split a string by the occurrences of pattern. If capturing parentheses are used in the regular expression pattern, then the text of all groups in the pattern are also returned as part of the resulting list. If max split is nonzero, at most max split splits occur, and the remainder of the string is returned as the final element of the list. Flags can again be used to modify the matches.

```
import re
str = 'It was a hot summer night' x
=re.split('\s', str)
print(x)
The output is
['It', 'was', 'a', 'hot', 'summer', 'night']
```

The sub() Function

The sub() function replaces occurrences of the regular expression pattern in the string with the repl string.

re.sub(pattern, repl, string, max=0)

This method replaces all occurrences of the regular expression pat- tern in string with repl, substituting all occurrences unless max is provided. This method returns the modified string.

```
import re
pattern = '(England|Wales|Scotland)'
input = 'England for football, Wales for Rugby
and Scotland for the Highland games'
print(re.sub(pattern, 'England', input ))
```

Which generates:

England for football, England for Rugby and England for the

Highland games

You can control the number of replacements by specifying the count parameter: The following code replaces the first 2 occurrences:

```
import re
pattern = '(England|Wales|Scotland)'
input = 'England for football, Wales for Rugby
and Scotland for the Highland games'
x = re.sub(pattern, 'Wales', input, 2)
print(x)
```

which produces

Wales for football,Wales for Rugby and Scotland for the

Highland games

You can also find out how many substitutions were made using the subn() function. This function returns the new string and the number of substitutions in a tuple:

```
import re
pattern = '(England|Wales|Scotland)'
input = 'England for football, Wales for Rugby
and Scotland for the Highland games'
print(re.subn(pattern,'Scotland', input ))
The output from this is:
('Scotland for football, Scotlandfor Rugby and
Scotlandfor the Highland games', 3)
```

The compile() Function

Most regular expression operations are available as both module-level functions (as described above) and as methods on a compiled regular expression object.

The module level functions are typically simplified or standardized ways to use the compiled regular expression. In many cases these functions are sufficient but if finer grained control is required then a compiled regular expression may be used.

```
re.compile(pattern, flags=0)
```

The compile() function compiles a regular expression pattern into a regular expression object, which can be used for matching using its match(), search() and other methods as described below.

The expression's behavior can be modified by specifying a flags value. V The statements:

```
prog = re.compile(pattern)
result = prog.match(string)
are equivalent to
result = re.match(pattern,string)
```

but using re.compile() and saving the resulting regular expression object for reuse is more efficient when the expression will be used several times in a single program.

Compiled regular expression objects support the following methods and attributes:

- Pattern.search(string, pos, end pos) Scan through string looking for the first location where this regular expression produces a match and return a corresponding Match object. Return None if no position in the string matches the pattern. Starting at pos if provided and ending at end pos if this is provided (otherwise process the whole string).
- Pattern.match(string, pos, end pos)If zero or more characters at the beginning of string match this regular expression,return a corresponding match object. Return None if the string does not match the pattern. The pos and end pos are optional and specify the start and end positions within which to search.
- Pattern.split(string, maxsplit = 0)Identical to the split()function, using the compiled pattern.
- Pattern.find all(string[, pos[, end pos]])Similar to the find all () function, but also accepts optional pos and

end pos parameters that limit the search region like for search().

- Pattern.finditer(string[, pos[, end pos]])Similar to the finditer() function, but also accepts optional pos and end pos parameters that limit the search region like for search().
- Pattern.sub(repl, string, count = 0)Identical to the sub()function, using the compiled pattern.
- Pattern.subn(repl,string, count = 0)Identical to the subn()function, using the compiled pattern.
- Pattern.pattern the pattern string from which the pattern object was compiled.

An example of using the compile() function is given below. The pattern to be compiled is defined as containing 1 or more digits (0 to 9):

```
import re
line1 = 'The price is 23.55' containsIntegers =
r'\d+'
rePattern = re.compile(containsIntegers)
matchLine1 = rePattern.search(line1)
if matchLine1:
print('Line 1 containsa number')
else:
print('Line 1 does not contain a number')
```

The compiled pattern can then be used to apply methods such as search() to a specific string (in this case held in line1). The output generated by this is:

Line 1 contains a number

Of course the compiler pattern object supports a range of methods in addition to search() as illustrated by the spilt method:

```
p = re.compile(r'\W+') s = '20 High Street'
print(p.split(s))
The output from this is
['20', 'High', 'Street']
```

Try

Write a Python function to verify that a given string only contains letters (upper case or lower case) and numbers. Thus spaces and under bars ('_') are not allowed. An example of the use of this function might be:

print(contains_only_characters_and_numbers(**'John'**)) # *True* print(contains_only_characters_and_numbers(**'John_Hunt'**)) # *False*
  print(contains_only_characters_and_numbers(**'42'**)) # *True* print(contains_only_characters_and_numbers(**'John42'**)) # *True* print(contains_only_characters_and_numbers(**'John 42'**)) # *False*

Write a function to verify a UK Postcode format (call it verify_postcode). The format of a Postcode is two letters followed by 1 or 2 numbers, followed by a space, followed by one or two numbers and finally two letters. An Example of a postcode is SY23 4ZZ another postcode might be BB1 3PO and finally we might have AA1 56NN (note this is a simplification of the UK Postcode system but is suitable for our purposes).

Using the output from this function you should be able to run the following test code:

```
# True
print("verify_postcode('SY23 3AA'):",
verify_postcode('SY23
33AA'))
# True
print("verify_postcode('SY23 4ZZ'):",
verify_postcode('SY23
4ZZ'))
# True
print("verify_postcode('BB1 3PO'):",
verify_postcode('BB1
3PO'))
# False
print("verify_postcode('AA111
NN56'):",verify_postcode('AA111
NN56'))
# True
print("verify_postcode('AA1 56NN'):",
verify_postcode('AA1
56NN'))
# False print("verify_postcode('AA156NN'):",
verify_postcode('AA156NN'))
# False
print("verify_postcode('AA NN'):",
verify_postcode('AA NN'))
```

Write a function that will extract the value held between

two strings or characters such as '<' and '>'. The function should take three parameters, the start character, the end character and the string to process. For example, the following code snippet:

```
print(extract_values('<', '>', '<John>'))
print(extract_values('<', '>', '<42>'))
print(extract_values('<', '>', '<John 42>'))
print(extract_values('<', '>', 'The <town> was in
the
<valley>'))
```

Should generate output such as:

['John']

['42']

['John 42']

['town', 'valley']

Introduction to Databases

Introduction

There are several different types of database system in common use today including Object databases, NoSQL databases and (probably the most common) Relational Databases. This chapter focuses on Relational Databases as typified by database systems such as Oracle, Microsoft SQL Server and MySQL. The database we will use in this book is MySQL.

What Is a Database?

A database is essentially a way to store and retrieve data. Typically, there is some form of query language used with the database to help select the information to retrieve such as SQL or Structured Query Language.

Inmost cases there is a structure defined that is used to hold the data (although this is not true of the newer NoSQL or non-relational unstructured databases such as CouchDB or MongoDB).

In a Relational Database the data is held in tables, where the columns define the properties or attributes of the data and each row defines the actual values being held, for example:

attribute

id	name	surname	subject	email
cs_18	Phoebe	Cooke	Animation	pc@my.com
cs_21	Gryff	Jones	Games	gj@my.com
cs_27	Adam	Fosh	Music	af@my.com
cs_29	Jasmine	Smith	Games	js@my.com

row

students

In this diagram there is a table called students; it is being used to hold information about students attending a meeting. The table has 5 attributes (or columns) defined for id, name, surname, subject and email.

In this case, the id is probably what is known as a primary key. The primary key is a property that is used to uniquely identify the student row; it cannot be omitted and must be unique (within the table). Obviously names and subjects may well be duplicated as there may be more than one student studying Animation or Games and students may have the same first name or surname. It is probable that the email column is also unique as students probably don't share an email address but again this may not necessarily be the case.

You might at this point wonder why the data in a Relational Database is called relational and not tables or tabular? The reason is because of a topic known as relational algebra that underpins Relational Database theory. Relational Algebra takes its name from the mathematical concept known as a relation. However, for the purposes of this chapter you don't need to worry about this and just need to remember that data is held in tables.

Data Relationships

When the data held in one table has a link or relationship to data held in another table then an index or key is used to link the values in one table to another. This is illustrated below for a table of addresses and a table of people who live in that address. This shows for example, that 'PhoebeGates' lives at address 'addr2' which is 12 Queen Street, Bristol, BS42 6YY.

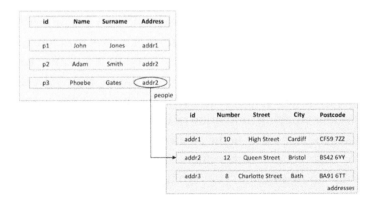

This is an example of a many to one (often written as many:1) relationship; that is there are many people who can live at one address (in the above Adam Smith also lives at address 'addr2'). In Relational Databases there can be several different types of relationship such as:

- one:one where only one row in one table references one and only one row in another table. An example of a one to one relationship might be from a person to an order for a unique piece of jewellery.
- one:many this is the same as the above address example, however in this case the direction of the relationship is reversed (that is to say that one address in the addresses table can reference multiple persons in the people table).
- many:many This is where many rows in one table may reference many rows in a second table. For example, many students may take a particular class and a student may take many classes. This relationship usually involves an intermediate (join) table to hold the associations between the rows.

The Database Schema

The structure of a Relational Database is defined using a Data Definition Language or Data Description Language (a DDL).

Typically, the syntax of such a language is limited to the semantics (meaning) required to define the structure of the tables. This structure is known as the database schema. Typically, the DDL has commands such as CREATETABLE, DROP TABLE (to delete a table) and ALTER TABLE (to modify the structure of an existing table).

Many tools provided with a database allow you to define the structure of the database without getting too bound up in the syntax of the DDL; however, it is useful to be aware of it and to understand that the database can be created in this way. For example, we will use the MySQL database in this chapter. The MySQL Workbench is a tool that allows you to work with MySQL databases to manage and query the data held within a particular database instance. For references for mySQL and the MySQL Workbench see the links at the end of this chapter.

As an example, within the MySQL Workbench we can create a new table using a menu option on a database:

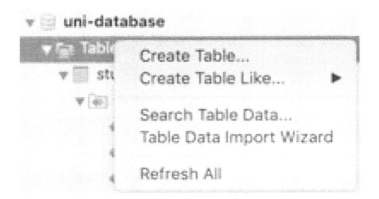

Using this we can interactively define the columns that will comprise the table:

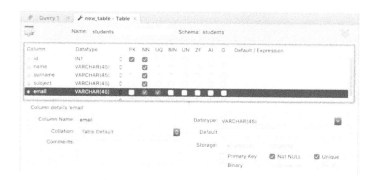

Here each column name, its type and whether it is the primary key (PK), not empty(or Not Null NN) or unique (UQ) have been specified. When the changes are applied, the tool also shows you the DDL that will be used to create the database:

```
1    CREATE TABLE  students . students  (
2        id   INT NOT NULL,
3        name   VARCHAR( ) NOT NULL,
4        surname   VARCHAR( ) NOT NULL,
5        subject   VARCHAR( ) NOT NULL,
6        email   VARCHAR( ) NOT NULL,
7       PRIMARY KEY ( id ),
8       UNIQUE INDEX  email_UNIQUE  ( email  ASC));
9
```

When this is applied a new table is created in the database as shown below:

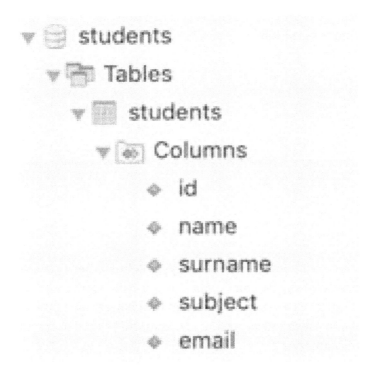

The tool also allows us to populate data into the table; this is done by entering data into a grid and hitting apply as shown below:

SQL and Databases

We can now use query languages to identify and return data held in the database often using specific criteria.

For example, let us say we want to return all the people who have the surname Jones from the following table:

id	name	surname	subject	email
cs_18	Phoebe	Cooke	Animation	pc@my.com
cs_21	Gryff	Jones	Games	gj@my.com
cs_27	Adam	Fosh	Music	af@my.com
cs_29	Jasmine	Smith	Games	js@my.com
cs_31	Tom	Jones	Music	tj@my.com

student_table

We can do this by specifying that data should be returned where the surname equals 'Jones'; in SQL this would look like:

```
SELECT * FROM students where surname='Jones';
```

The above SELECT statement states that all the properties (columns or attributes) in a row in the table students are to be returned where the surname equals 'Jones'. The result is that two rows are returned:

id	name	surname	subject	email
2	Gryff	Jones	Games	gj@my.com
5	Tom	Jones	Music	tj@my.com

Note we need to specify the table we are interested in and what data we want to return (the '*' after the select indicated we want all the data). If we were only interested in their first names then we could use:

```
SELECT name FROM students where surname='Jones';
```

This would return only the names of the students:

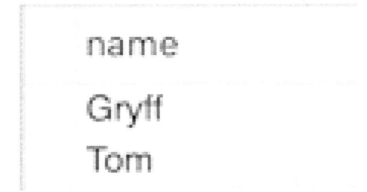

Data Manipulation Language

Data can also be inserted into a table or existing data in a table can be updated. This is done using the Data

Manipulation Language (DML).

For example, to insert data into a table we merely need to write an INSERT SQL statement providing the values to be added and how they map to the columns in the table:

```
INSERT INTO 'students'('id', 'name', 'surname',
'subject',
'email') VALUES ('6', 'James', 'Andrews', 'Games',
'ja@my.com');
```

This would add the row 6 to the table students with the result that the table would now have an additional row:

id	name	surname	subject	email
1	Phoebe	Cooke	Animation	pc@my.com
2	Gryff	Jones	Games	gj@my.com
3	Adam	Fosh	Music	af@my.com
4	Jasmine	Smith	Games	js@my.com
5	Tom	Jones	Music	tj@my.com
6	James	Andrews	Games	ja@my.com

Updating an existing row is a little more complicated as it is first necessary to identify the row to be updated and then the data to modify. Thus an UPDATE statement includes a where clause to ensure the correct row is modified:

```
UPDATE 'students' SET 'email'='grj@my.com' WHERE
'id'='2';
```

The effect of this code is that the second row in the students table is modified with the new email address:

id	name	surname	subject	email
1	Phoebe	Cooke	Animation	pc@my.com
2	Gryff	Jones	Games	grj@my.com
3	Adam	Fosh	Music	af@my.com
4	Jasmine	Smith	Games	js@my.com
5	Tom	Jones	Music	tj@my.com
6	James	Andrews	Games	ja@my.com

Transactions in Databases

Another important concept within a database is that of a Transaction. A Transaction represents a unit of work performed within a database management system (or similar system) against a database instance,and is independent of any other transaction.

Transactions in a database environment have two main purposes

- To provide a unit of work that allows recovery from failures and keeps a database consistent even in cases of system failure, when execution stops (completely or partially). This is because either all the operations within a transaction are performed or none of them are. Thus, if one operation causes an error then all the changes being made by the transaction thus far are rolled back and none of them will have been made.

- To provide isolation between programs accessing a database concurrently. This means that the work being done by one program will not interact with another programs work.

A database transaction, by definition, must be atomic, consistent, isolated and durable:

- Atomic This indicates that a transaction represents an atomic unit of work; that is either all the operations in the transaction are performed or none of them are performed.
- Consistent Once completed the transaction must leave the data in a consistent state with any data constraints met (such as a row in one table must not reference an non-existent row in another table in a one to many relationship etc.).
- Isolated This relates to the changes being made by concurrent transactions; these changes must be isolated from each other. That is, one transaction cannot see the changes being made by another transaction until the second transaction completes and all changes are permanently saved into the database.
- Durable This means that once a transaction completes then the changes it has made are permanently stored into the database (until some future transaction modifies that data).

Database practitioners often refer to these properties of database transactions using the acronym ACID (for Atomic,

Consistent, Isolated,Durable).

Not all databases support transactions although all commercial, production quality databases such as Oracle, Microsoft SQL Server and MySQL, do support transactions.

Further Reading

If you want to know more about databases and database management systems here are some online resources:

- https://en.wikipedia.org/wiki/Database which is the wikipedia entry for data- bases and thus acts as a useful quick reference and jumping off point for other material.
- https://en.wikibooks.org/wiki/Introduction_to_Computer_Information_Systems/Database which provides a short introduction to databases.
- https://www.techopedia.com/6/28832/enterprise/databases/introduction-to-data-bases another useful starting point for delving deeper into databases.
- https://en.wikipedia.org/wiki/Object_database for information on Object databases.
- https://en.wikipedia.org/wiki/NoSQL for an introduction to No SQL or non relational databases.
- https://www.mysql.com/ for the MySQL Database.
- https://dev.mysql.com/downloads/workbench The MySQL Workbench home page.
- https://www.mongodb.com/ for the home page of the MongoDBsite.

- http://couchdb.apache.org/ for the Apache Couch Database.

If you want to explore the subject of database design (that is design of the tables and links between tables in a database)then these references may help:

- https://en.wikipedia.org/wiki/Database_design the wikipedia entry for database design.
- https://www.udemy.com/cwdatabase-design-intro duction/ which covers most of the core ideas within database design.
- http://en.tekstenuitleg.net/articles/software/databas e-design-tutorial/intro.html which provides another tutorial that covers most of the core elements of data-base design.

If you wish to explore SQL more then see:

- https://en.wikipedia.org/wiki/SQL the wikipedia site for SQL
- https://www.w3schools.com/sql/sql_intro.asp which is the W3 school material on SQL and as such an excellent resource.
- https://www.codecademy.com/learn/learn-sql which is a code academy site for SQL.

Python DB-API

Accessing a Database from Python

The standard for accessing a database in Python is the Python DB-API. This specifies a set of standard interfaces for modules that wish to allow Python to access a specific database. The standard is described in PEP 249 (https://www.python.org/ dev/peps/pep-0249)—a PEP is a Python Enhancement Proposal.

Almost all Python database access modules adhere to this standard. This means that if you are moving from one database to another, or attempting to port a Python program from one database to another, then the APIs you encounter should be very similar (although the SQL processed by different database can also differ). There are modules available for most common databases such as MySQL, Oracle, Microsoft SQL Server etc.

TheDB-API

There are several key elements to the DB_API these are:

- The connect function. The connect() function that is used to connect to a database and returns a Connection Object.
- Connection Objects. Within the DB–API access to a database is achieved through connection objects. These connection objects provide access to cursor objects.
- Cursor objects are used to execute SQL statements on the database.
- The result of an execution. These are the results that can be fetched as a sequence of sequences (such a tuple of tuples). The standard can thus be used to select, insert or update information in the database.

These elements are illustrated below:

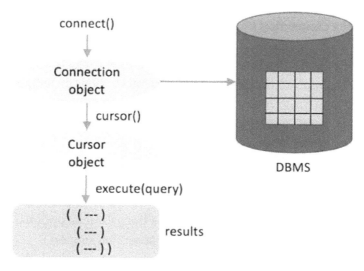

The standard specifies a set of functions and objects to be

used to connect to a database. These include the connection function, the Connection Object and the Cursor object.

The above elements are described in more detail below.

The Connect Function

The connection function is defined as:

```
connect(parameters...)
```

It is used to make the initial connection to the database. The connection returns a Connection Object. The parameters required by the connection function are data- base dependent.

The Connection Object

The Connection Object is returned by the connect() function. The Connection object provides several methods including:

- close() used to close the connection once you no longer need it. The connection will be unusable from this point on wards.
- commit() used to commit a pending transaction.
- rollback() used to rollback all the changes made to the database since the last transaction commit (optional as not all databases provide transaction support).
- cursor() returns a new Cursor object to use with the connection.

The Cursor Object

The Cursor object is returned from the connection.cusor() method. A Cursor Object represents a database cursor, which is used to manage the context of a fetch operation or the execution of a database command. Cursors support a variety of attributes and methods:

- cursor.execute(operation, parameters) Prepare and execute a database operation (such as a query statement or an update command). Parameters may be provided as a sequence or mapping and will be bound to variables in the operation. Variables are specified in a database specific notation.
- cursor.row count a read-only attribute providing the number of rows that the last cursor.execute() call returned (for select style statements) or affected (for update or insert style statements).
- cursor.description a read only attribute providing information on the columns present in any results returned from a SELECT operation.
- cursor.close() closes the cursor. From this point on the cursor will not be usable.

In addition, the Cursor object also provides several fetch style methods. These methods are used to return the results of a database query. The data returned is made up of a sequence of sequences (such as a tuple of tuples) where each inner sequence represents a single row returned by the SELECT statement. The fetch methods defined by the standard are:

- cursor.fetchone() Fetch the next row of a query result set, returning a single sequence, or None when no more data is available.
- cursor.fetchall()Fetch all (remaining) rows of a query result, returning them as a sequence of sequences.
- cursor.fetchman(size) Fetch the next set of rows of a query result, returning a sequence of sequences (e.g. a tuple of tuples). An empty sequence is returned when no more rows are available. The number of rows to fetch per call is specified by the parameter.

Mappings from Database Types to Python Types

The DB-API standard also specifies a set of mappings from the types used in a database to the types used in Python. For a full listing see the DB-API standard itself but the key mappings include:

Date(year, month, day)	Represents a database date
Time(hour, minute, second)	Represents a time database value
Timestamp(year, month, day, hour, minute, second)	Holds a database time stamp value
String	Used to represent string like database data (such as VARCHARs)

Generating Errors

The standard also specifies a set of Exceptions that can be thrown in different situations.

These are presented below and in the following table:

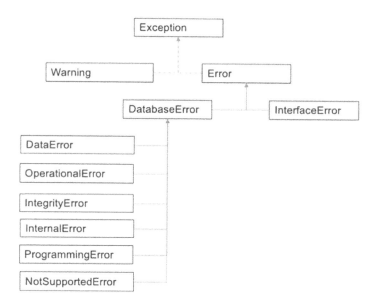

The above diagram illustrates the inheritance hierarchy for the errors and warning associated with the standard. Note that the DB–API Warning and Error both extend the Exception class from standard Python; however, depending on the specific implementation there may be one or more additional classes in the hierarchy between these classes. For example, in the PyMySQL module there is a MySQLError class that extends Exception and is then extended by both

Warning and Error.

Also note that Warning and Error have no relationship with each other. This is because Warnings are not considered

Errors and thus have a separate class hierarchies. However, the Error is the root class for all database Error classes.

A description of each Warning or Error class is provided below.

Warning	Used to warn of issues such as data truncations during inserting, etc.
Error	The base class of all other error exceptions
InterfaceError	Exception raised for errors that are related to the database interface rather than the database itself
Database Error	Exception raised for errors that are related to the database
Data Error	Exception raised for errors that are due to problems with the data such as division by zero, numeric value out of range, etc.
Operational Error	Exception raised for errors that are related to the database's operation and not necessarily under the control of the programmer, e.g. an unexpected disconnect occurs, etc.
Integrity Error	Exception raised when the relational integrity of the database is affected
Internal Error	Exception raised when the database encounters an internal error, e.g. the cursor is not valid anymore, the transaction is out of sync, etc.
ProgrammingError	Exception raised for programming errors, e.g. table not found, syntax error in the SQL statement, wrong number of parameters specified, etc.
NotSupportedError	Exception raised in case a method or database API was used which is not supported by the database, e.g. requesting a `rollback()` on a connection that does not support transactions or has transactions turned off

Row Descriptions

The Cursor object has an attribute description that provides a sequence of sequences; each sub sequence provides a description of one of the attributes of the data returned by a SELECT statement. The sequence describing the attribute is made up of up to seven items, these include:

- name representing the name of the attribute,
- type_code which indicates what Python type this at-

tribute has been mapped to,
- display_size the size used to display the attribute,
- internal_size the size used internally to represent the value,
- precision if a real numeric value the precision supported by the attribute,
- scale indicates the scale of the attribute,
- null_ok this indicates whether null values are acceptable for this attribute.

The first two items (name and type_code) are mandatory, the other five are optional and are set to None if no meaningful values can be provided.

Transactions in PyMySQL

Transactions are managed in PyMySQL via the database connection object. This object provides the following method:

- connection.commit()this causes the current transaction to commit all the changes made permanently to the database. A new transaction is then started.
- connection.rollback() this causes all changes that have been made so far (but not permanently stored into the database i.e. Not committed) to be removed. A new transaction is then started.

The standard does not specify how a database interface should manage turning on and off transaction (not least because not all databases support transactions). However,

MySQL does support transactions and can work in two modes; one supports the use of transactions as already described; the other uses an auto commit mode. In auto commit mode each command sent to the database (whether a SELECT statement or an INSERT/UPDATE statement) is treated as an independent transaction and any changes are automatically committed at the end of the statement. This auto commit mode can be turned on in PyMySQL using:

- connection.autocommit(True) turn on auto commit (False to turn off auto commit which is the default).

Other associated methods include

- connection.get_autocommit() which returns a boolean indicating whether auto commit is turned on or not.
- connection.begin() to explicitly begin a new transaction.

Online Resources

See the following online resources for more information on the Python Database API:

- https://www.python.org/dev/peps/pep-0249/ Python Database API Specification V2.0.
- https://wiki.python.org/moin/DatabaseProgramming Database Programming in Python.
- https://docs.python-guide.org/scenarios/db/ Databases and Python.

PyMySQL Module

The PyMySQL Module

The PyMySQL module provides access to a MySQL database from Python. It implements the Python DB-API v 2.0. This module is a pure Python database interface implementation meaning that it is portable across different operating systems; this is notable because some database interface modules are merely wrappers around other (native) implementations that may or may not be available on different operating systems. For example, a native Linux based database inter- face module may not be available for the Windows operating system. If you are never going to switch between different operating systems, then this is not a problem of course.

To use the PyMySQL module you will need to install it on your computer. This will involve using a tool such as Anaconda or adding it to your PyCharm project. You can also use pip to install it:

```
> pip install PyMySQL
```

Working with the PyMySQL Module

To use the PyMySQL module to access a database you will need to follow these steps.

1. Import the module.
2. Make a connection to the host machine running the database and to the database you are using.
3. Obtain a cursor object from the connection object.
4. Execute some SQL using the cursor.execute() method.
5. Fetch the result(s) of the SQL using the cursor object (e.g. fetchall,fetchmany or fetchone).
6. Close the database connection.

These steps are essentially boiler plate, code that is you will use them whenever you access a database via PyMySQL (or indeed any DB-API compliant module).

We will take each of these steps in turn.

Importing the Module

As the PyMySQL module is not one of the built-in modules provided by default with Python you will need to import the module into your code, for example using

```
import pymsql
```

Be careful with the case used here as the module name is pymysql in the code (if you try to import PyMySQL Python will not find it!).

Connect to the Database

Each database module will have their own specifics for connecting to the database server; these usually involve specifying the machine that the database is running on (as databases can be quiet resource intensive, they are often run on a separate physical computer), the user to use for the connection and any security information required such as a password and the database instance to connect to. In most cases a database is looked after by a database management system (a DBMS) that can manage multiple database instances and it is therefore necessary to specify which database instance you are interested in.

For MySQL, the MySQL database server is a DBMS that can indeed look after multiple database instances. The pymysql.connect function thus requires the following information when connecting to the database is:

- The name of the machine hosting the MySQL database servere.g. dbserver. mydomain.com. If you want to connect to the same machine as your Python program is running on, then you can use localhost. This is a special name reserved for the local machine and avoids you needing to worry about the name of your local computer.

The user name to use for the connection. Most databases limit access to their databases to named users. These are not necessary users such as humans that log into a system but rather entities that are allowed to connect to the database and perform certain operations. For example,one user may only be able to read data in the database where as another user is allowed to insert new data into the database. These users are authenticated by requiring them to provide a password.

· The password for the user.
· The database instance to connect to. As mentioned in the previous chapter a Database

Management System (DMS) can manage multiple database instances and thus it is necessary to say which database instance you are interested in.

For example:

```
# Open database connection connection =
pymysql.connect('localhost','username','password','uni-
database')
```

In this case the machine we are connecting to is 'localhost' (that is the same machine as the Python program itself is running on), the user is represented by 'username' and 'password' and the database instance of interest is called 'uni-database'.

This returns a Connection object as per the DB-API standard.

Obtaining the Cursor Object

You can obtain the cursor object from the connection using the cursor() method:

```
# prepare a cursor object using cursor()
method cursor = connection.cursor()
```

Using the Cursor Object

Once you have obtained the cursor object you can use it to execute an SQL query or a DML insert, update or delete statement. The following example uses a simple select statement to select all the attributes in the students table for all rows currently stored in the students table:

```
# execute SQL query using execute() method.
cursor.execute('SELECT * FROM students')
```

Note that this method executes the SELECT statement but does not return the set of results directly. Instead the execute method returns an integer indicating the number of rows either affected by the modification or returned as part of the query. In the case of a SELECT statement the number returned can be used to determine which type of fetch method to use.

Obtaining Information About the Results

The Cursor Object can also be used to obtain information about the results to be fetched such as how many rows there are in the results and what the type is of each attribute in the results:

- cusor.rowcount() this is a read-only property that indicates the number of rows returned for a SELECT statement or rows affected for a UPDATE or INSERT statement.
- cursor.description()this is a read-only property that provides a description of each attribute in the results set. Each description provides the name of the attribute and an indication of the type (via a type_code) as well as further information on whether the value can be null or not and for numbers scale, precision and size information.

An example of using these two properties is given below:

```
print('cursor.rowcount', cursor.rowcount)
print('cursor.description', cursor.description)
A sample of the output generated by these lines
is given below:
cursor.rowcount  6
cursor.description (('id', 3, None, 11, 11,
0, False), ('name', 253, None, 180, 180, 0,
 False), ('surname', 253, None, 180, 180, 0,
 False), ('subject', 253, None, 180, 180,
0, False), ('email', 253, None, 180, 180,
0, False))
```

Fetching Results

Now that a successful SELECT statement has been run against the database, we can fetch the results. The results are returned as a tuple of tuples. As mentioned in the last chapter there are several different fetch options available including fetchone (), fetchmany(size) and fetchall(). In the following example we use the fetchall() option as we know that there are only up to six rows that can be returned.

```
# Fetch all the rows and then iterate
over the data data = cursor.fetchall()
for row in data:
print('row:', row)
```

In this case we loop through each tuple within the data collection and print that row out. However, we could just as easily have extracted the information in the tuple into individual elements. These elements could then be used to construct an object that could then be processed within an application, for example:

```
for row in data:
id, name, surname, subject, email = row
student = Student(id, name, surname,
subject, email)
print(student)
```

Close the Connection

Once you have finished with the database connection it

should be closed.

```
# disconnect from server
connection.close()
```

Complete PyMySQL Query Example

A complete listing illustrating connecting up to the database, running a SELECT statement and printing out the results using a Student class is given below:

```
import pymysql
class Student:
def init (self, id, name, surname,
subject, email):
self.id = id
self.name = name
self.surname = surname
self.subject = subject
self.email = email
def str (self):
return 'Student[' + str(id) + '] ' + name
 + ' ' +
surname + ' - ' + subject + ' ' + email
# Open database connection
connection = pymysql.connect('localhost',
'user',
'password',
'uni-database')
# prepare a cursor object using cursor()
method cursor = connection.cursor()
# execute SQL query using execute() method.
cursor.execute('SELECT * FROM students')
print('cursor.rowcount', cursor.rowcount)
```

```
print('cursor.description', cursor.description)
# Fetch all the rows and then iterate
over the data data = cursor.fetchall()
for row in data:
student_id, name, surname, subject, email =
row
student = Student(student_id, name, surname,
 subject,
email)
print(student)
# disconnect from server connection.close()
```

The output from this program, for the database created in the last chapter is shown here:

```
cursor.rowcount  6
cursor.description (('id', 3, None, 11, 11,
0, False),
('name', 253, None, 180, 180, 0, False),
('surname', 253, None, 180, 180, 0, False),
('subject', 253, None, 180, 180,
0, False), ('email', 253, None, 180, 180,
0, False))
Student[1] Phoebe Cooke - Animation pc@my.com
Student[2] Gryff Jones - Games grj@my.com
Student[3] Adam Fosh - Music af@my.com
Student[4]Jasmine Smith - Games js@my.com
Student[5] Tom Jones - Music tj@my.com
Student[6] James Andrews - Games ja@my.com
```

Inserting Data to the Database

As well as reading data from a database many applications also need to add new data to the database. This is done via the DML (Data Manipulation Language) INSERT statement. The process for this is very similar to running a query against the database using a SELECT statement; that is, you need to make a connection, obtain a cursor object and execute the statement. The one difference here is that you do not need to fetch the results.

```python
import pymysql
# Open database connection connection =
pymysql.connect('localhost', 'user',
'password', 'uni-database')
# prepare a cursor object using cursor()
methodcursor = connection.cursor()
try:
# Execute INSERT command
cursor.execute("INSERT INTO students (id, name,
surname, subject, email) VALUES (7, 'Denise',
'Byrne', 'History',
'db@my.com')")
# Commit the changes to the database
connection.commit()
except:
# Something went wrong
# rollback the changes
connection.rollback()
# Close the database
connectionconnection.close()
```

The result of running this code is that the database is updated with a seventh row for 'Denise Byrne'. This can be seen in the MySQL Workbench if we look at the contents of the students table:

id	name	surname	subject	email
1	Phoebe	Cooke	Animation	pc@my.com
2	Gryff	Jones	Games	grj@my.com
3	Adam	Fosh	Music	af@my.com
4	Jasmine	Smith	Games	js@my.com
5	Tom	Jones	Music	tj@my.com
6	James	Andrews	Games	ja@my.com
7	Denise	Byrne	History	db@my.com

There are a couple of points to note about this code example. The first is that we have used the double quotes around the string defining the INSERT command— this is because a double quotes string allows us to include single quotes within that string. This is necessary as we need to quote any string values passed to the database (such as 'Denise').

The second thing to note is that by default the PyMySQL database interface requires the programmer to decide when to commit or rollback a transaction. A transaction was introduced in the last chapter as an atomic unit of work that must either be completed or as a whole or rollback so that no changes are made. However, the way in which we indicate that a transaction is completed is by calling the commit() method on the database connection. In turn we can indicate that we want to rollback the current transaction by calling rollback(). In either case, once the method has been invoked a new transaction is started for any further database activity.

In the above code we have used a try block to ensure that if everything succeeds, we will commit the changes made, but if an exception is thrown (of any kind) we will rollback the transaction—this is a common pattern.

Updating Data in the Database

If we are able to insert new data into the database, we may also want to update the data in a database, for example to correct some information. This is done using the UPDATE statement which must indicate which existing row is being updated as well as what the new data should be.

```python
import pymysql
# Open database connection
connection = pymysql.connect('localhost',
'user',
'password',
'uni-database')
# prepare a cursor object using cursor()
method cursor = connection.cursor()
try:
# Execute UPDATE command
cursor.execute("UPDATE students SET email =
'denise@my.com' WHERE id = 7")
# Commit the changes to the database
connection.commit()
except:
# rollback the changes if an exception /
error
connection.rollback()
# Close the database connection
connection.close()
```

In this example we are updating the student with id 7 such that their email address will be changed to 'denise

@my.com'. This can be verified by examining the contents of the students table in the MySQL Workbench:

id	name	surname	subject	email
1	Phoebe	Cooke	Animation	pc@my.com
2	Gryff	Jones	Games	grj@my.com
3	Adam	Fosh	Music	af@my.com
4	Jasmine	Smith	Games	js@my.com
5	Tom	Jones	Music	tj@my.com
6	James	Andrews	Games	ja@my.com
7	Denise	Byrne	History	denise@my.com

Deleting Data in the Database

Finally, it is also possible to delete data from a database, for example if a student leaves their course. This follows the same format as the previous two examples with the difference that the DELETE statement is used instead:

```
import pymysql
# Open database connection
connection = pymysql.connect('localhost',
'user',
'password',
'uni-database')
# prepare a cursor object using cursor()
method cursor = connection.cursor()
try:
# Execute DELETE command
cursor.execute("DELETE FROM studentsWHERE id = 7")
# Commit the changes to the database
connection.commit()
except:
# rollback the changes if an exception /
```

```
error
connection.rollback()
# Close the database connection
connection.close()
```

In this case we have deleted the student with id 7. We can see that again in the MySQL Workbench by examining the contents of the students table after this code has run:

id	name	surname	subject	email
1	Phoebe	Cooke	Animation	pc@my.com
2	Gryff	Jones	Games	grj@my.com
3	Adam	Fosh	Music	af@my.com
4	Jasmine	Smith	Games	js@my.com
5	Tom	Jones	Music	tj@my.com
6	James	Andrews	Games	ja@my.com

Result Grid | Filter Rows: | Edit:

Creating Tables

It is not just data that you can add to a database; if you wish you can programmatically create new tables to be used with an application. This process follows exactly the same pattern as those used for INSERT, UPDATE and DELETE. The only difference is that the command sent to the database contains a CREATE statement with a description of the table to be created. This is illustrated below:

```
import pymysql
# Open database connection
connection = pymysql.connect('localhost',
'user',
```

```
'password',
'uni-database')
# prepare a cursor object using cursor()
method cursor = connection.cursor()
try:
# Execute CREATE command
cursor.execute("CREATE TABLE log (message
VARCHAR(100) NOT NULL)")
# Commit the changes to the database
connection.commit()
except:
# rollback the changes if an exception /
error
connection.rollback()
# Close the database connection
connection.close()
```

This creates a new table log within the uni-database; this can be seen by looking at the tables listed for the uni-database within the MySQL Workbench.

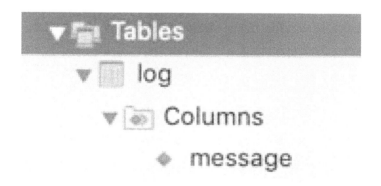

Online Resources

See the following online resources for more information on the Python Database API:

- https://pymysql.readthedocs.io/en/latest/PyMySQL Documentation site.
- https://github.com/PyMySQL/PyMySQL Git hub repository for the PyMySQL library.

Try

In this exercise you will create a database and tables based on a set of transactions stored in a current account. You can use the account class you created in the CSV and Excel chapter for this.

You will need two tables, one for the account information and one for the transaction history. The primary key of the account information table can be used as the foreign key for the transaction history table. Then write a function that takes an Account object and populates the tables with the appropriate data.

To create the account information table you might use the following DDL:

```
CREATE TABLE acc_info (idacc_info INT NOT NULL,
name
VARCHAR(255) NOT NULL, PRIMARY KEY (idacc_info))
```

While for the transactions table you might use:

```
CREATE TABLE transactions (idtransactions INT NOT
NULL, type
VARCHAR(45) NOT NULL, amount VARCHAR(45) NOT
NULL, account INT
NOT NULL, PRIMARY KEY (idtransactions))"
```

Remember to be careful with integers and decimals if you
are creating an SQL string such as:

```
statement  =  "INSERT  into  transactions
(idtransactions,  type, amount,  account)  VALUES
 ("  +  str(id)  +  ",  '"  +  action  +  "',  "
+ str(amount)  +  ",  "  +  str(account_number)
+  ")"
```

Introduction to Logging

Introduction

Many programming languages have common logging libraries including Java and C# and of course Python also has a logging module. Indeed the Python logging module has been part of the built in modules since Python 2.3.

This chapter discusses why you should add logging to your programs, what you should (and should not) log and why just using the print() function is not sufficient.

Why Log?

Logging is typically a key aspect of any production application; this is because it is important to provide appropriate information to allow future investigation following some event or issue in such applications. These investigations include:

- Diagnosing failures; that is why did an application fail/crash.

- Identifying unusual or unexpected behavior; which might not cause the application to fail but which may leave it in an unexpected state or where data may be corrupted etc.
- Identifying performance or capacity issues; in such situations the application is performing as expected by it is not meeting some non-functional requirements associated with the speed at which it is operating or its ability to scale as the amount of data or the number of users grows.
- Dealing with attempted malicious behavior in which some outside agent is attempting to affect the behavior of the system or to acquire information which they should not have access to etc. This could happen for example, if you are creating a Python web application and a user tries to hack into your web server.
- Regulatory or legal compliance. In some cases records of program execution may be required for regulatory or legal reasons. This is particularly true of the financial sector where records must be kept for many years in case there is a need to investigate the organizations' or individuals' behavior.

What Is the Purpose of Logging?

In general there are therefore two general reason to log what an application is doing during it operation:

- For diagnostic purposes so that recorded events/steps can be used to analyze the behavior of the system when something goes wrong.

· Auditing purposes that allow for later analysis of the behavior of the system for business, legal or regulatory purposes. For example, in this case to determine who did what with what and when.

Without such logged information it is impossible after the event to know what happened. For example, if all you know is that an application crashed (unexpectedly stopped executing) how can you determine what state the application was in, what functions, methods etc. were being executed and which statements run?

Remember that although a developer may have been using an IDE to run their applications during development and may possibly been using the debugging facilities available that allow you to see what functions or methods, statements and even variable values are place; this is not how most production systems are run. In general a production Python system will be run either from a command line or possibly through a short cut (on a Windows box) to simplify running the program. All the user will know is that something failed or that the behavior they expected didn't occur—if in fact they are aware of any issue at all!

Logs are therefore key to after the event analysis of failures, unexpected behavior or for analysis of the operation of the system for business reasons.

What Should You Log?

One question that you might be considering at this point is 'what information should I log?'. An application should log enough information so that post event investigators can understand what was happening, when and where. In general this means that you will want to log the time of the log message, the module/filename, function name or method name executing, potentially the log level being used (see later) and in some cases the parameter values/state of the environment, program or class involved.

In many cases developers log the entry (and to a lesser extent) the exit from a function or method. However, it may also be useful to log what happens at branch points within a function or method so that the logic of the application can be followed.

All applications should log all errors/exceptions. Although care is needed to ensure that this is done appropriately. For example if an exception is caught and then re thrown several times it is not necessary to log it every time it is caught. Indeed doing this can make the log files much larger, cause confusion when the problem is being investigated and result in unnecessary overheads. One common approach is to log an exception where it is first raised and caught and not to log it after that.

What Not to Log

The follow on question to consider is 'what information should I not log?'. One general area not to log is any personal or sensitive information including any information that can be used to identify an individual. This sort of information is known as PII or Personally Identification Information.

Such information includes

- user ids and passwords,
- email addresses,
- data of birth, birth place,
- personally identifiable financial information such as bank account details,credit card details etc.,
- bio metric information,
- medical/health information,
- government issued personal information such as passport details,drivers license number, social security numbers, National Insurance numbers etc.,
- official organizational information such as professional registrations and membership numbers,
- physical addresses, phone (land-line) numbers, mobile phone numbers,
- verification elated information such as mother's maiden name, pets' names, high school, first school, favorite film, etc.,
- it also increasing includes online information relating to social media such as

Facebook or LinkedIn accounts.

All of the above is sensitive information and much of it can be used to identify an individual; none of this information should be logged directly.

That does not mean that you cannot and shouldn't log that a user logged in; you may well need to do that. However, the information should at least be obfuscated and should not include any information not required. For example you may record that a user represented by some id attempted to log in at a specific time and whether they were successful or not. However, you should not log their password and may not log the actual user id instead you may log an id that can be used to map to their actual user id.

You should also be careful about directly logging data input too an application directly into a log file. One way in which a malicious agent can attack an application (particularly a web application) is by attempting to send very large amounts of data to it (as part of a field or as a parameter to an operation). If the application blindly logs all data submitted to it, then the log files can fill up very quickly. This can result in the file store being used by the application filling up and causing potential problems for all software using the same file store. This form of attack is known as a log (or log file) injection attack and is well documented (see https:// www.owasp.org/index.php/Log_Injection which is part of the well respected Open Web Application Security Project).

Another point to note is that it is not merely enough to log an error. This is not error handling; logging an error does not mean you have handled it; only that you have noted it. An application should still decide how it should manage the error or exception.

In general you should also aim for empty logs in a production system; that is only information that needs to be logged in a production system should be logged (often information about errors, exceptions or other unexpected behavior). However, during testing much more detail is required so that the execution of the system should be followed. It should therefore be possible to select how much information is logged depending on the environment the code is running in (that is within a test environment or within a production environment).

A final point to note is that it is important to log information to the correct place. Many applications (and organizations) log general information to one log file, errors and exceptions to another and security information to a third. It is therefore important to know where your log information is being sent and not to send information to the wrong log.

Why Not Just Use Print?

Assuming that you want to log information in your application then next question is how should you do that? Through this book we have been using the Python print() function to print out information that indicates results generated by our code but also at times what is happening with a function or a method etc.

Thus we need to consider whether using the print() function the best way to log information.

In actual fact, using print() to log information in a production system is almost never the right answer, this is for several reasons:

- The print()function by default writes strings out to the standard output (stdout) or standard error output (stderr) which by default directs output to the console/ terminal. For example, when you run an application within an IDE, the output is displayed in the Console window. If you run an application from the command line then the output is directed back to that command/terminal window. Both of these are fine during development, but what if the program is not run from a command window, perhaps instead it is started up by the operating system automatically (as is typical of numerous services such as a print service or a web server). In this case there is no terminal/console window to send the data to; instead the data is just lost. As it happens the stdout and stderr output streams can be directed to a file (or files). However, this is typically done when the program is launched and may be easily omitted. In addition there is only the option of sending all stdout to a specific file or all error output to the stderr.

- Another issue with using the print()function is that all calls to print will be output. When using most loggers it is possible to specify the log level required. These different log levels allow different amounts of information to be generated depending upon the scenario. For example, in a well tested reliable production system we may only want error related or critical information to be logged. This will reduce the amount of information we are collecting and reduce any performance impact introduced by logging into the application. However, during testing phases we may want a far more detailed level of logging.

· In other situations we may wish to change the log level being used for a running production system without needing to modify the actual code (as this has the potential to introduced errors into the code). Instead we would like to have the facility to externally change the way in which the logging system behaves, for example through a configuration file. This allows system administrators to modify the amount and the detail of the information being logged. It typically also allows the designation of the log information to be changed.

· Finally, when using the print()function a developer can use whatever format they like, they can include a timestamp on the message or not, they can include the module or function/method name or not they can include parameters of not. Using a logging system usually standardizes the information generated along with the log message. Thus all log messages will have (or not have) a times- tamp,or all messages will include (or not include) information on the function or method in which they were generated etc.

Logging in Python

The Logging Module

Python has included a builtin logging module since Python 2.3. This module, the logging module, defines functions and classes which implement a flexible logging framework that can be used in any Python application/script or in Python libraries/modules.

Although different logging frameworks differ in the specific details of what they offer; almost all offer the same core elements (although different names are sometimes used). The Python logging module is no different and the core elements that make up the logging framework and its processing pipeline are shown below (note that a very similar diagram could be drawn for login frameworks in Java, Scala, C++ etc.).

The following diagram illustrates a Python program that uses the built-in Python logging framework to log messages to a file.

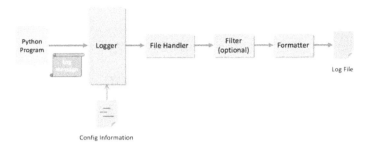

Config Information

The core elements of the logging framework (some of which are optional) are shown above and described below:

- Log Message The is the message to be logged from the application.
- Logger Provides the programmers entry point/interface to the logging system.

The Logger class provides a variety of methods that can be used to log messages at different levels.

- Handler Handlers determine where to send a log message, default handlers include file handlers that send messages to a file and HTTP handlers that send messages to a web server.
- Filter This is an optional element in the logging pipeline. They can be used to further filter the information to be logged providing fine grained control of which log messages are actually output (for example to a log file).
- For matter These are used to format the log message as required. This may involve adding timestamps, module

and function/method information etc. to the original log message.

- Configuration Information The logger (and associated handlers, filters and for matters) can be configured either programmatically in Python or through configuration files. These configuration files can be written using key-value pairs or in a YAML file (which is a simple mark up language). YAML stands for Yet Another Markup Language!

It is worth noting that much of the logging framework is hidden from the developer who really only sees the logger; the remainder of the logging pipeline is either configured by default or via log configuration information typically in the form of a log configuration file.

The Logger

The Logger provides the programmers interface to the logging pipeline. A Logger object is obtained from the getLogger() function defined in the logging module. The following code snippet illustrates acquiring the default logger and using it to log an error message. Note that the logging module must be imported:

```
import logging
logger = logging.getLogger()
logger.error('This should be used with
somethingunexpected'
```

The output from this short application is logged to the console as this is the default configuration:

This should be used with something unexpected

Controlling the Amount of Information Logged

Log messages are actually associated with a log level.These log levels are intended to indicate the severity of the message being logged. There are six different log levels associated with the Python logging framework, these are:

- NOTSET At this level no logging takes place and logging is effectively turned off.
- DEBUG This level is intended to provide detailed information, typically of interest when a developer is diagnosing a bug or issues within an application.
- INFO This level is expected to provide less detail than the DEBUG log level as it is expected to provide information that can be used to confirm that the application is working as expected.
- WARNING This is used to provide information on an unexpected event or an indication of some likely problem that a developer or system administration might wish to investigate further.
- ERROR This is used to provide information on some serious issue or problem that the application has not been able to deal with and that is likely to mean that the application cannot function correctly.
- CRITICAL This is the highest level of issue and is reserved for critical situations such as ones in which

the program can no longer continue executing.

The log levels are relative to one another and defined in a hierarchy. Each log level has a numeric value associated with it as shown below (although you should never need to use the numbers). Thus INFO is a higher log level than DEBUG, in turn ERROR is a higher log level than WARNING, INFO, DEBUG etc.

	CRITICAL	50
	ERROR	40
	WARNING	30
	INFO	20
	DEBUG	10
Increasing log levels	NOTSET	0

Associated with the log level that a message is logged with, a logger also has a log level associated with it. The logger will process all messages that are at the loggers log level or above that level. Thus if a logger has a log level of WARNING then it will log all messages logged using the warning, error and critical log levels.

Generally speaking, an application will not use the DEBUG level in a production system. This is usually considered inappropriate as it is only intended for debug scenarios. The

INFO level may be considered appropriate for a production system although it is likely to produce large amounts of information as it typically traces the execution of functions and methods. If an application has been well tested and verified then it is only really warnings and errors which should occur/be of concern. It is therefore not uncommon to default to the WARNING level for production systems (indeed this is why the default log level is set to WARNING within the Python logging system).

If we now look at the following code that obtains the default logger object and then uses several different logger methods, we can see the effect of the log levels on the output:

```python
import logging
logger = logging.getLogger()
logger.debug('This is to help with debugging')
logger.info('This is just for information')
logger.warning('This is a warning!')
logger.error('This should be used with something
unexpected')
logger.critical('Something serious')
```

The default log level is set to warning, and thus only messages logged at the warning level or above will be printed out:

This is a warning!
This should be used with something unexpected
Something serious

As can be seen from this, the messages logged at the debug and info level have been ignored.

However, the Logger object allows us to change the log level programmatically using the setLevel() method, for example logger.setLevel(logging. DEBUG) or via the logging.basicConfig(level = logging.DEBUG) function; both of these will set the logging level to DEBUG. Note that the log level must be set before the logger is obtained.

If we add one of the above approaches to setting the log level to the previous program we will change the amount of log information generated:

```
import  logging
logging.basicConfig(level=logging.DEBUG)
logger  =  logging.getLogger()
logger.warning('This is a warning!')
logger.info('This is just for information')
logger.debug('This is to help with debugging')
logger.error('This should be used with something
unexpected logger.critical('Something serious')
```

This will now output all the log messages as debug is the lowest logging level. We can of course turn off logging by setting the log level to NOTSET

```
logger.setLevel(logging.NOTSET)
Alternativelyyou can set the Loggers disabled
attribute to True:
logging.Logger.disabled  =  True
```

Logger Methods

The Logger class provides a number of methods that can
be used to control what is logged including:

- setLevel(level) Sets this loggers log level.
- getEffectiveLevel() Returns this loggers log level.
- isEnabledFor(level) Checks to see if this logger is enabled for the log level specified.
- debug(message) logs messages at the debug level.
- info(message) logs messages at the info level.
- warning(message) logs messages at the warning level.
- error(message) logs messages at the error level.
- critical(message) logs messages at the critical level.
- exception(message) This method logs a message at the error level.

However, it can only be used within an exception handler
and includes a stack trace of any associated exception, for
example:

```
import logging
logger = logging.getLogger()
try:
print('starting')
x = 1 / 0 print(x)
except:
logger.exception('an exception message')
print('Done')
```

- log(level, message) logs messages at the log level specified as the first parameter.

In addition there are several methods that are used to manage handlers and filters:

- addFilter(filter) This method adds the specified filter filter to this logger.
- removeFilter(filter) The specified filter is removed from this logger object.
- addHandler(handler) The specified handler is added to this logger.
- removeHandler(handler) Removes the specified handler from this logger.

Default Logger

A default (or root) logger is always available from the logging framework. This logger can be accessed via the functions defined in the logging module. These functions allow messages to be logged at different levels using methods such as info(), error(), warning() but without the need to obtain a reference to a logger object first. For example:

```
import logging
# Set the root logger level
logging.basicConfig(level=logging.DEBUG)
# Use root (default)logger
logging.debug('This is to help with debugging')
```

```
logging.info('This is just for information')
logging.warning('This is a warning!')
logging.error('This shouldbe used with something
unexpected'
logging.critical('Something serious')
```

This example sets the logging level for the root or default logger to DEBUG (the default is WARNING). It then uses the default logger to generate a range of log messages at different levels (from DEBUG up to CRITICAL). The output from this program is given below:

```
DEBUG:root:This  is  to  help  with  debugging
INFO:root:This  is  just  for
informationWARNING:root:This  is  a  warning!
ERROR:root:This  should  be  used  with
something  unexpected
CRITICAL:root:Something  serious
```

Note that the format used by default with the root logger prints the log level, the name of the logger generating the output and the message. From this you can see that it is the root longer that is generating the output.

Module Level Loggers

Most modules will not use the root logger to log information, instead they will use a named or module level logger. Such a logger can be configured independently of the root logger. This allows developers to turn on logging just for

446

a module rather than for a whole application.This can be useful if a developer wishes to investigate an issue that is located within a single module.

Previous code examples in this chapter have used the getLogger() function with no parameters to obtain a logger object, for example:

```
logger = logging.getLogger()
```

This is really just another way of obtaining a reference to the root logger which is used by the stand alone logging functions such as logging.info(), logging.debug()function, thus:

```
logging.warning('my warning')
and
logger=logging.getlogger()
logger.warning('my warning'
```

Have exactly the same effect; the only difference is that the first version involves less code.

However, it is also possible to create a named logger. This is a separate logger object that has its own name and can potentially have its own log level, handlers and formatters etc. To obtain a named logger pass a name string into the getLogger() method:

```
logger1 = logging.getLogger('my logger')
```

This returns a logger object with the name 'my logger'. Note that this may be a brand new logger object, however if any other code within the current system has previously requested a logger called 'my logger' then that logger object will be returned to the current code. Thus multiple calls to getLogger() with the same name will always return a reference to the same Logger object.

It is common practice to use the name of the module as the name of the logger; as only one module with a specific name should exist within any specific system. The name of the module does not need to be hard coded as it can be obtained using the _name_ module attribute, it is thus common to see:

```
logger2  =  logging.getLogger(      name      )
```

We can see the effect of each of these statements by printing out each logger:

```
logger  =  logging.getLogger()
print('Root logger:',  logger)
logger1  =  logging.getLogger('my logger')
print('Named logger:',  logger1)
logger2  =  logging.getLogger(      name   )
print('Module logger:',  logger2)
When the above code is run the output is:
Root  logger:  <RootLogger  root  (WARNING)>
Named  logger:  <Logger  my  logger  (WARNING)>
Module  logger:  <Logger      main
```

```
(WARNING)>
```

This shows that each logger has their own name (the code was run in the main module and thus the module name was main_) and all three loggers have an effective log level of WARNING (which is the default).

Logger Hierarchy

There is in fact a hierarchy of loggers with the root logger at the top of this hierarchy. All named loggers are below the root logger. The name of a logger can actually be a period-separated hierarchical value such as util, util.lib and util.lib.printer. Loggers that are further down the hierarchy are children of loggers further up the logger hierarchy.

For example given a logger called lib, then it will be below the root logger but above the logger with the name util.lib. This logger will in turn be above the logger called util.lib.printer. This is illustrated in the following diagram:

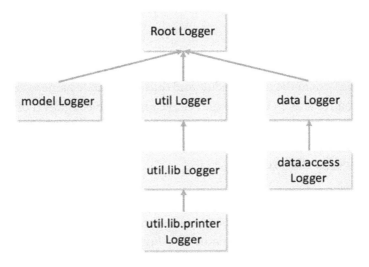

The logger name hierarchy is analogous to the Python package hierarchy, and identical to it if you organize your loggers on a per-module basis using the recommended construction logging.getLogger(_name_).

This hierarchy is important when considering the log level. If a log level has not been set for the current logger then it will look to its parent to see if that logger has a log level set. If it does that will be the log level used. This search back up the logger hierarchy will continue until either an explicit log level is found or the root logger is encountered which has a default log level of WARNING.

This is useful as it is not necessary to explicitly set the log level for every logger object used in an application. Instead it is only necessary to set the root log level (or fora module hierarchy an appropriate point in the module hierarchy).

This can then be overridden where specifically required.

For matters

The are two levels at which you can format the messages logged, these are within the log message passed to a logging method(such as info() or warn()) and via the top level configuration that indicates what additional information may be added to the individual log message.

Formatting Log Messages

The log message can have control characters that indicate what values should be placed within the message, for example:

```
logger.warning('%s is set to %d', 'count', 42)
```

This indicates that the format string expects to be given a string and a number. The parameters to be substituted into the format string follow the format string as a comm separated list of values.

Formatting Log Output

The logging pipeline can be configured to incorporate standard information with each log message. This can be done globally for all handlers. It is also possible to programmatically set a specific for matter on a individual handler;this is discussed in the next section.

To globally set the output format for log messages use the logging. basicConfig() function using the named parameter format.

The format parameter takes a string that can contain LogRecord attributes organized as you see fit. There is a comprehensive list of LogRecord attributes which can be referenced at https://docs.python.org/3/library/logging. html#logrecord-attributes. The key ones are:

- args a tuple listing the arguments used to call the associated function or method.
- asctime indicates the time that the log message was created.
- filename the name of the file containing the log statement.
- module the module name (the name portion of the filename).
- funcName the name of the function or method containing the log statement.
- levelname the log level of the log statement.
- message the log message itself as provided to the log method.

The effect of some of these are illustrated below.

```
import logging
logging.basicConfig(format='%(asctime)s
%(message)s', level=logging.DEBUG)
logger = logging.getLogger(   name   )
```

```
def do_something():
logger.debug('This is to help with debugging')
logger.info('This is just for information')
logger.warning('This is a warning!')
logger.error('This should be used with something
unexpected')
logger.critical('Something serious')
do_something()
```

The above program generates the following log statements:

2019-02-20 16:50:34,084 This is to help with debugging
    2019-02-20 16:50:34,084 This is just for information
    2019-02-20 16:50:34,085 This is a warning!
    2019-02-20 16:50:34,085 This should be used with some-
thing unexpected
    2019-02-20 16:50:34,085 Something serious

However, it might be useful to know the log level associated with the log statements, as well as the function that the log statements were called from. It is possible to obtain this information by changing the format string passed to the logging.basicConfig() function:

```
logging.basicConfig(format='%(asctime)s[%(levelname)s]
%(funcName)s:  %(message)s',  level=logging.DEBUG)
```

Which will now generate the output within log level information and the function involved:

453

2019-02-20 16:54:16,250[DEBUG] do_something: This is to help with debugging

2019-02-20 16:54:16,250[INFO] do_something: This is just for information

2019-02-20 16:54:16,250[WARNING] do_something: This is a warning!

2019-02-20 16:54:16,250[ERROR] do_something: This should be used with something unexpected

2019-02-20 16:54:16,250[CRITICAL] do_something: Something serious

We can even control the format of the date time information associated with the log statement using the data fmt parameter of the logging.basic Config() function:

```
logging.basicConfig(format='%(asctime)s
%(message)s', datefmt='%m/%d/%Y %I:%M:%S%p',
level=logging.DEBUG)
```

This format string uses the formatting options used by the datetime.strp- time() function (see https://docs.python.o rg/3/library/datetime.html#strftime- strptime-behavior) for information on the control characters, in this case

- %m—Month as a zero-padded decimal number e.g. 01, 11, 12.
- %d—Day of the month as a zero-padded decimal number e.g. 01, 12 etc.

- %Y—Year with century as a decimal number e.g. 2020.
- %I—Hour (12-h clock) as a zero-padded decimal number e.g. 01, 10 etc.
- %M—Minute as a zero-padded decimal number e.g. 0, 01, 59 etc.
- %S—Second as a zero-padded decimal number e.g. 00, 01, 59 etc.
- %p—Either AM or PM.

Thus the output generated using the above date fmt string is:

02/20/2019 05:05:18 PM This is to help with debugging
02/20/2019 05:05:18 PM This is just for information
02/20/2019 05:05:18 PM This is a warning!
02/20/2019 05:05:18 PM This should be used with something unexpected
02/20/2019 05:05:18 PM Something serious

To set a for matter on an individual handler see the next section.

Online Resources

For further information on the Python logging framework see the following:

- https://docs.python.org/3/library/logging.html The standard library documentation on the logging facilities in Python.

- https://docs.python.org/3/howto/logging.html A how to guide on logging from the Python standard library documentation.
- https://pymotw.com/3/logging/index.html Python Module of the Week logging page.

Advanced Logging

Introduction

In this chapter we go further into the configuration and modification of the Python logging module. In particular we will look at Handlers (used to determine the destination fo log messages), Filters which can be used by Handlers to provide finer grained control of log output and logger configuration files. We conclude the chapter by considering performance issues associated with logging.

Handlers

Within the logging pipeline, it is a handlers that send the log message to their final destination. By default the handler is set up to direct output to the console/terminal associated with the running program. However, this can be changed to send the log messages to a file, to an email service, to a web server etc. Or indeed to any combination of these as there can be multiple handlers configured for a logger. This is shown in the diagram below:

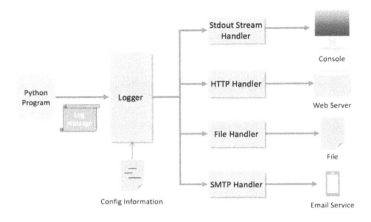

In the above diagram the logger has been configured to send all log messages to four different handlers which allow a log message to be written to the console, to a web server to a file and to an email service. Such a behavior may be required because:

- The web server will allow developers access to a web interface that allows them to seethe log files even if they do not have permission to access a production server.
- The log file ensures that all the log data is permanently stored in a file within the file store.
- An email message may be sent to a notification system so that someone will be notified that there is an issue to be investigated.
- The console may still be available to the system administrators who may wish to look at the log messages generated.

The Python logging framework comes with several differ-ent handlers as suggested above and listed below:

- logging.Stream Handler sends messages to outputs such as stdout, stderr etc.
- logging.FileHandler sends log messages to files. There are several varieties of File Handler in addition to the basic FileHandler, these include the logging.han-dlers.RotatingFileHandler (which will rotate log files based on a maximum file size) and logging.handlers. TimeRotatingFileHandler (which rotates the log file at specified time intervals e.g. daily).
- logging.handlers.SocketHandler which sends mes-sages to a TCP/IP socket where it can be received by a TCP Server.
- logging.handlers.SMTPHandler that sends messages by the SMTP (Simple Mail Transfer Protocol) to a email server.
- logging.handlers.SysLogHandler that sends log mes-sages to a Unix syslog program.
- logging.handlers.NTEventLogHandler that sends mes-sage to a Windows event log.
- logging.handlers.HTTPHandler which sends messages to a HTTP server.
- logging.NullHandler that does nothing with error mes-sages. This is often used by library developers who want to include logging in their applications but expect developers to set up an appropriate handler when they use the library.
- All of these handlers can be configured programmati-cally or via a configuration file.

Setting the Root Output Handler

The following example, uses the logging.basicConfig() function to set up the root logger to use a FileHandler that will write the log messages to a file called 'example.log':

```
import logging
# Sets a file handler on the root logger to
# save log messages to the example.log file
logging.basicConfig(filename='example.log'
,level=logging.DEBUG)
# If no handler is explicitly set on the name
logger
# it will delegate the messages to the parent
logger to handle
logger = logging.getLogger(  name  )
logger.debug('This is to help with debugging' )
logger.info('This is just for information' )
logger.warning('This is a warning!' )
logger.error('This shouldbe used with something
unexpected'  )
logger.critical('Something serious' )
```

Note that if no handler is specified for a named logger then it delegates output to the parent (in this case the root) logger. The file generated for the above program is shown below:

```
 example.log
1     DEBUG:__main__:This is to help with debugging
2     INFO:__main__:This is just for information
3     WARNING:__main__:This is a warning!
4     ERROR:__main__:This should be used with something unexpected
5     CRITICAL:__main__:Something serious
```

As can be seen from this the default for matter is now configured for a File Handler. This File Handler adds the log message level before the log message itself.

Programmatically Setting the Handler

It is also possible to programmatically create a handler and set it for the logger. This is done by instantiating one of the existing handler classes (or by sub classing an existing handler such as the root Handler class or the FileHander etc.). The instantiated handler can then be added as a handler to the logger (remember the logger can have multiple handlers this is why the method is called add Handler ()rather than something such as setHandler).

An example of explicitly setting the FileHandler for a logger is given below:

```
import logging
#Empty  basic  config  turns  off  default
console  handler logging.basicConfig()
logger  =  logging.getLogger(    name    )
logger.setLevel(logging.DEBUG)
#createfile handler which logs to the
specifiedfile
file_handler  =
logging.FileHandler('detailed.log')
#Add the handler to the Logger
logger.addHandler(file_handler)
#'application' code
def do_something(): logger.debug('debug message')
logger.info('info message') logger.warning('warn
message') logger.error('error message')
```

```
logger.critical('critical message')
logger.info('Starting') do_something()
logger.info('Done')
```

The result of running this code is that a log file is created with the logged messages:

```
LOG detailed.log

1        Starting
2        debug message
3        info message
4        warn message
5        error message
6        critical message
7        Done
```

Given that this is a lot more code than using the basicConfig() function; the question here might be 'Why bother?'. The answer is two fold:

- You can have different handlers for different loggers rather than setting the handler to be used centrally.
- Each handler can have its own format set so that logging to a file has a different format to logging to the console.

We can set the format for the handler by instantiating the logging. For matter class with an appropriate format string. The for matter object can then be applied to a handler using the set For matter() method on the handler object.

For example, we can modify the above code to include a for matter that is then set on the file handler as shown below.

```
# create file handler which logs to the specified
file
file_handler = logging.FileHandler('detailed.log'
)
# Create formatter for the file_handler
formatter = logging.Formatter('%(asctime)s -
%(funcName)s -
%(message)s' )
file_handler.setFormatter(formatter)
logger.addHandler(file_handler)
```

The log file now generated is modified such that each message includes a time stamp, the function name (or module if at the module level) as well as the log message itself.

```
detailed.log
1     2019-02-21 09:53:49,160 - <module> - Starting
2     2019-02-21 09:53:49,160 - do_something - debug message
3     2019-02-21 09:53:49,160 - do_something - info message
4     2019-02-21 09:53:49,160 - do_something - warn message
5     2019-02-21 09:53:49,160 - do_something - error message
6     2019-02-21 09:53:49,160 - do_something - critical message
7     2019-02-21 09:53:49,160 - <module> - Done
```

Multiple Handlers

As suggested in the previous section we can create multiple handlers to send log messages to different locations; for example from the console, to files and even email servers. The following program illustrates setting up both a file handler and a console handler for a module level logger.

To do this we create two handlers the file_handler and the con- sole_handler. As a side effect we can also give them different log levels and different for matters. In this case the file_handler inherits the log level of the logger itself (which is DEBUG) while the console_handler has its log level set explicitly at WARNING. This means different amounts of information will be logged to the log file than the console output.

We have also set different for matters on each handler; in this case the log file handler's for matter provides more information than the console handlers for matter.

Both handlers are then added to the logger before it is used.

```
# MultipleHandlers and formatters
import logging
# Set up the defaultroot logger to do nothing
logging.basicConfig(handlers=[logging.NullHandler()])
# Obtain the module level logger and set level to
DEBUG logger  =  logging.getLogger(    name    )
logger.setLevel(logging.DEBUG)
# Create file handler
file_handler  =
logging.FileHandler('detailed.log')
```

```
# Create consolehandler with a higher log level
console_handler  =  logging.StreamHandler()
console_handler.setLevel(logging.WARNING)
# Create formatterfor the file handler
fh_formatter  =  logging.Formatter(
%(name)s.%(funcName)s: %(message)s',
datefmt='%M-%d-%Y %I:%M:%S
%P')
file_handler.setFormatter(fh_formatter)
# Create formatter for the console handler
console_formatter  =
logging.Formatter('%(asctime)s
%(funcName)s - %(message)s')-
console_handler.setFormatter(console_formatter)
# Add the handlers to logger
logger.addHandler(console_handler)
logger.addHandler(file_handler)
# 'application' code
def do_something():
logger.debug('debug message')
logger.info('info message') logger.warning('warn
message') logger.error('error message')
logger.critical('critical message')
logger.info('Starting') do_something()
logger.info('Done')
```

The output from this program is now split between the log file and the console out, as shown below:

```
detailed.log
1      02-21-2019 10:00:33 AM [INFO] __main__.<module>: Starting
2      02-21-2019 10:00:33 AM [DEBUG] __main__.do_something: debug message
3      02-21-2019 10:00:33 AM [INFO] __main__.do_something: info message
4      02-21-2019 10:00:33 AM [WARNING] __main__.do_something: warn message
5      02-21-2019 10:00:33 AM [ERROR] __main__.do_something: error message
6      02-21-2019 10:00:33 AM [CRITICAL] __main__.do_something: critical message
7      02-21-2019 10:00:33 AM [INFO] __main__.<module>: Done
```

```
Run:      logging_example8
          /Library/Frameworks/Python.framework/Versions/3.7/bin/python3.7
          2019-02-21 10:00:33,970 - do_something - warn message
          2019-02-21 10:00:33,970 - do_something - error message
          2019-02-21 10:00:33,970 - do_something - critical message
```

Filters

Filters can be used by Handlers to provide finer grained control of the log output. A filter can be added to a logger using the logger.addFilter() method. A Filter can be created by extending the logging.Filter class and implementing the filter() method. This method takes a log record. This log record can be validated to determine if the record should be output or not. If it should be output then True is returned, if the record should be ignored False should be returned.

In the following example, a filter called MyFilter is defined that will filter out all log messages containing the string 'John'. It is added as a filter to the logger and then two log messages are generated.

```python
import logging
class MyFilter(logging.Filter):
def filter(self,  record):
if 'John' in record.msg:
return False
else:
return True
logging.basicConfig(format='%(asctime)s
%(message)s', level=logging.DEBUG)
logger =  logging.getLogger()
logger.addFilter(MyFilter())
```

```
logger.debug('This is to help with debugging')
logger.info('This is information on John')
```

The output shows that only the log message that does not contain the string

'John' is output:

2019-02-20 17:23:22,650 This is to help with debugging

Logger Configuration

All the examples so far in this chapter have used programmatic configuration of the logging framework. This is certainly feasible as the examples show, but it does require a code change if you wish to alter the logging level for any particular logger, or to change where a particular handler is routing the log messages.

For most production systems a better solution is to use an external configuration file which is loaded when the application is run and is used to dynamically configure the logging framework. This allows system administrators and others to change the log level, the log destination, the log format etc. without needing to change the code.

The logging configuration file can be written using several standard formats from JSON (the Java Script ObjectNotation), to YAML (Yet Another Markup Language) format, or as a set of key-value pairs in a conf file. For further information on the different options available see the Python logging module documentation.

In this book we will briefly explore the YAML file format used to configure loggers.

```
version:  1 formatters:
myformatter:
format:  '%(asctime)s  [%(levelname)s]
%(name)s.%(funcName)s:
%(message)s'
handlers:
console:
class:  logging.StreamHandler level:  DEBUG
formatter:  myformatter stream:  ext://sys.stdout
loggers:
myLogger: level:  DEBUG handlers:  [console]
propagate:  no
root:
level:  ERROR
handlers:  [console]
```

The above YAML code is stored in a file called log-ging.conf.yaml; however you can call this file anything that is meaningful.

The YAML file always starts with a version number. This is an integer value representing the YAML schema version (currently this can only be the value 1). All other keys in the file are optional, they include:

- for matters—this lists one or more for matters; each

for matter has a name which acts as a key and then a format value which is a string defining the format of a log message.

- filters—this is a lit of filter names and a set of filter definitions.
- handlers—this is a list of named handlers.Each handler definition is made up of a set of key value pairs where the keys define the class used for the filter (mandatory),the log level of the filter (optional), the for matter to use with the handler (optional) and a list of filters to apply (optional).
- loggers—provides one or more named loggers. Each logger can indicate the log level (optional) and a list of handlers (optional). The propagate option can be used to stop messages propagating to a parent logger (by setting it to False).
- root—this is the configuration for the root logger.

This file can be loaded into a Python application using the PyYAML module. This provides a YAML parser that can load a YAML file as a dictionary structure that can be passed to the logging.config.dictConfig() function. As this is a file it must be opened and closed to ensure that the resource is handled appropriately; it is therefore best managed using the with-as statement as shown below:

```
with open('logging.config.yaml' , 'r')as f:
config = yaml.safe_load(f.read())
logging.config.dictConfig(config)
```

This will open the YAML file in read-only mode and close it when the two statements have been executed. This snippet is used in the following application that loads the logger configuration from the YAML file:

```
import logging
import logging.config
import yaml
with open('logging.config.yaml',  'r')  as f:
config  =  yaml.safe_load(f.read())
logging.config.dictConfig(config)
logger  =  logging.getLogger('myLogger')
# 'application' code
def do_something(): logger.debug('debug message')
logger.info('info message') logger.warning('warn
message') logger.error('error message')
logger.critical('critical message')
logger.info('Starting') do_something()
logger.info('Done')
```

The output from this using the earlier YAML file is:

2019-02-21 16:20:46,466 [INFO] myLogger.<module>: Starting
  2019-02-21 16:20:46,466 [DEBUG] myLogger.do_something: debug message
  2019-02-21 16:20:46,466 [INFO] myLogger.do_something: info message
  2019-02-21 16:20:46,466 [WARNING] myLogger.do_something: warn message
  2019-02-21 16:20:46,466 [ERROR] myLogger.do_something: error message
  2019-02-21 16:20:46,466 [CRITICAL] myLogger.do_some-

thing: critical message

    2019-02-21 16:20:46,466 [INFO] myLogger.<module>:
Done

Performance Considerations

Performance when logging should always be a consideration. In general you should aim to avoid performing any
unnecessary work when logging is disabled (or disabled
for the level being used). This may seem obvious but it can
occur in several unexpected ways.

One example is string concatenation. If a message to
be logged involves string concatenation; then that string
concatenation will always be performed when a log method
is being invoked. For example:

```
logger.debug('Count: ' + count + ', total:' +
total)
```

This will always result in the string being generated for
count and total before the call is made to the debug function;
even if the debug level is not turned on. However using
a format string will avoid this. The formatting involved
will only be performed if the string is to be used in a
log message. You should therefore always use string
formatting to populate log messages. For example:

```
logger.debug(' Count: %d, total: %d ', count, 42)
```

Another potential optimization is to use the logger.is En-abled For (level) method as a guard against running the log statement. This can be useful insinuations where an associated operation must be performed to support the logging operation and this operation is expensive. For example:

```
if logger.isEnabledFor(logging.DEBUG):
logger.debug('Message with %s,%s',
expensive_func1(), expensive_func2())
```

Now the two expensive functions will only be executed if the DEBUG log level is set.

Try

Using the logging you dded to the Account class int he last chapter, you should load the log configuration information from a YAML file similar to that used in this chapter.

This should be loaded into the application program used to drive the account classes.

Introduction to Concurrency and Parallelism

Introduction

In this chapter we will introduce the concepts of concurrency and parallelism. We will also briefly consider the related topic of distribution. After this we will consider process synchronization, why object oriented approaches are well suited to con- currency and parallelism before finishing with a short discussion of threads versus processes.

Concurrency

Concurrency is defined by the dictionary as two or more events or circumstances happening or existing at the same time. In Computer Science concurrency refers to the ability of different parts or units of a program, algorithm or problem to be executed at the same time, potentially on multiple processors or multiple cores.

Here a processor refers to the central processing unit (or CPU) or a computer while core refers to the idea that a CPU chip can have multiple cores or processors on it.

Originally a CPU chip had a single core. That is the CPU chip had a single processing unit on it. However, over time, to increase computer performance, hardware manufacturers added additional cores or processing units to chips. Thus a dual-core CPU chip has two processing units while a quad-core CPU chip has four processing units. This means that as far as the operating system of the computer is concerned, it has multiple CPUs on which it can run programs.

Running processing at the same time, on multiple CPUs, can substantially improve the overall performance of an application.

For example, let us assume that we have a program that will call three independent functions, these functions are:

- make a backup of the current data held by the program,
- print the data currently held by the program,
- run an animation using the current data.

Let us assume that these functions run sequentially, with the following timings:

- the backup function takes 13 s,
- the print function takes 15 s,
- the animation function takes 10 s.

This would result in a total of 38 s to perform all three operations. This is illustrated graphically below:

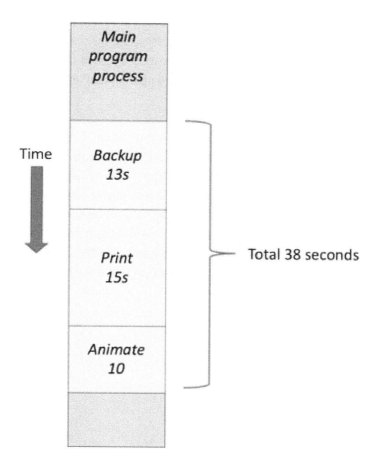

However, the three functions are all completely independent of each other. That is they do not rely on each other for any results or behavior; they do not need one of the other functions to complete before they can complete etc. Thus we can run each function concurrently.

If the underlying operating system and program language being used support multiple processes, then we can potentially run each function in a separate process at the same time and obtain a significant speed up in overall execution time.

If the application starts all three functions at the same time, then the maximum time before the main process can continue will be 15s, as that is the time taken by the longest function to execute. However, the main program may be able to continue as soon as all three functions are started as it also does not depend on the results from any of the functions; thus the delay may be negligible (although there will typically be some small delay as each process is set up). This is shown graphically below:

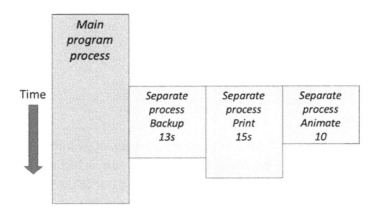

Parallelism

A distinction its often made in Computer Science between concurrency and parallelism. In concurrency, separate independent tasks are performed potentially at the same time. In parallelism, a large complex task is broken down into a set of sub tasks. The sub tasks represent part of the overall problem.Each sub task can be executed at the same time. Typically it is necessary to combine the results of the sub tasks together to generate an overall result.These sub tasks are also very similar if not functionally exactly the same (although in general each sub task invocation will have been supplied with different data).

Thus parallelism is when multiple copies of the same functionality are run at the same time, but on different data. Some examples of where parallelism can be applied include:

- A web search engine. Such a system may look at many, many web pages. Each time it does so it must send a request to the appropriate web site, receive the result and process the data obtained. These steps are the same whether it is the BBC web site, Microsoft's web site or the web site of Cambridge University. Thus the requests can be run sequentially or in parallel.
- Image Processing. A large image maybe broken down into slices so that each slice can be analyzed in parallel.

The following diagram illustrates the basic idea behind parallelism; a main program fires off three sub tasks each of which runs in parallel. The main program then waits for all the sub tasks to complete before combining together the results from the sub tasks before it can continue.

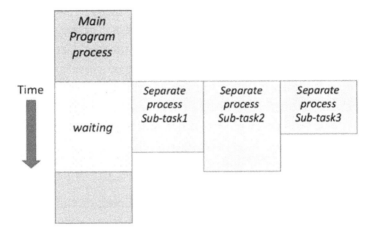

Distribution

When implementing a concurrent or parallel solution, where the resulting processes run is typically an implementation detail. Conceptually these processes could run on the same processor, physical machine or on a remote or distributed machine. As such distribution, in which problems are solved or processes executed by sharing the work across multiple physical machines, is often related to concurrency and parallelism.

However, there is no requirement to distribute work across physical machines, indeed in doing so extra work is usually involved.

To distribute work to a remote machine, data and in many cases code, must be transferred and made available to the remote machine. This can result in significant delays in running the code remotely and may offset any potential performance advantages of using a physically separate computer. As a result many concurrent/ parallel technologies default to executing code in a separate process on the same machine.

Grid Computing

Grid Computing is based on the use of a network of loosely coupled computers, in which each computer can have a job submitted to it, which it will run to completion before returning a result.

In many cases the grid is made up of a heterogeneous set of computers (rather than all computers being the same) and may be geographically dispersed. These computers may be comprised of both physical computers and virtual machines.

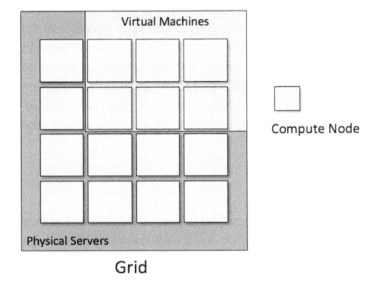

Grid

A Virtual Machine is a piece of software that emulates a whole computer and runs on some underlying hardware that is shared with other virtual machines. Each Virtual Machine thinks it is the only computer on the hardware;however the virtual machines all share the resources of the physical computer. Multiple virtual machines can thus run simultaneously on the same physical computer. Each virtual machine provides its own virtual hardware,including CPUs, memory, hard drives, network interfaces and other devices.The virtual hardware is then mapped to the real hardware on the physical machine which saves costs by reducing the need for physical hardware systems along with the associated maintenance costs, as well as reducing the power and cooling demands of multiple computers.

Within a grid, software is used to manage the grid nodes and to submit jobs to those nodes. Such software will receive the jobs to perform (programs to run and information about the environment such as libraries to use) from clients of the grid. These jobs are typically added to a job queue before a job scheduler submits them to a node within the grid. When any results are generated by the job they are collected from the node and returned to the client. This is illustrated below:

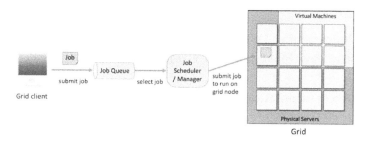

The use of grids can make distributing concurrent/parallel processes amongst a set of physical and virtual machines much easier.

Concurrency and Synchronization

Concurrency relates to executing multiple tasks at the same time. In many cases these tasks are not related to each other such as printing a document and refreshing the User Interface. In these cases, the separate tasks are completely independent and can execute at the same time without any interaction.

In other situations multiple concurrent tasks need to interact; for example, where one or more tasks produce data and one or more other tasks consume that data. This is often referred to as a producer-consumer relationship. In other situations, all parallel processes must have reached the same point before some other behaviour is executed.

Another situation that can occur is where we want to ensure that only one concurrent task executes a piece of sensitive code at a time; this code must therefore be protected from concurrent access.

Concurrent and parallel libraries need to provide facilities that allow for such synchronization to occur.

Object Orientation and Concurrency

The concepts behind object-oriented programming lend themselves particularly well to the concepts associated with concurrency. For example, a system can be described as a set of discrete objects communicating with one another when necessary. In Python, only one object may execute at any one moment in time within a single interpreter. However, conceptually at least, there is no reason why this restriction should be enforced. The basic concepts behind object orientation still hold, even if each object executes within a separate independent process

Traditionally a message send is treated like a procedural call, in which the calling object's execution is blocked until a response is returned. However, we can extend this model quite simply to view each object as a concurrently executable program, with activity starting when the object is created and continuing even when a message is sent to another object (unless the response is required for further processing). In this model, there may be very many (concurrent) objects executing at the same time. Of course, this introduces issues associated with resource allocation, etc. but no more so than in any concurrent system.

One implication of the concurrent object model is that objects are larger than in the traditional single execution thread approach, because of the overhead of having each object as a separate thread of execution. Overheads such as the need for a scheduler to handling these execution threads and resource allocation mechanisms means that it is not feasible to have integers, characters, etc. as separate processes.

Threads V Processes

As part of this discussion it is useful to understand what is meant by a process. A process is an instance of a computer program that is being executed by the operating system. Any process has three key elements; the program being executed, the data used by that program (such as the variables used by the program) and the state of the process (also known as the execution context of the program).

A (Python) Thread is a preemptive lightweight process.

A Thread is considered to be preemptive because every thread has a chance to run as the main thread at some point.

When a thread gets to execute then it will execute until

- completion,
- until it is waiting for some form of I/O (Input/Output),
- sleeps for a period of time,
- it has run for 15 ms (the current threshold in Python 3).

If the thread has not completed when one of the above situations occurs, then it will give up being the executing thread and another thread will be run instead. This means that one thread can be interrupted in the middle of performing a series of related steps.

thread is a considered a lightweight process because it does not possess its own address space and it is not treated as a separate entity by the host operating system. Instead, it exists within a single machine process using the same address space.

It is useful to get a clear idea of the difference between a thread (running within a single machine process) and a multi process system that uses separate processes on the underlying hardware.

Some Terminology

The world of concurrent programming is full of terminology that you may not be familiar with. Some of those terms and concepts are outlined below:

- Asynchronous versus Synchronous invocations. Most

of the method, function or procedure invocations you will have seen in programming represent synchronous invocations. A synchronous method or function call is one which blocks the calling code from executing until it returns. Such calls are typically within a single thread of execution. Asynchronous calls are ones where the flow of control immediately returns to the caller and the caller is able to execute in its own thread of execution. Allowing both the caller and the call to continue processing.

· Non-Blocking versus Blocking code. Blocking code is a term used to describe the code running in one thread of execution, waiting for some activity to complete which causes one of more separate threads of execution to also be delayed. For example, if one thread is the producer of some data and other threads are the consumers of that data, then the consumer treads cannot continue until the producer generates the data for them to consume. In contrast, non-blocking means that no thread is able to indefinitely delay others.

· Concurrent versus Parallel code. Concurrent code and parallel code are similar, but different in one significant aspect. Concurrency indicates that two or more activities are both making progress even though they might not be executing at the same point in time. This is typically achieved by continuously swapping competing processes between execution and non-execution. This process is repeated until at least one of the threads of execution (Threads) has completed their task. This may occur because two threads are sharing the same physical processor with each is being

485

given a short time period in which to progress before the other gets a short time period to progress. The two threads are said to be sharing the processing time using a technique known as time slicing. Parallelism on the other hand implies that there are multiple processors available allowing each thread to execute on their own processor simultaneously.

Online Resources

See the following online resources for information on the topics in this chapter:

- https://en.wikipedia.org/wiki/Concurrency_(computer_science) Wikipedia page on concurrency.
- https://en.wikipedia.org/wiki/Virtual_machine Wikipedia page on Virtual Machines.
- https://en.wikipedia.org/wiki/Parallel_computing Wikipedia page on parallelism.
- http://tutorials.jenkov.com/java-concurrency/concurrency-vs-parallelism.html Concurrency versus Parallelism tutorial.
- https://www.redbooks.ibm.com/redbooks/pdfs/sg246778.pdf IBM Red Book on an Introduction to Grid Computing.

Threading

Introduction

Threading is one of the ways in which Python allows you to write programs that multitask; that is appearing to do more than one thing at a time. This chapter presents the threading module and uses a short example to illustrate how these features can be used.

Threads

In Python the Thread class from the threading module represents an activity that's run in a separate thread of execution within a single process. These threads of execution are lightweight, preemptive execution threads. A thread is lightweight because it does not possess its own address space and it is not treated as a separate entity by the host operating system; it is not a process. Instead, it exists within a single machine process using the same address space as other threads.

Thread States

When a thread object is first created it exists, but it is not yet runnable; it must be started. Once it has been started it is then runnable; that is, it is eligible to be scheduled for execution. It may switch back and forth between running and being runnable under the control of the scheduler. The scheduler is responsible for managing multiple threads that all wish to grab some execution time.

A thread object remains runnable or running until its run() method terminates;

at which point it has finished its execution and it is now dead. All states between unstated and dead are considered to indicate that the Thread is alive (and therefore may run at some point). This is shown below:

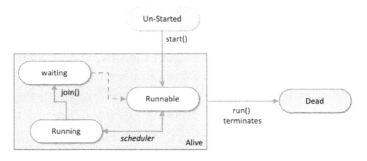

A Thread may also be in the waiting state; for example, when it is waiting for another thread to finish its work before continuing (possibly because it needs the results produced by that thread to continue). This can be achieved using the join() method and is also illustrated above. Once the second thread completes the waiting thread will again become runnable.

The thread which is currently executing is termed the active thread. There are a few points to note about thread states:

- A thread is considered to be alive unless its run() method terminates after which it can be considered dead.
- A live thread can be running, runnable, waiting, etc.
- The runnable state indicates that the thread can be executed by the processor, but it is not currently executing. This is because an equal or higher priority process is already executing, and the thread must wait until the processor becomes free. Thus the diagram shows that the scheduler can move a thread between the running and runnable state. In fact,this could happen many times as the thread executes for a while, is then removed from the processor by the scheduler and added to the waiting queue, before being returned to the processor again at a later date.

Creating a Thread

There are two ways in which to initiate a new thread of execution:

- Pass a reference to a callable object (such as a function or method) into the Thread class constructor. This reference acts as the target for the Thread to execute.
- Create a subclass of the Thread class and redefine the

run() method to perform the set of actions that the thread is intended to do.

We will look at both approaches.

As a thread is an object, it can be treated just like any other object: it can be sent messages, it can have instance variables and it can provide methods. Thus, the multi-threaded aspects of Python all conform to the object-oriented model. This greatly simplifies the creation of multi-threaded systems as well as the maintain- ability and clarity of the resulting software.

Once a new instance of a thread is created, it must be started.Before it is started, it cannot run, although it exists.

Instantiating the Thread Class

The Thread class can be found in the threading module and therefore must be imported prior to use. The class Thread defines a single constructor that takes up to six optional arguments:

```
class threading.Thread(group=None,
target=None,
name=None,
args=(),
kwargs={},
daemon=None)
```

The Thread constructor should always be called using

keyword arguments; the meaning of these arguments is:

- group should be None; reserved for future extension when a ThreadGroup class is implemented.
- target is the callable object to be invoked by the run() method. Defaults to None, meaning nothing is called.
- name is the thread name. By default, a unique name is constructed of the form "Thread-N" where N is an integer.
- args is the argument tuple for the target invocation. Defaults to (). If a single argument is provided the tuple is not required. If multiple arguments are provided then each argument is an element within the tuple.
- kwargs is a dictionary of keyword arguments for the target invocation. Defaults to {}.
- daemon indicates whether this thread runs as a daemon thread or not. If not None, daemon explicitly sets whether the thread is daemonic. If None (the default), the daemonic property is inherited from the current thread.

Once a Thread is created it must be started to become eligible for execution using the Thread.start() method. The following illustrates a very simple program that creates a Thread that will run the simple_worker() function:

```
from threading import Thread
def simple_worker():
print('hello')
# Createa new thread and start it
# The threadwill run the functionsimple_worker
```

```
t1 = Thread(target=simple_worker)
t1.start()
```

In this example, the thread t1 will execute the function simple_worker. The main code will be executed by the main thread that is present when the program starts; there are thus two threads used in the above program; main and t1.

The Thread Class

The Thread class defines all the facilities required to create an object that can execute within its own lightweight process. The key methods are:

- start() Start the thread's activity. It must be called at most once per thread object. It arranges for the object's run() method to be invoked in a separate thread of control. This method will raise a RuntimeError if called more than once on the same thread object.
- run() Method representing the thread's activity. You may override this method in a subclass. The standard run() method invokes the callable object passed to the object's constructor as the target argument, if any, with positional and keyword arguments taken from the args and kwargs arguments, respectively. You should not call this method directly.
- join(timeout= None) Wait until the thread sent this message terminates.

This blocks the calling thread until the thread whose join()method is called terminates. When the timeout argument is present and not None, it should be a floating-point number specifying a timeout for the operation in seconds (or fractions thereof). A thread can be join()ed many times.

- name A string used for identification purposes only. It has no semantics. Multiple threads may be given the same name. The initial name is set by the constructor. Giving a thread a name can be useful for debugging purposes.
- ident The 'thread identifier' of this thread or None if the thread has not been started. This is a nonzero integer.
- is_alive() Return whether the thread is alive. This method returns True just before the run() method starts until just after the run() method terminates. The module function threading.enumerate() re- turns a list of all alive threads.
- daemon A boolean value indicating whether this thread is a daemon thread (True) or not (False). This must be set before start() is called, otherwise a Runtime Error is raised. Its default value is inherited from the creating thread. The entire Python program exits when no alive non-daemon threads are left.

An example illustrating using some of these methods is given below:

```
from threading import Thread
def simple_worker():
print('hello')
t1 = Thread(target=simple_worker)
t1.start()
print(t1.getName()) print(t1.ident)
print(t1.is_alive())
```

This produces:

hello

Thread-1

123145441955840

True

The join() method can cause one thread to wait for another to complete. For example, if we want the main thread to wait until a thread completes before it prints the done message; then we can make it join that thread:

```
from threading import Thread
from time import sleep
def worker():
for i in range(0,10):
print('.', end='', flush=True)
sleep(1)
print('Starting')
# Createread object with referenceto worker
function
t = Thread(target=worker)
# Start the thread object
t.start()
```

```
# Wait for the thread to complete
t.join()
print('\nDone')
```

Now the 'Done' message should not be printed out until after the worker thread has finished as shown below:

Starting

  ....

  Done

The Threading Module Functions

There are a set of threading module functions which support working with threads; these functions include:

- threading.active_count() Return the number of Thread objects currently alive. The returned count is equal to the length of the list returned by enumerate().
- threading.current_thread() Return the current Thread object, cor- responding to the caller's thread of control. If the caller's thread of control was not created through the threading module, a dummy thread object with limited functionality is returned.
- threading.get_ident() Return the 'thread identifier' of the current thread. This is a nonzero integer. Thread identifiers may be recycled when a thread exits and another thread is created.
- threading.enumerate()Return a list of all Thread objects currently alive. The list includes daemon threads,

dummy thread objects created by current_thread() and the main thread. It excludes terminated threads and threads that have not yet been started.

- threading.main_thread()Return the main Thread object.

Passing Arguments to a Thread

Many functions expect to be given a set of parameter values when they are run; these arguments still need to be passed to the function when they are run via a separate thread. These parameters can be passed to the function to be executed via the args parameter, for example:

```
from threading import Thread
from time import sleep
def worker(msg):
for i in range(0,10):
print(msg, end='', flush=True)
sleep(1)
print('Starting')
t1 = Thread(target=worker,args='A') t2 =
Thread(target=worker, args='B') t3 =
Thread(target=worker, args='C') t1.start()
t2.start()
t3.start()
print('Done')
```

In this example, the worker function takes a message to be printed 10 times within a loop. Inside the loop the thread will print the message and then sleep for a second. This allows other threads to be executed as the Thread must wait for the sleep timeout to finish before again becoming runnable.

Three threads t1, t2 and t3 are then created each with a different message. Note that the worker() function can be reused with each Thread as each invocation of the function will have its own parameter values passed to it.

The three threads are then started. This means that at this point there is the main thread, and three worker threads that are Runnable (although only one thread will run at a time). The three worker threads each run the worker() function printing out either the letter A,B or C ten times. This means that once started each thread will print out a string,sleep for 1 s and then wait until it is selected to run again, this is illustrated in the following diagram:

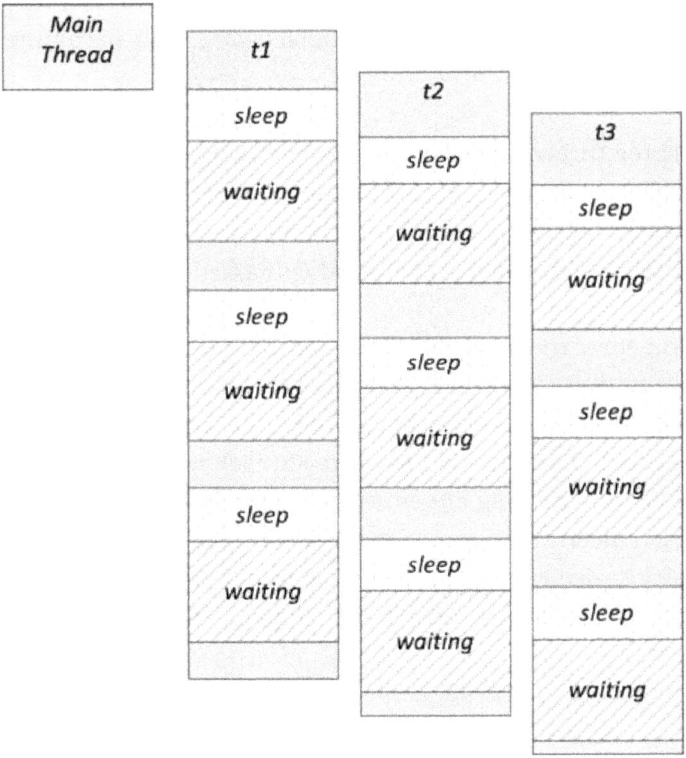

The output generated by this program is illustrated below:

Starting ABCDone
   ABCACBABCABCCBAABCABCABCBAC

Notice that the main thread is finished after the worker threads have only printed out a single letter each; however as long as there is at least one non-daemon thread running the program will not terminate; as none of these threads are marked as a daemon thread the program continues until the last thread has finished printing out the tenth of its letters.

Also notice how each of the threads gets a chance to run on the processor before it sleeps again; thus we can see the letters A, B and C all mixed in together.

Extending the Thread Class

The second approach to creating a Thread mentioned earlier was to subclass the

Thread class. To do this you must

1. Define a new subclass of Thread.
2. Override the run() method.
3. Define a new _init_() method that calls the parent class init_()

method to pass the required parameters up to the Thread class constructor.

This is illustrated below where the WorkerThread class passes the name, target and daemon parameters up to the Thread super class constructor.

```python
from threading import Thread
from time import sleep

class WorkerThread(Thread):
    def __init__(self, daemon=None, target=None, name=None):
        super().__init__(daemon=daemon, target=target,
                         name=name)

    def run(self):
        for i in range(0, 10):
            print('.', end='', flush=True)
            sleep(1)
```

Once you have done this you can create an instance of the new WorkerThread class and then start that instance.

```python
print('Starting')
t = WorkerThread()
t.start()
print('\nDone')
```

The output from this is:

Starting
  . Done
  ....

Note that it is common to call any sub classes of the Thread class, Something Thread, to make it clear that it is a subclass of the Thread class and should be treated as if it was a Thread (which of course it is).

Daemon Threads

A thread can be marked as a daemon thread by setting the daemon property to true either in the constructor or later via the access or property.

For example:

```python
from threading import Thread
from time import sleep
def worker(msg):
for i in range(0,10):
print(msg, end='',flush=True)
sleep(1)
print('Starting')
# Createa daemon thread
d = Thread(daemon=True, target=worker, args='C')
d.start()
sleep(5)
print('Done')
```

This creates a background daemon thread that will run the function worker(). Such threads are often used for house keeping tasks (such as background data backups etc.).

As mentioned above a daemon thread is not enough on its own to keep the current program from terminating. This means that the daemon thread will keep looping until the main thread finishes. As the main thread sleeps for 5 s that allows the daemon thread to print out about 5 strings before the main thread terminates. This is illustrated by the output below:

Starting
CCCCCDone

Naming Threads

Threads can be named; which can be very useful when debugging an application with multiple threads.

In the following example,three threads have been created; two have been explicitly given a name related to what they are doing while the middle one has been left with the default name. We then start all three threads and use the threading.enumerate() function to loop through all the currently live threads printing out their names:

```python
import threading
from threading import Thread
from time import sleep

def worker(msg):
    for i in range(0, 10):
        print(msg, end='', flush=True)
        sleep(1)

t1 = Thread(name='worker', target=worker, args='A')
t2 = Thread(target=worker, args='B')  # use default name e.g.
Thread-1
d = Thread(daemon = True, name='daemon', target=worker,
args='C')

t1.start()
t2.start()
d.start()

print()
for t in threading.enumerate():
    print(t.getName())
```

The output from this program is given blow:

ABC MainThread worker Thread-1 daemon
ABCBACACBCBACBAABCCBACBACBA

As you can see in addition to the worker thread and the daemon thread there is a MainThread (that initiates the whole program) and Thread-1 which is the thread referenced by the variable t2 and uses the default thread name.

Thread Local Data

In some situations each Thread requires its own copy of the data it is working with; this means that the shared (heap) memory is difficult to use as it is inherently shared between all threads.

To overcome this Python provides a concept known as Thread-Local data. Thread-local data is data whose values are associated with a thread rather than with the shared memory. This idea is illustrated below:

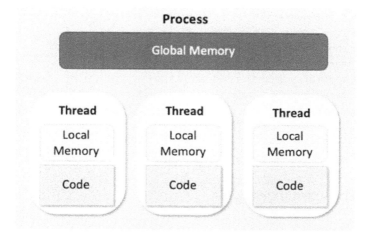

To create thread-local data it is only necessary to create an instance of threading. local (or a subclass of this) and store attributes into it. The instances will be thread specific; meaning that one thread will not see the values stored by another thread.

```
For example:
from threading import Thread,local, currentThread
from random import randint
def show_value(data):
try:
val = data.value
except AttributeError:
print(currentThread().name, ' - No value yet')
else:
print(currentThread().name, ' - value =', val)
def worker(data):
show_value(data)
data.value = randint(1, 100)
show_value(data)
print(currentThread().name, ' - Starting')
local_data = local()
show_value(local_data)
for i in range(2):
t = Thread(name='W' + str(i),
target=worker, args=[local_data])
t.start()
show_value(local_data)
print(currentThread().name, ' - Done')
```

The output from this is

```
MainThread - Starting

MainThread - No value yet W0 - No value yet
```

```
W0 - value = 20
W1 - No value yet
W1 - value = 90
MainThread - No value yet
MainThread - Done
```

The example presented above defines two functions.

- The first function attempts to access a value in the thread local data object. If the value is not present an exception is raised (AttributeError). The show_value() function catches the exception or successfully processes the data.
- The worker function calls show_value()twice, once before it sets a value in the local data object and once after. As this function will be run by separate threads the current Thread name is printed by the show_value() function.

The main function creates a local data object using the local() function from the threading library. It then calls show_value() itself. Next it creates two threads to execute the worker function in passing the local_data object into them; each thread is then started.Finally, it calls show_value() again.

As can be seen from the output one thread cannot see the data set by another thread in the local_data object (even when the attribute name is the same).

Timers

The Timer class represents an action (or task) to run after a certain amount of time has elapsed. The Timer class is a subclass of Thread and as such also functions as an example of creating custom threads.

Timers are started,as with threads, by calling their start() method. The timer can be stopped (before its action has begun) by calling the cancel() method.The interval the timer will wait before executing its action may not be exactly the same as the interval specified by the user as another thread may be running when the timer wishes to start.

The signature of the Timer class constructor is:

```
Timer(interval, function, args = None, kwargs
=None)
An example of using the Timer class is given
below:
from threading  import Timer
def hello():
print('hello')
print('Starting')
t  =  Timer(5,  hello)
t.start()
print('Done')
```

In this case the Timer will run the hello function after an initial delay of 5 s.

The Global Interpreter Lock

The Global Interpreter Lock(or the GIL) is a global lock within the underlying CPython interpreter that was designed to avoid potential deadlocks between multiple tasks. It is designed to protect access to Python objects by preventing multiple threads from executing at the same time.

For the most part you do not need to worry about the GIL as it is at a lower level than the programs you will be writing. However, it is worth noting that the GIL is controversial because it prevents multi threaded Python programs from taking full advantage of multiprocessor systems in certain situations.

This is because in order to execute a thread must obtain the GIL and only one thread at a time can hold the GIL (that is the lock it represents). This means that Python acts like a single CPU machine; only one thing can run at a time. A Thread will only give up the GIL if it sleeps, has to wait for something (such as some I/O) or it has held the GIL for a certain amount of time. If the maximum time that a thread can hold the GIL has been met the scheduler will release the GIL from that thread (resulting it stopping execution and now having to wait until it has the GIL returned to it) and will select another thread to gain the GIL and start to execute.

It is thus impossible for standard Python threads to take advantage of the multiple CPUs typically available on modern computer hardware. One solution to this is to use the Python multiprocessing library described in the next chapter.

Multiprocessing

Introduction

The multiprocessing library supports the generation of separate (operating system level) processes to execute behavior (such as functions or methods) using an API that is similar to the Threading API presented in the last chapter.

It can be used to avoid the limitation introduced by the Global Interpreter Lock (the GIL) by using separate operating system processes rather than lightweight threads (which run within a single process).

This means that the multiprocessing library allows developers to fully exploit the multiple processor environment of modern computer hardware which typically has multiple processor cores allowing multiple operations/behaviors to run in parallel; this can be very significant for data analytics, image processing, animation and games applications.

The multiprocessing library also introduces some new features, most notably the Pool object for parallelizing execution of a callable object (e.g. functions and methods) that has no equivalent within the Threading API.

The Process Class

The Process class is the multiprocessing library's equivalent to the Thread class in the threading library. It can be used to run a callable object such as a function in a separate process. To do this it is necessary to create a new instance of the Process class and then call the start() method on it. Methods such as join() are also available so that one process can wait for another process to complete before continuing etc.

The main difference is that when a new Process is created it runs within a separate process on the underlying operating systems (such as Window, Linux or Mac OS). In contrast a Thread runs within the same process as the original program. This means that the process is managed and executed directly by the operating system on one of the processors that are part of the underlying computer hardware.

The up side of this is that you are able to exploit the underlying parallelism inherent in the physical computer hardware. The downside is that a Process takes more work to set up than the lighter weight Threads. The constructor for the Process class provides the same set of arguments as the Thread class, namely:

```
class multiprocessing.Process(group=None,
 target=None,
name=None,
args=(),
kwargs={}, daemon=None)
```

- group should always be None; it exists solely for compatibility with the Threading API.
- target is the callable object to be invoked by the run() method. It defaults to None, meaning nothing is called.
- name is the process name.
- args is the argument tuple for the target invocation.
- kwargs is a dictionary of keyword arguments for the target invocation.
- daemon argument sets the process daemon flag to True or False.

If None (the default), this flag will be inherited from the creating process.

As with the Thread class, the Process constructor should always be called using keyword arguments.

The Process class also provides a similar set of methods to the Thread class

- start() Start the process's activity. This must be called

at most once per process object. It arranges for the object's run() method to be invoked in a separate process.

- join([timeout]) If the optional argument timeout is None (the default), the method blocks until the joined process terminates. If timeout is positive number, it blocks at most timeout seconds. Note that the method returns None if its process terminates or if the method times out.

- is_alive() Return whether the process is alive.Roughly, a process object is alive from the moment the start() method returns until the child process terminates.

The process class also has several attributes:

- name The process's name. The name is a string used for identification purposes only. It has no semantics. Multiple processes may be given the same name. It can be useful for debugging purposes.

- daemon The process's daemon flag, a boolean value. This must be set before start() is called. The default value is inherited from the creating process. When a process exits, it attempts to terminate all of its dae-monic child processes. Note that a daemonic process is not allowed to create child processes.

- pid Return the process ID. Before the process is spawned, this will be None.

- exit code The process exit code. This will be None if the process has not yet terminated. A negative value -N indicates that the child was terminated by signal N.

In addition to these methods and attributes, the Process class also defines additional process related methods including:

- terminate() Terminate the process.
- kill() Same as terminate() except that on Unix the SIGKILL signal is used instead of the SIGTERM signal.
- close() Close the Process object, releasing all resources associated with it. ValueError is raised if the underlying process is still running. Once close() returns successfully,most of the other methods and attributes of the Process object will raise a ValueError.

Working with the Process Class

The following simple program creates three Process objects; each runs the function worker(), with the string arguments A, B and C respectively. These three process objects are then started using the start() method.

```
from multiprocessing import Process
from time import sleep
def worker(msg):
for i in range(0,10):
print(msg, end='',flush=True)
sleep(1)
print('Starting')
t2 = Process(target=worker, args='A') t3=
Process(target=worker,args='B') t4 =
Process(target=worker, args='C')
t2.start() t3.start() t4.start()
```

```
print('Done')
```

It is essentially the same as the equivalent program for threads but with the

Process class being used instead of the Thread class.
    The output from this application is given below:
    Starting Done ABCABCABCABCABCABCABCACBACBACB

The main difference between the Thread and Process versions is that the Process version runs the worker function in separate processes whereas in the Thread version all the Threads share the same process.

Alternative Ways to Start a Process

When the start() method is called on a Process, three different approaches to starting the underlying process are available. These approaches can be set using the multiprocessing.set_start_method() which takes a string indicating the approach to use. The actual process initiation mechanisms available depend on the underlying operating system:

- 'spawn' The parent process start a fresh Python interpreter process. The child process will only inherit those resources necessary to run the process objects run() method. In particular, unnecessary file descriptors and handles from the parent process will not be inherited. Starting a process using this method is rather slow compared to using fork or fork server. Available on Unix and Windows. This is the default on Windows.

· 'fork' The parent process uses os.fork() to fork the Python interpreter. The child process, when it begins, is effectively identical to the parent process. All resources of the parent are inherited by the child process. Available only on Unix type operating systems. This is the default on Unix, Linux and Mac OS.

· 'fork server' In this case a server process is started. From then on, whenever a new process is needed, the parent process connects to the server and requests that it fork a new process.The fork server process is single threaded so it is safe for it to use os.fork(). No unnecessary resources are inherited. Available on Unix style platforms which support passing file descriptors over Unix pipes.

The set_start_method() should be used to set the start method (and this should only be set once within a program).

This is illustrated below, where the spawn start method is specified:

```
from multiprocessing import Process
from multiprocessing import set_start_method
from time import sleep
import os
def worker(msg):
print('module name:',   name ) print('parent
process:', os.getppid()) print('process id:',
os.getpid())
for i in range(0,10):
print(msg, end='', flush=True)
```

```
sleep(1)
def main():
print('Starting')
print('Root application process id:', os.getpid())
set_start_method('spawn')
t = Process(target=worker, args='A')
t.start()
print('Done')
if_name_=='_main_':
main()
```

The output from this is shown below:

```
Starting
Root application process id: 6281
Done
module name: _main_
parent process: 6281 process id: 6283
AAAAAAAAAA
```

Note that the parent process and current process ids are printed out for the worker () function, while the main() method prints out only its own id. This shows that the main application process id is the same as the worker process parents' id.

Alternatively, it is possible to use the get_context() method to obtain a context object. Context objects have the same API as the multiprocessing module and allow you to use multiple start methods in the same program, for example:

```
ctx = multiprocessing.get_context('spawn')
q = ctx.Queue()
p = ctx.Process(target = foo, args = (q,))
```

Using a Pool

Creating Processes is expensive in terms of computer resources. It would therefore be useful to be able to reuse processes within an application. The Pool class provides such reusable processes.

The Pool class represents a pool of worker processes that can be used to perform a set of concurrent, parallel operations. The Pool provides methods which allow tasks to be offloaded to these worker processes.

The Pool class provides a constructor which takes a number of arguments:

```
class multiprocessing.pool.Pool(processes,
initializer, initargs, maxtasksperchild, context)
```

These represent:

- processes is the number of worker processes to use. If processes is None then the number returned by os.cpu_count() is used.

- initializer If initializer is not None then each worker process will call initializer(*initargs) when it starts.
- max tasks per child is the number of tasks a worker process can complete before it will exit and be replaced with a fresh worker process, to enable unused resources to be freed. The default max tasks per child is None, which means worker processes will live as long as the pool.
- context can be used to specify the context used for starting the worker processes. Usually a pool is created using the function multiprocessing. Pool(). Alternatively the pool can be created using the Pool() method of a context object.

The Pool class provides a range of methods that can be used to submit work to the worker processes managed by the pool. Note that the methods of the Pool object should only be called by the process which created the pool.

The following diagram illustrates the effect of submitting some work or task to the pool. From the list of available processes, one process is selected and the task is passed to the process. The process will then execute the task. On completion any results are returned and the process is returned to the available list. If when a task is submitted to the pool there are no available processes then the task will be added to a wait queue until such time as a process is available to handle the task.

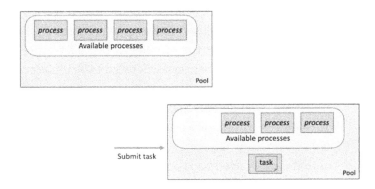

The simplest of the methods provided by the Pool for work submission is the map method:

```
pool.map(func, iterable, chunksize=None)
```

This method returns a list of the results obtained by executing the function in parallel against each of the items in the iterable parameter.

- The func parameter is the callable object to be executed (such as a function or a method).
- The iteratable is used to pass in any parameters to the function.
- This method chops the iterable into a number of chunks which it submits to the process pool as separate tasks. The (approximate) size of these chunks can be specified by setting chunk size to a positive integer. The method

blocks until the result is ready.

The following sample program illustrates the basic use of the Pool and the map() method.

```
from multiprocessing import Pool
def worker(x):
print('In worker with: ', x)
return x * x
def main():
with Pool(processes=4) as pool:
print(pool.map(worker, [0, 1, 2, 3, 4, 5]))
if_name_== '_main_':
main()
```

Note that the Pool object must be closed once you have finished with it; we are therefore using the 'with as' statement described earlier in this book to handle the Pool resource cleanly (it will ensure the Pool is closed when the block of code within the with as statement is completed).

The output from this program is

In worker with:0

In worker with:1

In worker with:2

In worker with:3

In worker with:4

In worker with:5 [0, 1, 4, 9, 16, 25]

As can be seen from this output the map() function is used to run six different instances of the worker() function with the values provided by the list of integers. Each instance is executed by a worker process managed by the Pool.

However, note that the Pool only has 4 worker processes, this means that the last two instances of the worker function must wait until two of the worker Processes have finished the work they are doing and can be reused. This can act as a way of throttling, or controlling, how much work is done in parallel.

A variant on the map() method is the imap_unordered() method. This method also applies a given function to an iterable but does not attempt to maintain the order of the results. The results are accessible via the iterable returned by the function. This may improve the performance of the resulting program.

The following program modified the worker() function to return its result rather than print it. These results are then accessible by iterating over them as they are produced via a for loop:

```python
from multiprocessing import Pool
def worker(x):
    print('In worker with: ', x)
    return x * x

def main():
    with Pool(processes=4) as pool:
        for result in pool.imap_unordered(worker,
                                          [0, 1, 2, 3, 4, 5]):
            print(result)

if __name__ == '__main__':
    main()
```

As the new method obtains results as soon as they are
available, the order in which the results are returned may
be different, as shown below:

In worker with:0

In worker with:1

In worker with:3

In worker with:2

In worker with:4

In worker with:5

0

1

9

16

4

25

A further method available on the Pool class is the Pool.ap-
ply_async() method. This method allows operations/func-
tions to be executed asynchronously allowing the method
calls to return immediately. That is as soon as the method
call is made, control is returned to the calling code which

can continue immediately. Any results to be collected from the asynchronous operations can be obtained either by providing a callback function or by using the blocking get() method to obtain a result.

Two examples are shown below, the first uses the blocking get() method. This method will wait until a result is available before continuing. The second approach uses a callback function. The callback function is called when a result is available; the result is passed into the function.

```python
from multiprocessing  import Pool
def collect_results(result):
print('In collect_results: ',  result)
def worker(x):
print('In worker with: ',  x)
return x  *  x
def main():
with Pool(processes=2)  as pool:
# get based example
res  =  pool.apply_async(worker,  [6])
print('Result from async: ',  res.get(timeout=1))
with Pool(processes=2)  as pool:
# callback based example
pool.apply_async(worker,  args=[4],
callback=collect_results)
if_name_ == '_main_':
main()
```

The output from this is:
   In worker with:6
   Result from async: 36
   In worker with:4

In collect_results: 16

Exchanging Data Between Processes

In some situations it is necessary for two processes to exchange data. However, the two process objects do not share memory as they are running in separate operating system level processes. To get around this the multiprocessing library provides the Pipe() function.

The Pipe() function returns a pair of connection.Connection objects connected by a pipe which by default is duplex (two-way). The two connection objects returned by Pipe() represent the two ends of the pipe. Each connection object has send() and recv() methods (among others). This allows one process to send data via the send() method of one end of the connection object. In turn a second process can receive that data via the receive () method of the other connection object. This is illustrated below:

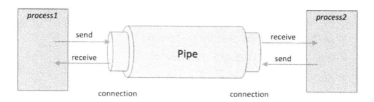

Once a program has finished with a connection is should be closed using close ().

The following program illustrates how pipe connections

are used:

```python
from multiprocessing import Process, Pipe
from time import sleep

def worker(conn):
    print('Worker - started now sleeping for 1 second')
    sleep(1)
    print('Worker - sending data via Pipe')
    conn.send('hello')
    print('Worker - closing worker end of connection')
    conn.close()

def main():
    print('Main - Starting, creating the Pipe')
    main_connection, worker_connection = Pipe()
    print('Main - Setting up the process')
    p = Process(target=worker, args=[worker_connection])
    print('Main - Starting the process')
    p.start()
    print('Main - Wait for a response from the child process')
    print(main_connection.recv())
    print('Main - closing parent process end of connection')
    parent_connection.close()
    print('Main - Done')

if __name__ == '__main__':
    main()
```

The output from this Pipe example is:

Main - Starting, creating the Pipe

Main - Setting up the process

Main - Starting the process

Main - Wait for a response from the child process

Worker - started now sleeping for 1 second

Worker - sending data via Pipe

Worker - closing worker end of connection hello

Main - closing parent process end of connection

Main - Done

Note that data in a pipe may become corrupted if two

processes try to read from or write to the same end of the pipe at the same time. However, there is no risk of corruption from processes using different ends of the pipe at the same time.

Sharing State Between Processes

In general, if it can be avoided, then you should not share state between separate processes. However, if it is unavoidable then the multiprocessing library provides two ways in which state (data) can be shared, these are Shared Memory (as supported by multiprocessing.Value and multiprocessing.Array) and Server Process.

Process Shared Memory

Data can be stored in a shared memory map using a multiprocessing.Value or multiprocessing.Array. This data can be accessed by multiple processes.

The constructor for the multiprocessing.Value type is:

```
multiprocessing.Value
(typecode_or_type, *args, lock = True)
```

Where:

- typecode_or_type determines the type of the returned object:it is either a ctypes type or a one character type code. For example, 'd' indicates a double precision float and 'i' indicates a signed integer.

- *args is passed on to the constructor for the type.
- lock If lock is True (the default) then a new recursive lock object is created to synchronize access to the value. If lock is False then access to the returned object will not be automatically protected by a lock, so it will not necessarily be process-safe.

The constructor for multiprocessing.Array is

```
multiprocessing.Array
multiprocessing.Array(typecode_or_type,
size_or_initializer, lock=True)
```

Where:

- typecode_or_type determines the type of the elements of there turned array.
- size_or_initializer If size_or_initializer is an integer,then it determines the length of the array, and the array will be initially zeroed. Otherwise, size_or_initializer is a sequence which is used to initialize the array and whose length determines the length of the array.
- If lock is True (the default) then a new lock object is created to synchronize access to the value.If lock is False then access to the returned object will not be automatically protected by a lock, so it will not

necessarily be "process-safe".

An example using both the Value and Array type is given below:

```
from multiprocessing import Process,Value, Array
def worker(n, a):
n.value = 3.1415927
for i in range(len(a)):
a[i] = -a[i]
def main():
print('Starting')
num = Value('d', 0.0)
arr = Array('i', range(10))
p = Process(target=worker, args=(num, arr))
p.start() p.join() print(num.value) print(*arr)
print('Done')
if_name_=='_main_':
main()
```

Try

Write a program that can find the factorial of any given number. For example, find the factorial of the number 5 (often written as 5!) which is 1 * 2 * 3 * 4 * 5 and equals 120.

The factorials not defined for negative numbers and the factorial of Zero is 1; that is 0! = 1.

Next modify the program to run multiple factorial calculations in parallel. Collect all the results together in a list and print that list out.

You an use whichever approach you like to running multiple processes although a Pool could be a good approach to use. Your program should compute the factorials of 5, 8, 10, 15, 3, 6, and 4 in parallel.

Inter Thread/Process Synchronization

Introduction

In this chapter we will look at several facilities supported by both the threading and multiprocessing libraries that allow for synchronization and cooperation between Threads or Processes.

In the remainder of this chapter we will look at some of the ways in which Python supports synchronization between multiple Threads and Processes.Note that most of the libraries are mirrored between threading and multiprocessing so that the same basic ideas hold for both approaches with, in the main, very similar APIs. However, you should not mix and match threads and processes. If you are using Threads then you should only use facilities from the threading library. In turn if you are using Processes than you should only use facilities in the multiprocessing library. The examples given in this chapter will use one or other of the technologies but are relevant for both approaches.

Using a Barrier

Using a threading.Barrier (or multiprocessing.Barrier) is one of the simplest ways in which the execution of a set of Threads (or Processes) can be synchronized. The threads or processes involved in the barrier are known as the parties that are taking part in the barrier. Each of the parties in the barrier can work independently until it reaches the barrier point in the code.

The barrier represents an end point that all parties must reach before any further behavior can be triggered. At the point that all the parties reach the barrier it is possible to optionally trigger a post-phase action (also known as the barrier call- back). This post phase action represents some behavior that should be run when all parties reach the barrier but before allowing those parties to continue. The post-phase action (the callback) executes in a single thread (or process).Once it is completed then all the parties are unblocked and may continue.

This is illustrated in the following diagram. Threads t1, t2 and t3 are all involved in the barrier. When thread t1 reaches the barrier it must wait until it is released by the barrier. Similarly when t2 reaches the barrier it must wait. When t3 finally reaches the barrier the callback is invoked. Once the callback has completed the barrier releases all three threads which are then able to continue.

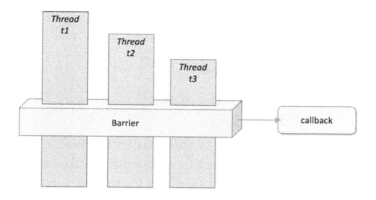

An example of using a Barrier object is given below. Note that the function being invoked in each Thread must also cooperate in using the barrier as the code will run up to the barrier.wait() method and then wait until all other threads have also reached this point before being allowed to continue.

The Barrier is a class that can be used to create a barrier object. When the Barrier class is instantiated, it can be provided with three parameters:

where

- parties the number of individual parties that will participate in the Barrier.
- action is a callable object (such as a function) which, when supplied, will be called after all the parties have entered the barrier and just prior to releasing them all.
- timeout If a 'timeout' is provided, it is used as the

default for all subsequent wait() calls on the barrier.

Thus, in the following code

```
b = Barrier(3, action=callback)
```

Indicates that there will be three parties involved in the Barrier and that the callback function will be invoked when all three reach the barrier (however the timeout is left as the default value None).

The Barrier object is created outside of the Threads (or Processes) but must be made available to the function being executed by the Thread (or Process). The easiest way to handle this is to pass the barrier into the function as one of the parameters; this means that the function can be used with different barrier objects depending upon the context.

An example using the Barrier class with a set of Threads is given below:

```
from threading  import Barrier,  Thread
from time  import sleep
from random  import randint
def print_it(msg,  barrier): print('print_it
for:',  msg) for i  in range(0,  10):
print(msg,  end='',  flush=True)
sleep(1)
sleep(randint(1,  6))
print('Wait for barrier with:',  msg)
barrier.wait()
```

```
print('Returning from print_it:',  msg)
def callback():
print('Callback Executing')
print('Main - Starting')
b = Barrier(3, callback)
t1  =  Thread(target=print_it,args=('A',  b)) t2
=  Thread(target=print_it,args=('B',  b)) t3 =
Thread(target=print_it, args=('C', b)) t1.start()
t2.start()
t3.start()
print('Main - Done')
The output from this is:
Main - Starting print_it for: A print_it for: B
print_it for: C ABC
Main  -  Done
ABCACBACBABCACBCABACBACBBAC Wait  for  barrier
with:  B Wait  for  barrier  with:  A Wait  for
barrier  with:  C Callback  Executing
Returning  from  print_it:  A
Returning  from  print_it:  B
Returning  from  print_it:  C
```

From this you can see that the print_it()function is run three times con- currently; all three invocations reach the barrier.wait() statement but in a different order to that in which they were started. Once the three have reached this point the callback function is executed before the print_it() function invocations can proceed.

The Barrier class itself provides several methods used to manage or find out information about the barrier:

Method	Description
wait(timeout=None)	Wait until all threads have notified the barrier (unless timeout is reached)—returns the number of threads that passed the barrier
reset()	Return barrier to default state
abort()	Put the barrier into a broken state
parties	Return the number of threads required to pass the barrier
n_waiting	Number of threads currently waiting

A Barrier object can be reused any number of times for the same number of Threads.

The above example could easily be changed to run using Process by altering the import statement and creating a set of Processes instead of Threads:

```
from multiprocessing  import Barrier,  Process
...
print('Main  -  Starting')
b  =  Barrier(3,  callback)
t1  =  Process(target=print_it,  args=('A',  b))
```

Note that you should only use threads with a threading.Barrier. In turn you should only use Processes with a multiprocessing.Barrier.

Event Signaling

Although the point of using multiple Threads or Processes is to execute separate operations concurrently, there are times when it is important to be able to allow two or more Threads or Processes to cooperate on the timing of their behavior. The Barrier object presented above is a relatively high-level way to do this; however, in some cases finer grained control is required. The threading.Event or multiprocessing.Event classes can be used for this purpose.

An Event manages an internal flag that callers can either set()or clear(). Other threads can wait() for the flag to be set(), effectively blocking their own progress until allowed to continue by the Event. The internal flag is initially set to False which ensures that if a task gets to the Event before it is set then it must wait.

You can in fact invoke wait with an optional timeout. If you do not include the optional timeout then wait() will wait forever while wait(timeout) will wait up to the timeout given in seconds. If the time out is reached,then the wait method returns False; otherwise wait returns True.

As an example,the following diagram illustrates two pro-cesses sharing an event object. The first process runs a function that waits for the event to be set. In turn the second process runs a function that will set the event and thus release the waiting process.

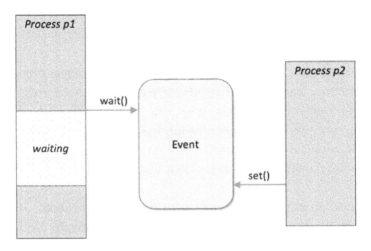

The following program implements the above scenario:

```
from multiprocessing  import Process,  Event
from time  import sleep
def wait_for_event(event):
print('wait_for_event - Entered and waiting')
event_is_set = event.wait()
print('wait_for_event - Event is set: ',
event_is_set)
def set_event(event):
print('set_event - Entered but about to sleep')
sleep(5)
print('set_event - Waking up and setting event')
event.set()
print('set_event - Event set')
print('Starting')
#  Create  the  event  object
event = Event()
#  Start  a  Process  to  wait  for  the  event
notification p1  =
Process(target=wait_for_event,  args=[event])
```

```
p1.start()
# Set up a process to set the event
p2 = Process(target=set_event, args=[event])
p2.start()
# Wait for the first process to complete
p1.join()
print('Done')
```

The output from this program is:

Starting
wait_for_event - Entered and waiting
set_event - Entered but about to sleep
set_event - Waking up and setting event
set_event - Event set
wait_for_event - Event is set: True
Done

To change this to use Threads we would merely need to change the import and to create two Threads:

```
from threading import Thread, Event
... print('Starting') event = Event()
t1 = Thread(target=wait_for_event,
args=[event])
t1.start()
t2 = Thread(target=set_event, args=[event])
t2.start()
t1.join()
print('Done')
```

Synchronizing Concurrent Code

It is not uncommon to need to ensure that critical regions of code are protected from concurrent execution by multiple Threads or Processes. These blocks of code typically involve the modification of, or access to, shared data. It is therefore necessary to ensure that only one Thread or Process is updating a shared object at a time and that consumer threads or processes are blocked while this update is occurring.

This situation is most common where one or more Threads or Processes are the producers of data and one or more other Threads or Processes are the consumers of that data. This is illustrated in the following diagram.

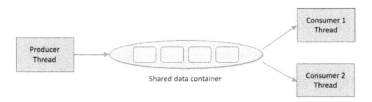

In this diagram the Producer is running in its own Thread (although it could also run in a separate Process) and places data onto some common shared data container. Subsequently a number of independent Consumers can consume that data when it is available and when they are free to process the data. However, there is no point in the consumers repeatedly checking the container for data as that would be a waste of resources (for example in terms of executing code on a processor and of context switching between multiple Threads or Processes).

We therefore need some form of notification or synchronization between the Producer and the Consumer to manage this situation.

Python provides several classes in the threading (and also in the multi- processing) library that can be used to manage critical code blocks. These classes include Lock, Condition and Semaphore.

Python Locks

The Lock class defined (both in the threading and the multiprocessing libraries) provides a mechanism for synchronizing access to a block of code. The Lock object can be in one of two states locked and unlocked (with the initial state being unlocked). The Lock grants access to a single thread at a time; other threads must wait for the Lock to become free before progressing.

The Lock class provides two basic methods for acquiring the lock (acquire()) and releasing (release()) the lock.

- When the state of the Lock object is unlocked, then acquire() changes the state to locked and returns immediately.
- When the state is locked, acquire() blocks until a call to release() in another thread changes it to unlocked, then the acquire() call resets it to locked and returns.
- The release() method should only be called in the locked state; it changes the state to unlocked and returns immediately. If an attempt is made to release an

unlocked lock, a Runtime Error will be raised.

An example of using a Lock object is shown below:

```
from threading import Thread, Lock
class SharedData(object):
def   init (self): self.value = 0 self.lock=
Lock()
def read_value(self):
try:
print('read_value Acquiring Lock')
self.lock.acquire()
return self.value
finally:
print('read_value releasing Lock')
self.lock.release()
def change_value(self): print('change_value
acquiring lock') with self.lock:
self.value = self.value + 1 print('change_value
lock released')
```

The SharedData class presented above uses locks to control access to critical blocks of code, specifically to the read_value() and the change_value() methods. The Lock object is held internally to the ShareData object and both methods attempt to acquire the lock before performing their behavior but must then release the lock after use.

The read_value() method does this explicitly using try: finally: blocks while the change_value() method uses a with statement (as the Lock type supports the Context Manager Protocol). Both approaches achieve the same result but the with statement style is more concise.

The SharedData class is used below with two simple functions. In this case the SharedData object has been defined as a global variable but it could also have been passed into the reader() and updater() functions as an argument. Both the reader and updater functions loop, attempting to call the read_value() and change_value() methods on the shared_data object.

As both methods use a lock to control access to the methods, only one thread can gain access to the locked area at a time. This means that the reader() function may start to read data before the updater() function has changed the data (or vice versa).

This is indicated by the output where the reader thread accesses the value '0' twice before the updater records the value '1'. However, the updater() function runs a second time before the reader gains access to locked block of code which is why the value 2 is missed. Depending upon the application this may or may not be an issue.

```
shared_data = SharedData()
def reader():
while True:
print(shared_data.read_value())
def updater():
while True:
shared_data.change_value()
print('Starting')
t1 = Thread(target=reader)
t2 = Thread(target=updater)
```

```
t1.start()
t2.start()
print('Done')
The output from this is:
Starting
read_value  Acquiring  Lock read_value  releasing
 Lock
0
read_value  Acquiring  Lock read_value  releasing
 Lock
0
Done
change_valueacquiring  lock change_value  lock
released
1
change_valueacquiring  lock change_value  lock
released change_value  acquiring  lock
change_value  lock  released
3
change_valueacquiring  lock change_value  lock
released
4
```

Lock objects can only be acquired once; if a thread attempts to acquire a lock on the same Lock object more than once then a Runtime Error is thrown.

If it is necessary to re-acquire a lock on a Lock object then the threading. RLock class should be used. This is a Re-entrant Lock and allows the same Thread (or Process) to acquire a lock multiple times. The code must however release the lock as many times as it has acquired it.

Python Conditions

Conditions can be used to synchronize the interaction between two or more Threads or Processes. Conditions objects support the concept of a notification model; ideal fora shared data resource being accessed by multiple consumers and producers.

A Condition can be used to notify one or all of the waiting Threads or Processes that they can proceed(for example to read data from a shared resource). The methods available that support this are:

- notify() notifies one waiting thread which can then continue
- notify_all() notifies all waiting threads that they can continue
- wait() causes a thread to wait until it has been notified that it can continue

A Condition is always associated with an internal lock which must be acquired and released before the wait() and notify() methods can be called. The Condition supports the Context Manager Protocol and can therefore be used via a with statement (which is the most typical way to use a Condition) to obtain this lock. For example, to obtain the condition lock and call the wait method we might write:

```
with condition:
condition.wait()
print('Now we can proceed')
```

The condition object is used in the following example to illustrate how a producer thread and two consumer threads can cooperate. A DataResource class has been defined which will hold an item of data that will be shared between a consumer and a set of producers. It also (internally) defines a Condition attribute. Note that this means that the Condition is completely internalized to the DataResource class; external code does not need to know, or be concerned with, the Condition and its use. Instead external code can merely call the consumer() and producer() functions in separate Threads as required.

The consumer() method uses a with statement to obtain the (internal) lock on the Condition object before waiting to be notified that the data is available. In turn the producer() method also uses a with statement to obtain a lock on the condition object before generating the data attribute value and then notifying anything waiting on the condition that they can proceed. Note that although the consumer method obtains a lock on the condition object; if it has to wait it will release the lock and re obtain the lock once it is notified that it can continue. This is a subtly that is often missed.

```
from threading  import Thread,  Condition,
currentThread
from time  import sleep
from random  import randint
class DataResource:
def  init    (self):
print('DataResource - Initialising the empty
data')
self.data  =  None
```

```
print('DataResource - Setting up the Condition
object')
self.condition = Condition()
def consumer(self):
"""wait   for   the   condition   and   use   the
resource"""
print('DataResource - Starting consumer method
in', currentThread().name)
with self.condition:
self.condition.wait()
print('DataResource - Resource is available to',
currentThread().name)
print('DataResource - Data read in',
currentThread().name,   ':',   self.data)
def producer(self):
"""set   up   the   resource   to   be   used   by   the
consumer"""
print('DataResource - Starting producer method')
with self.condition:
print('DataResource - Producer setting data')
self.data  =   randint(1,   100)
print('DataResource - Producer notifying all
waiting threads')
self.condition.notifyAll()
print('Main - Starting')
print('Main - Creating the DataResource object')
resource  =  DataResource()
print('Main - Create the Consumer Threads') c1   =
 Thread(target=resource.consumer) c1.name   =
'Consumer1'
c2  =  Thread(target=resource.consumer)
c2.name  =  'Consumer2'
print('Main - Create the Producer Thread')
p  =  Thread(target=resource.producer)
print('Main - Starting consumer threads')
c1.start()
c2.start()
```

```
sleep(1)
print('Main - Starting producer thread')
p.start()
print('Main - Done')
```

The output from an example run of this program is:

Main - Starting

Main - Creating the DataResource object DataResource - Initializing the empty data DataRes

Main - Create the Producer Thread

Main - Starting consumer threads

DataResource - Starting consumer method in Consumer1

DataResource - Starting consumer method in Consumer2

Main - Starting producer thread DataResource - Starting producer method DataResource - P

Main - Done

DataResource - Producer notifying all waiting threads

DataResource - Resource is available to Consumer1

DataResource - Data read in Consumer1 : 36

DataResource - Resource is available to Consumer2

DataResource - Data read in Consumer2 : 36

Python Semaphores

The Python Semaphore class implements Dijkstra's counting semaphore model.

In general, a semaphore is like an integer variable, its value is intended to represent a number of available resources of some kind. There are typically two operations available on a semaphore; these operations are acquire() and re- lease()

(although in some libraries Dijkstra's original names of p() and v() are used, these operation names are based on the original Dutch phrases).

- The acquire() operation subtracts one from the value of the semaphore, unless the value is 0, in which case it blocks the calling thread until the semaphore's value increases above 0 again.
- The signal() operation adds one to the value, indicating a new instance of the resource has been added to the pool.

Both the threading.Semaphore and the multiprocessing.Semaphore classes also supports the Context Management Protocol. An optional parameter used with the Semaphore constructor gives the initial value for the internal counter; it defaults to 1. If the value given is less than 0, ValueError is raised.

The following example illustrates 5 different Threads all running the same worker() function. The worker() function attempts to acquire a semaphore; if it does then it continues into the with statement block; if it doesn't, it waits until it can acquire it. As the semaphore is initialized to 2 there can only be two threads that can acquire the Semaphore at a time.

The sample program however, starts up five threads, this therefore means that the first 2 running Threads will acquire the semaphore and the remaining thee will have to wait to acquire the semaphore. Once the first two release the semaphore a further two can acquire it and so on.

```
from threading  import Thread,  Semaphore,
currentThread
from time  import sleep
def worker(semaphore):
with semaphore:
print(currentThread().getName()  +  "  - entered")
sleep(0.5)
print(currentThread().getName()  +  "  - exiting")
print('MainThread  -  Starting')
semaphore = Semaphore(2)
for i  in range(0,  5):
thread  =  Thread(name='T'  +  str(i),
target=worker, args=[semaphore])
thread.start()
print('MainThread  -  Done')
```

The output from a run of this program is given below:

```
MainThread  -  Starting
T0  -  entered T1  -
entered MainThread  -
Done T0  -
exiting
T2 - entered
T1 - exiting
T3 - entered
T2 - exiting
T4 - entered
T3 - exiting
T4 - exiting
```

The Concurrent Queue Class

As might be expected the model where a producer Thread or Process generates data to be processed by one or more Consumer Threads or Processes is so common that a higher level abstraction is provided in Python than the use of Locks, Conditions or Semaphores; this is the blocking queue model implemented by the threading.Queue or multiprocessing.Queue classes.

Both these Queue classes are Thread and Process safe. That is they work appropriately (using internal locks) to manage data access from concurrent Threads or Processes.

An example of using a Queue to exchange data between a worker process and the main process is shown below.

The worker process executes the worker() function sleeping, for 2 s before putting a string 'Hello World' on the queue. The main application function sets up the queue and creates the process. The queue is passed into the process as one of its arguments. The process is then started. The main process then waits until data is available on the queue via the (blocking) get() methods. Once the data is available it is retrieved and printed out before the main process terminates.

```
from multiprocessing  import Process,  Queue
from time  import sleep
def worker(queue):
print('Worker  -  going  to  sleep')
sleep(2)
print('Worker  -  woken  up  and  putting  data
```

```
on  queue')
queue.put('Hello World')
def main():
print('Main  -  Starting')
queue = Queue()
p  =  Process(target=worker,  args=[queue])
print('Main  -  Starting  the  process')
p.start()
print('Main  -  waiting  for  data')
print(queue.get())
print('Main  -  Done')
if_name_=='_main_':
main()
```

The output from this is shown below:

Main - Starting

Main - Starting the process

Main - wait for data

Worker - going to sleep

Worker - woken up and putting data on queue

Hello World

Main – Done

However, this does not make it that clear how the execution of the two processes interweaves. The following diagram illustrates this graphically:

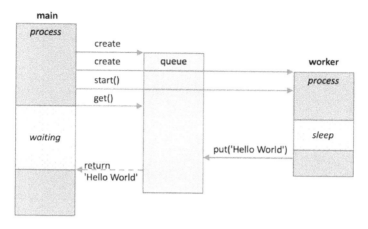

In the above diagram the main process waits for a result to be returned from the queue following the call to the get() method; as it is waiting it is not using any system resources. In turn the worker process sleeps for two seconds before putting some data onto the queue (via put('Hello World')). After this value is sent to the Queue the value is returned to the main process which is woken up (moved out of the waiting state) and can continue to process the rest of the main function.

Futures

Introduction

A future is a thread (or process) that promises to return a value in the future; once the associated behavior has completed. It is thus a future value. It provides a very simple way of firing off behavior that will either be time consuming to execute or which may be delayed due to expensive operations such as Input/Output and which could slow down the execution of other elements of a program. This chapter discusses futures in Python.

The Need for a Future

In a normal method or function invocation, the method or function is executed in line with the invoking code (the caller) having to wait until the function or method (the caller) returns. Only after this is the caller able to continue to the next line of code and execute that. In many (most) situations this is exactly what you want as the next line of code may depend on a result returned from the previous line of code etc.

However, in some situations the next line of code is independent of the previous line of code. For example, let us assume that we are populating a User Interface (UI). The first line of code may read the name of the user from some external data source (such as a database)and then display it within a field in the UI. The next line of code may then add today's data to another field in the UI. These two lines of code are independent of each other and could be run concurrently/in parallel with each other.

In this situation we could use either a Thread or a Process to run the two lines of code independently of the caller, thus achieving a level of concurrency and allowing the caller to carry onto the third line of code etc. However, neither the Thread or the Process by default provide a simple mechanism for obtaining a result from such an independent operation. This may not be a problem as operations may be self-contained; for example they may obtain data from the database or from today's date and then updated a UI. However, in many situations the calculation will return a result which needs to be handled by the original invoking code (the caller).This could involve performing a long running calculation and then using the result returned to generate another value or update another object etc.

A Future is an abstraction that simplifies the definition and execution of such concurrent tasks. Futures are available in many different languages including Python but also Java, Scala, C++ etc. When using a Future; a callable object(such as a function) is passed to the Future which executes the behavior either as a separate Thread or as a separate Process and then can return a result once it is generated. The result can either be handled by a call back function(that is invoked when the result is available) or by using a operation that will wait for a result to be provided.

Futures in Python

The concurrent.futures library was introduced into Python in version 3.2 (and is also available in Python 2.5 on wards). The concurrent.futures library provides the Future class and a high level API for working with Futures. The concurrent.futures.Future class encapsulates the asynchronous execution of a callable object (e.g. a function or method). The Future class provides a range of methods that can be used to obtain information about the state of the future,retrieve results or cancel the future:

- cancel() Attempt to cancel the Future. If the Future is currently being executed and cannot be canceled then the method will return False, otherwise the call will be canceled and the method will return True.
- canceled() Returns True if the Future was successfully canceled.
- running() Returns True if the Future is currently being executed and cannot be canceled.
- done() Returns True if the Future was successfully canceled or finished running.
- result(timeout=None) Return the value returned by the Future. If the Future hasn't yet completed then this method will wait up to timeout seconds. If the call hasn't completed in timeout seconds, then a Timeout

Error will be raised. timeout can be an int or float. If timeout is not specified or None, there is no limit to the wait time. If the future is canceled before completing then the Canceled Error will be raised. If the call raised, this method will raise the same exception.

It should be noted however, that Future instances should not be created directly, rather they should be created via the submit method of an appropriate executor.

Future Creation

Futures are created and executed by Executors. An Executor provides two methods that can be used to execute a Future (or Futures) and one to shut down the executor.

At the root of the executor class hierarchy is the concurrent.futures. Executor abstract class. It has two sub classes:

· the ThreadPoolExecutor and
· the ProcessPoolExecutor.

The ThreadPoolExecutor uses threads to execute the futures while the ProcessPoolExecutor uses separate processes. You can therefore choose how you want the Future to be executed by specifying one or other of these executors.

Simple Example Future

To illustrate these ideas, we will look at a very simple

example of using a Future. To do this we will use a simple worker function; similar to that used in the previous chapters:

```
from time import sleep
# define function to be used with future
def worker(msg):
for i in range(0, 10):
print(msg, end='', flush=True)
sleep(1)
return i
```

The only difference with this version of worker is that it also returns a result which is the number of times that the worker printed out the message.

We can of course invoke this method inline as follows:

```
res = worker('A')
print(res)
```

We can make the invocation of this method into a Future. To do this we use a ThreadPoolExecutor imported from the concurrent.futures module. We will then submit the worker function to the pool for execution. This returns a reference to a Future which we can use to obtain the result:

```
from time import sleep
from concurrent.futures import ThreadPoolExecutor
print('Setting up the ThreadPoolExecutor')
pool = ThreadPoolExecutor(1)
# Submit the function ot the pool to run
```

```
# concurrently - obtain a future from pool
print('Submitting the worker to the pool') future
=pool.submit(worker, 'A')
print('Obtained a reference to the future
object', future)
# Obtain the result from the future - wait if
necessary
print('future.result():', future.result())
print('Done')
```

The output from this is:

Setting up the ThreadPoolExecutor

  Submitting the worker to the pool

  AAObtained a reference to the future object <Future at

  0x1086ea8d0 state=running>

  AAAAAAAA future.result(): 9

  Done

Notice how the output from the main program and the worker is interwoven with two 'A's being printed out before the message starting 'Obtained a...'.

In this case a new ThreadPoolExecutor is being created with one thread in the pool (typically there would be multiple threads in the pool but one is being used here for illustrative purposes). The submit() method is then used to submit the function worker with the parameter 'A' to the ThreadPoolExecutor for it to schedule execution of the function. The submit() method returns a Future object.

The main program then waits for the future object to return a result (by calling the result() method on the future). This method can also take a timeout.

To change this example to use Processes rather than Threads all that is needed is to change the pool executor to a ProcessPoolExecutor:

```
from concurrent.futures import ProcessPoolExecutor
print('Setting up the ThreadPoolExecutor')
pool = ProcessPoolExecutor(1)
print('Submitting the worker to the pool')
future = pool.submit(worker, 'A')
print('Obtained a reference to the future
object', future1)
print('future.result():', future.result())
print('Done')
```

The output from this program is very similar to the last one:

Setting up the ThreadPoolExecutor
  Submitting the worker to the pool
  Obtained a reference to the future object <Future at
  0x109178630 state=running>
  AAAAAAAAAAfuture.result(): 9
  Done

The only difference is that in this particular run the message starting 'Obtained a..' is printed out before any of the 'A's are printed; this may be due to the fact that a Process initially takes longer to set up than a Thread.

Running Multiple Futures

Both the ThreadPoolExecutor and the ProcessPoolExecutor can be configured to support multiple Threads/Processes via the pool. Each task that is submitted to the pool will then run within a separate Thread/Process. If more tasks are submitted than there are Threads/Processes available, then the submitted task will wait for the first available Thread/Process and then be executed. This can act as a way of managing the amount of concurrent work being done.

For example, in the following example, the worker() function is submitted to the pool four times, but the pool is configured to use threads. Thus the fourth worker will need to wait until one of the first three completes before it is able to execute:

from concurrent.futures **import** ThreadPoolExecutor

```
print('Starting...')
pool = ThreadPoolExecutor(3) future1 =
pool.submit(worker, 'A') future2 =
pool.submit(worker, 'B') future3 =
pool.submit(worker, 'C') future4 =
pool.submit(worker, 'D')
print('\nfuture4.result():', future4.result())
print('All Done')
```

When this runs we can see that the Futures for A, B and C all run concurrently but D must wait until one of the others finishes:

```
Starting...
ABCACBCABCBABCACBACABCBACABCBADDDDDDDDDDD
future4.result(): 9
All Done
```

The main thread also waits for future4 to finish as it requests the result which is a blocking call that will only return once the future has completed and generates a result.

Again, to use Processes rather than Threads all we need to do is to replace the ThreadPoolExecutor with the ProcessPoolExecutor:

```
from concurrent.futures import ProcessPoolExecutor
print('Starting...')
pool = ProcessPoolExecutor(3) future1 =
pool.submit(worker, 'A') future2 =
pool.submit(worker, 'B') future3 =
pool.submit(worker, 'C') future4 =
pool.submit(worker, 'D')
print('\nfuture4.result():', future4.result())
print('All Done')
```

Waiting for All Futures to Complete

It is possible to wait for all futures to complete before progressing. In the previous section it was assumed that future4 would be the last future to complete; but in many cases it may not be possible to know which future will be the last to complete. In such situations it is very useful to be able to wait for all the futures to complete before continuing. This can be done using the concurrent.futures.wait function. This function takes a collection of futures and optionally a timeout and a return_when indicator.

```
wait(fs, timeout=None, return_when=ALL_COMPLETED)
```

where:

- timeout can be used to control the maximum number of seconds to wait before returning. timeout can be an int or float. If timeout is not specified or None, there is no limit to the wait time.
- return_when indicates when this function should return. It must be one of the following constants:

– FIRST_COMPLETED The function will return when any future finishes or is canceled.

– FIRST_EXCEPTION The function will return when any future finishes by raising an exception. If no future raises an exception,then it is equivalent to ALL_COMPLETED.

– ALL_COMPLETED The function will return when all futures finish or are canceled.

The wait() function returns two sets done and not_done. The first set contains the futures that completed (finished or were canceled) before the wait completed. The second set, the not_dones, contains uncompleted futures.

We can use the wait() function to modify out previous example so that we no longer rely on future4 finishing last:

```
from concurrent.futures import ProcessPoolExecutor
from concurrent.futures import wait from time
import sleep
def worker(msg):
for i in range(0,10):
print(msg,end='',flush=True) sleep(1)
return i
print('Starting...setting up pool') pool =
ProcessPoolExecutor(3) futures = []
print('Submitting futures')
future1 = pool.submit(worker, 'A')
futures.append(future1)
future2 = pool.submit(worker, 'B')
futures.append(future2)
future3 = pool.submit(worker, 'C')
futures.append(future3)
future4 = pool.submit(worker, 'D')
futures.append(future4)
print('Waiting for futures to complete')
wait(futures)
print('\nAll Done')
```

The output from this is:

Starting...setting up pool

Submitting futures

Waiting for futures to complete

ABCABCABCABCABCABCABCBCACBACBABCADDDDDDDDDDD

All Done

Note how each future is added to the list of futures which is then passed to the wait() function.

Processing Results as Completed

What if we want to process each of the results returned by our collection of futures? We could loop through the futures list in the previous section once all the results have been generated. However, this means that we would have to wait for them all to complete before processing the list.

In many situations we would like to process the results as soon as they are generated without being concerned if that is the first, third, last or second etc. The concurrent.futures.as_completed() function does preciously this; it will serve up each future in turn as soon as they are completed; with all futures eventually being returned but without guaranteeing the order (just that as soon as a future is finished generating a result it will be immediately available).

For example, in the following example, the is_even() function sleeps for a random number of seconds(ensuring that different invocations of this function will take different duration) then calculates a result:

```
from concurrent.futures import
ThreadPoolExecutor, as_completed from time import
sleep
from random import randint
def is_even(n):
print('Checking if', n , 'is even')
sleep(randint(1, 5))
return str(n) + ' ' + str(n % 2 == 0)
print('Started')
data = [1, 2, 3, 4, 5, 6]
pool = ThreadPoolExecutor(5)
futures = []
for v in data:
futures.append(pool.submit(is_even, v))
for f in as_completed(futures):
print(f.result())
print('Done')
```

The second for loop will loop through each future as they
complete printing out the result from each, as shown below:

Started

Checking if 1 is even

Checking if 2 is even

Checking if 3 is even

Checking if 4 is even

Checking if 5 is even

Checking if 6 is even

1 False

4 True

5 False

3 False

2 True

6 True

Done

As you can see from this output although the six futures were started in sequence the results returned are in a different order (with the returned order being 1, 4, 5, 3, 2 and finally 6).

Processing Future Results Using a Callback

An alternative to the as_complete() approach is to provide a function that will be called once a result has been generated. This has the advantage that the main program is never paused; it can continue doing whatever is required of it.

The function called once the result is generated is typically known as a callback function; that is the future calls back to this function when the result is available.

Each future can have a separate call back as the function to invoke is set on the future using the add_done_callback() method. This method takes the name of the function to invoke.

For example, in this modified version of the previous example, we specify a call back function that will be used to print the futures result. This call back function is called print_future_result(). It takes the future that has completed as its argument:

```python
from concurrent.futures import ThreadPoolExecutor
from time import sleep
from random import randint
def is_even(n):
print('Checking if', n, 'is even')
sleep(randint(1, 5))
return str(n) + ' ' + str(n % 2 == 0)
def print_future_result(future):
print('In callback Future result: ',
future.result())
print('Started')
data = [1, 2, 3, 4, 5, 6]
pool = ThreadPoolExecutor(5)
for v in data:
future = pool.submit(is_even, v)
future.add_done_callback(print_future_result)
print('Done')
```

When we run this, we can see that the call back function is called after the main thread has completed. Again, the order is unspecified as the is_even() function still sleeps for a random amount of time.

Started

Checking if 1 is even

Checking if 2 is even

Checking if 3 is even

Checking if 4 is even

Checking if 5 is even

Done

In callback Future result: 1 False

Checking if 6 is even

In callback Future result: 5 False

In callback Future result: 4 True

In callback Future result: 3 False

In callback Future result: 2 True

In callback Future result: 6 True

Concurrency with AsyncIO

Introduction

The Async IO facilities in Python are relatively recent additions originally introduced in Python 3.4 and evolving up to and including Python 3.7. They are comprised (as of Python 3.7) of two new keywords async and await (introduced in Python 3.7) and the Async IO Python package.

In this chapter we first discuss Asynchronous IO before introducing the Async and await keywords. We then present Async IO Tasks, how they are created used and managed.

Asynchronous IO

Asynchronous IO (or Async IO) is a language agnostic concurrent programming model (or paradigm) that has been implemented in several different programming language (such as C# and Scala) as well as in Python.

Asynchronous IO is another way in which you can build concurrent applications in Python. It is in many ways an alternative to the facilities provided by the Threading library in Python. However, were as the Threading library is more susceptible to issues associated with the GIL (The Global Interpreter Lock) which can affect performance, the Async IO facilities are better insulated from this issue.

The way in which Async IO operates is also lighter weight then the facilities provide day the multiprocessing library since the asynchronous tasks in Async IO run within a single process rather than requiring separate processes to be spawned on the underlying hardware.

Async IO is therefore another alternative way of implementing concurrent solutions to problems. It should be noted that it does not build on either Threading or Multi Processing; instead Async IO is based on the idea of cooperative multitasking. These cooperating tasks operate asynchronously; by this we mean that the tasks:

- are able to operate separately from other tasks,
- are able to wait for another task to return a result when required,
- and are thus able to allow other tasks to run while they are waiting.

The IO (Input/Output) aspect of the name Async IO is because this form of concurrent program is best suited to I/O bound tasks.

In an I/O bound task a program spends most of its time sending data to, or reading data from, some form of external device (for example a database or set of files etc.).

This communication is time consuming and means that the program spends most of its time waiting for a response from the external device.

One way in which such I/O bound applications can (appear to) speed up is to overlap the execution of different tasks; thus, while one task is waiting for a database to respond with some data, another task can be writing data to a log file etc.

AsyncIO Event Loop

When you are developing code using the Async IO facilities you do not need to worry about how the internals of the Async IO library work; however at least at the conceptual level it is useful to understand one key concept; that of the Async IO Event Loop; This loop control show and when each task gets run. For the purposes of this discussion a task represents some work that can be run independently of other pieces of work.

The Event Loop knows about each task to be run and what the state of the task currently is (for example whether it is waiting for something to happen/complete). It selects a task that is ready to run from the list of available tasks and executes it. This task has complete control of the CPU until it either completes its work or hands back control to the Event Loop (for example, because it must now wait for some data to be supplied from a database).

The Event Loop now checks to see if any of the waiting tasks are ready to continue executing and makes a note of their status. The Event Loop then selects another task that is ready to run and starts that task off. This loop continues until all the tasks have finished. This is illustrated below:

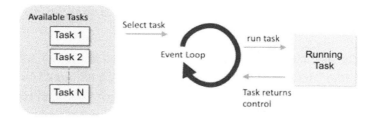

An important point to note in the above description is that a task does not give up the processor unless it decides to, for example by having to wait for something else. They never get interrupted in the middle of an operation; this avoids the problem that two threads might have when being time sliced by a separate scheduler as they may both be sharing the same resource.This can greatly simplify your code.

The Async and Await Keywords

The Async keyword, introduced in Python 3.7 is used to mark a function as being something that uses the await keyword (we will come back to this below as there is one other use of the Async keyword).A function that uses the await keyword can be run as a separate task and can give up control of the processor when it calls await against another Async function and must wait for that function to complete.

The invoked async function can then run as a separate task etc.

To invoke an Async function it is necessary to start the Async IO Event Loop and for that function to be treated as a task by the Event Loop. This is done by calling the asyncio.run() method and passing in the root async function.

The asyncio.run() function was introduced in Python 3.7 (older versions of Python such as Python 3.6 required you to explicitly obtain a reference to the Event Loop and to run the root Async function via that). One point to note about this function is that it has been marked as being provisional in Python 3.7. This means that future versions of Python may or may not support the function or may modify the function in some way. You should therefore check the documentation for the version of Python you are using to see whether the run method has been altered or not.

Using Async and Await

We will examine a very simple Async IO program from the top down. The main() function for the program is given below:

```
def main()   :
print('Main  -  Starting')
asyncio.run(do_something())
print('Main  -  Done')
```

```
if_name_== '_main_':
main()
```

The main() function is the entry point for the program and calls:

```
asyncio.run(do_something())
```

This starts the Async IO Event Loop running and results in the do_some- thing() function being wrapped up in a Task that is managed by the loop. Note that you do not explicitly create a Task in Async IO; they are always created by some function however it is useful to be aware of Tasks as you can interact with them to check their status or to retrieve a result.

The do_something() function is marked with the keyword Async:

```
async def do_something():
print('do_something - will wait for worker')
result = await worker()
print('do_something - result:', result)
```

As previously mentioned this indicates that it can be run as a separate Task and that it can use the keyword await to wait for some other function or behavior to complete. In this case the do_something() asynchronous function must wait for the worker() function to complete.

The await keyword does more than merely indicate that the do_something() function must wait for the worker to complete. It triggers another Task to be created that will execute the worker() function and releases the processor allowing the Event Loop to select the next task to execute (which may or may not be the task running the worker() function). The status of the do_something task is now waiting while the status of the worker() task is ready (to run).

The code for the worker task is given below:

```
async def worker():
print('worker - will take some time')
time.sleep(3)
print('worker - Done it')
return  42
```

The Async keyword again indicates that this function can be run as a separate task. However, this time the body of the function does not use the await keyword. This is because this is a special case known as an Async IO coroutine function. This is a function that returns a value from a Task (it is related to the idea of a standard Python coroutine which is a data consumer).

Sadly, Computer Science has many examples where the same term has been used for different things as well as examples where different terms have been used for the same thing. In this case to avoid confusion just stick with Async IO coroutines are functions marked with Async that can be run as a separate task and may call await.

The full listing for the program is given below:

```
import asyncio
import time
async def worker():
print('worker - will take some time')
time.sleep(3)
print('worker - done it')
return 42
async def do_something():
print('do_something - will wait for worker')
result  =  await worker()
print('do_something - result:',  result)
def main():
print('Main - Starting')
asyncio.run(do_something())
print('Main - Done')
if_name_=='_main_':
main()
```

When this program is executed the output is:

Main - Starting

do_something - will wait for worker worker - will take some time

worker - done it do_something – result: 42

Main – Done

When this is run there is a pause between the two worker printouts as it sleeps. Although it is not completely obvious here, the do_something() function was run as one task, this task then waited when it got to the worker() function which was run as another Task. Once the worker task completed the do_some- thing task could continue and complete its operation. Once this happened the

Async IO Event Loop could then terminate as no further tasks were available.

AsyncIO Tasks

Tasks are used to execute functions marked with the async keyword concurrently. Tasks are never created directly instead they are created implicitly via the keyword await or through functions such as asyncio.run described above or asyncio.create_task(), asyncio.gather() and asyncio.as_-completed(). These additional task creation functions are described below:

- asyncio.create_task() This function takes a function marked with async and wraps it inside a Task and schedules it for execution by the Async IO Event Loop. This function was added in Python 3.7.
- asyncio.gather(*aws)This function runs all the async functions passed to it as separate Tasks.It gathers the results of each separate task together and returns them as a list. The order of the results corresponds to the order of the async functions in the aws list.
- asyncio.as_completed(aws) Runs each of the async functions passed to it.

A Task object supports several useful methods

- cancel() cancels a running task. Calling this method will cause the Task to throw a CancelledError exception.
- cancelled() returns True if the Task has been canceled.
- done() returns True if the task has completed, raised an exception or was canceled.
- result() returns the result of the Task if it is done. If the Tasks result is not yet available, then the method raises the InvalidState Error exception.
- exception() return an exception if one was raised by the Task. If the task was canceled then raises the Cancelled Error exception. If the task is not yet done, then raises an InvalidStateError exception.

It is also possible to add a callback function to invoke once the task has completed (or to remove such a function if it has been added):

- add_done_callback(callback) Add a callback to be run when the Task is done.
- remove_done_callback(callback) Remove callback from the call- backs list.

Note that the method is called 'add' rather than 'set' implying that there can be multiple functions called when the task has completed (if required).

The following example illustrates some of the above:

```python
import asyncio
async def  worker():
print('worker - will take some time')
await asyncio.sleep(1) print('worker - Done it')
return  42
def print_it(task):
print('print_it result:',  task.result())
async def do_something():
print('do_something - create  task  for
worker')
task = asyncio.create_task(worker())
print('do_something - add  a  callback')
task.add_done_callback(print_it)
await  task
# Information  on  task
print('do_something - task.cancelled():',
task.cancelled())
print('do_something - task.done():',
task.done()) print('do_something -
task.result():',  task.result())
print('do_something - task.exception():',
task.exception())
print('do_something - finished')
def main()  :
print('Main - Starting')
asyncio.run(do_something())
print('Main - Done')
if_name_=='_main_':
main()
```

In this example, the worker() function is wrapped within a task object that is returned from the asyncio.create_task(worker()) call.

A function (print_it()) is registered as a callback on the task using the asyncio.create_task(worker()) function. Note that the worker is passed the task that has completed as a parameter. This allows it to obtain information from the task such as any result generated.

In this example the async function do_something() explicitly waits on the task to complete. Once this happens several different methods are used to obtain information about the task (such as whether it was canceled or not).

One other point to note about this listing is that in the worker() function we have added an await using the asyncio.sleep(1) function; this allows the worker to sleep and wait for the triggered task to complete; it is an Async IO alternative to time.sleep(1).

The output from this program is:

```
Main - Starting
    do_something - create task for worker do_something - add a callback
    worker - will take some time worker - Done it
    print_it result: 42
    do_something - task.cancelled(): False do_something - task.done(): True do_something -
    Main - Done
```

Running Multiple Tasks

In many cases it is useful to be able to run several tasks concurrently. There are two options provided for this the asyncio.gather()and the asyncio. as_completed() function; we will look at both in this section.

Collating Results from Multiple Tasks

It is often useful to collect all the results from a set of tasks together and to continue only once all the results have been obtained.When using Threads or Processes this can be achieved by starting multiple Threads or Processes and then using some other object such as a Barrier to wait for all the results to be available before continuing. Within the Async IO library all that is required is to use the asyncio.gather()function with a list of the async functions to run, for example:

```python
import asyncio
import random
async def worker():
print('Worker - will take some time')
await asyncio.sleep(1)
result  =  random.randint(1,10)
print('Worker - Done it')
return result
async def do_something():
print('do_something - will wait for worker')
#  Run  three  calls  to  worker  concurrently
and  collect
results
results  =  await asyncio.gather(worker(),
worker(), worker())
print('results from calls:',  results)
def main()  :
print('Main - Starting')
asyncio.run(do_something()) print('Main - Done')
if_name_=='_main_':
main()
```

In this program the do_something() function uses

```
results  =  await asyncio.gather(worker(),
worker(),  worker())
```

to run three invocations of the worker() function in three separate Tasks and to wait for the results of all three to be made available before they are returned as a list of values and stored in the results variable.

This makes is very easy to work with multiple concurrent tasks and to collate their results.

Note that in this code example the worker async function returns a random number between 1 and 10.

The output from this program is:

```
Main - Starting
    do_something - will wait for worker
    Worker - will take some time Worker - will take some time Worker - will take some time Wo
    Worker - Done it
    Worker - Done it
    results from calls: [5, 3, 4] Main – Done
```

As you can see from this all three of the worker invocations are started but then release the processor while they sleep. After this the three tasks wake up and complete before the results are collected together and printed out.

Handling Task Results as They Are Made Available

Another option when running multiple Tasks is to handle the results as they become available, rather than wait for all the results to be provided before continuing. This option is supported by the asyncio.as_completed() function. This function returns an iterator of async functions which will be served up as soon as they have completed their work.

The for-loop construct can be used with the iterator returned by the function; however within the for loop the code must call await on the async functions returned so that the result of the task can be obtained.For example:

```
async def do_something():
print('do_something - will wait for worker')
# Run three calls to worker concurrently
and collect
results
for async_func in
asyncio.as_completed((worker('A'),
worker('B'), worker('C'))):
result = await async_func
print('do_something - result:', result)
```

Note that the asyncio.as_completed() function takes a container such as a tuple of async functions.

We have also modified the worker function slightly so that

a label is added to the random number generated so that it is clear which invocation of the worker function return which result:

```
async def worker(label):
print('Worker - will take some time')
await asyncio.sleep(1)
result = random.randint(1,10)
print('Worker - Done it')
return label + str(result)
```

When we run this program

```
def main() :
print('Main - Starting')
asyncio.run(do_something())
print('Main - Done')
```

The output is

Main - Starting

  do_something - will wait for worker

  Worker - will take some time Worker - will take some time Worker - will take some time Wo

  Worker - Done it

  Worker - Done it

  do_something - result: C2 do_something - result: A1 do_something - result: B10

  Main – Done

As you can see from this, the results are not returned in the order that the tasks are created, task 'C' completes first followed by 'A' and 'B'. This illustrates the behavior of the asyncio.as_completed() function.

583

Try

This exercise will use the facilities in the AsyncIOlibrary to calculate a set of factorial numbers.

The factorial of a positive integer is the product of all positive integers less than or equal to n. For example,

$5! = 5 \times 4 \times 3 \times 2 \times 1 = 120$

Note that the value of 0! is 1,

Create an application that will use the async and await keywords to calculate the factorials of a set of numbers. The factorial function should await for 0.1 of a second(using asyncio.sleep(0.1)) each time round the loop used to calculate the factorial of a number.

You can use with asyncio.as_completed() or asyncio.gather() to collect the results up. You might also use a list comprehension to create the list of calls to the factorial function.

The main function might look like:

```
def main():
print('Main - Starting')
asyncio.run(calculate_factorials([5,  7, 3, 6]))
print('Main - Done')
if_name_== '_main_':
main()
```

Reactive Programming Introduction

Introduction

In this chapter we will introduce the concept of Reactive Programming. Reactive programming is a way of write programs that allow the system to reactive to data being published to it. We will look at the RxPy library which provides a Python implementation of the ReactiveX approach to Reactive Programming.

What Is a Reactive Application?

A Reactive Application is one that must react to data; typically either to the presence of new data, or to changes in existing data. The Reactive Manifesto presents the key characteristics of Reactive Systems as:

- Responsive. This means that such systems respond in a timely manner. Here of course timely will differ depending upon the application and domain; in one situation a second may be timely in another it may be far too slow.
- Resilient. Such systems stay responsive in the face of

failure. The systems must therefore be designed to handle failure gracefully and continue to work appropriately following the failure.

· Elastic. As the workload grows the system should continue to be responsive.

· Message Driven. Information is exchanged between elements of a reactive system using messages. This ensures loose coupling, isolation and location transparency between these components.

As an example, consider an application that lists a set of Equity Stock Trade values based on the latest market stick price data. This application might present the current value of each trade within a table. When new market stock price data is published, then the application must update the value of the trade within the table. Such an application can be described as being reactive.

Reactive Programming is a programming style (typically supported by libraries) that allows code to be written that follow the ideas of reactive systems. Of course just because part of an application uses a Reactive Programming library does not make the whole application reactive; indeed it may only be necessary for part of an application to exhibit reactive behavior.

The ReactiveX Project

ReactiveX is the best known implementation of the Reactive Programming paradigm. ReactiveX is based on the

Observer-Observable design pattern. However it is an extension to this design pattern as it extends the pattern such that the approach supports sequences of data and/or events and adds operators that allow developers to compose sequences together declaratively while abstracting away concerns associated with low-level threads,synchronization, concurrent data structures and non-blocking I/O.

The ReactiveX project has implementations for many languages including RxJava, RxScala and RxPy; this last is the version we are looking at as it is for the Python language.

RxPy is described as:

A library for composing asynchronous and event-based programs using Observable collections and query operator functions in Python

The Observer Pattern

The Observer Pattern is one of the Gang of Four set of Design Patterns. The Gang of Four Patterns (as originally described in Gamma et al. 1995) are so called because this book on design patterns was written by four very famous authors namely; Erich Gamma, Richard Helm, Ralph Johnson and John Vlis sides.

The Observer Pattern provides a way of ensuring that a set of objects is notified whenever the state of another object changes. It has been widely used in a number of languages (such as Small talk and Java) and can also be used with

587

Python.

The intent of the Observer Pattern is to manage a one to many relationship between an object and those objects interested in the state, and in particular state changes, of that object. Thus when the objects' state changes, the interested (dependent) objects are notified of that change and can take whatever action is appropriate.

There are two key roles within the Observer Pattern, these are the Observable and the Observer roles.

- Observable. This is the object that is responsible for notifying other objects that a change in its state has occurred
- Observer. An Observer is an object that will be notified of the change in state of the Observable and can take appropriate action (such as triggering a change in their own state or performing some action).

In addition the state is typically represented explicitly:

- State. This role may be played by an object that is used to share information about the change in state that has occurred within the Observable. This might be as simple as a String indicating the new state of the Observable or it might be a data oriented object that provides more detailed information.

These roles are illustrated in the following figure.

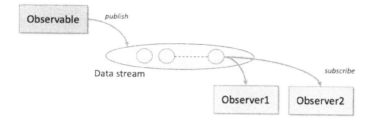

In the above figure, the Observable object publishes data to a Data Stream.The data in the Data Stream is then sent to each of the Observers registered with the Observable. In this way data is broadcast to all Observers of an Observable.

It is common for an Observable to only publish data once there is an Observer available to process that data. The process of registering with an Observable is referred to as subscribing. Thus an Observable will have zero or more subscribers (Observers).

If the Observable publishes data at a faster rate than can be processed by the Observer then the data is queued via the Data Stream.This allows the Observer to process the data receive done at a time at its own pace; without any concern for data loss (as long as sufficient memory is available for the data stream).

Hot and Cold Observables

Another concept that it is useful to understand is that of Hot and Cold Observables.

- Cold Observables are lazy Observables. That is, a Cold Observable will only publish data if at least one Observer is subscribed to it.
- Hot Observables, by contrast, publish data whether there is an Observer subscribed or not.

Cold Observables

A Cold Observable will not publish any data unless there is at least one Observer subscribed to process that data. In addition a cold Observable only provides data to an Observer when that Observer is ready to process the data; this is because the Observable-Observer relationship is more of a pull relationship. For example, given an Observable that will generate a set of values based on a range, then that Observable will generate each result lazily when requested by an Observer.

If the Observer takes some time to process the data emitted by the Observable, then the Observable will wait until the Observer is ready to process the data before emitting another value.

Hot Observables

Hot Observables by contrast publish data whether there is an Observer subscribed or not. When an Observer registers with the Observable, it will start to receive data at that point, as and when the Observable publishes new data. If the Observable has already published previous data items, then these will have been lost and the Observer will not receive that data.

The most common situation in which a Hot Observable is created is when the source producer represents data that may be irrelevant if not processed immediately or may be superseded by subsequent data. For example, data published by a Stock Market Price data feed would fall into this category. When an Observable wraps around this data feed it can publish that data whether or not an Observer is subscribed.

Implications of Hot and Cold Observables

It is important to know whether you have a hot or cold Observable because this can impact on what you can assume about the data supplied to the Observers and thus how you need to design your application.If it is important that no data is lost then care is needed to ensure that the subscribers are in place before a Hot Observable starts to publish data (where as this is not a concern for a cold Observable).

Differences Between Event Driven Programming and Reactive Programming

In Event Driven programming, an event is generated in response too something happening; the event then represents this with any associated data. For example, if the user clicks the mouse then an associated MouseClickEvent might be generated. This object will usually hold information about the x and y coordinates of the mouse along with which button was clicked etc. It is then possible to associate some behavior (such as a function or a method) with this event so that if the event occurs, then the associated operation is invoked and the event object is provided as a parameter. This is certainly the approach used in the wxPython library presented earlier in this book:

From the above diagram, when a MoveEvent is generated the on_move() method is called and the event is passed into the method.

In the Reactive Programming approach, an Observer is associated with an Observable. Any data generated by the Observable will be received and handled by the Observer. This is true whatever that data is, as the Observer is a handler of data generated by the Observable rather than a handler of a specific type of data (as with the Event driven approach).

Both approaches could be used in many situations. For example, we could have a scenario in which some data is to be processed whenever a stock price changes.

This could be implemented using a StockPriceChangeEvent associated with a StockPriceEventHandler. It could also be implemented via Stock PriceChangeObserverable and a StockPriceChangeObserver. In either case one element handles the data generated by another element. However, the RxPy library simplifies this process and allows the Observer to run in the same thread as, or a separate thread from, the Observable with just a small change to the code.

Advantages of Reactive Programming

There are several advantages to the use of a Reactive Programming library these include:

- It avoids multiple callback methods. The problems associated with the use of callbacks are sometimes referred to as callback hell. This can occur when there are multiple callbacks, all defined to run in response to some data being generated or some operation complet-ing. It can be hard to understand, maintain and debug such systems.
- Simpler asynchronous, multi threaded execution. The approach adopted by RxPy makes it very easy to execute operations/ behavior within a multi threaded environ-ment with independent asynchronous functions.
- Available Operators. The RxPy library comes pre built with numerous operators that make processing the data produced by an Observable much easier.
- Data Composition. It is straight forward to compose new data streams (Observables) from data supplied by two or more other Observables for asynchronous processing.

Disadvantages of Reactive Programming

Its easy to over complicate things when you start to chain operators together. If you use too many operators, or too complex a set of functions with the operators,it can become hard to understand what is going on.

Many developers think that Reactive programming is inherently multi-threaded; this is not necessarily the case; in fact RxPy (the library explored in the next two chapters) is single threaded by default. If an application needs the behavior to execute asynchronously then it is necessary to explicitly indicate this.

Another issue for some Reactive programming frameworks is that it can become memory intensive to store streams of data so that Observers can processes that data when they are ready.

The RxPy Reactive Programming Framework

The RxPy library is a part of the larger ReactiveX project and provides an implementation of ReactiveX for Python. It is built on the concepts of Observables, Observers, Subjects and operators. In this book we use RxPy version 3.

In the next chapter we will discuss Observables, Observers, Subjects and subscriptions using the RxPy library.The following chapter will explore various RxPy operators.

Reference

For more information on the Observer Observable design

pattern see the "Patterns" book by the Gang of Four

- E. Gamma, R. Helm, R. Johnson, J. Vlissades, Design patterns: elements of reusable object-oriented software, Addison-Wesley (1995).

Rxpy Observables, Observers and Subjects

Introduction

In this chapter we will discuss Observables,Observers and Subjects. We also consider how observers may or may not run concurrently.

In the remainder of this chapter we look at RxPy version 3 which is a major update from RxPy version 1 (you will therefore need to be careful if you are looking on the web for examples as some aspects have changed; most notably the way in which operators are chained).

Observables in RxPy

An Observable is a Python class that publishes data so that it can be processed by one or more Observers(potentially running in separate threads).

An Observable can be created to publish data from static data or from dynamic sources. Observables can be chained tougher to control how and when data is published, to transform data before it is published and to restrict what data is actually published.

For example, to create an Observable from a list of values we can use the rx.from_list() function. This function (also known as an RxPy operator) is used to create the new Observable object:

```
import rx
Observable = rx.from_list([2, 3, 5, 7])
```

Observers in RxPy

We can add an Observer to an Observable using the sub-scribe() method. This method can be supplied with a lambda function, a named function or an object whose class implements the Observer protocol.

For example,the simplest way to create an Observer is to use a lambda function:

```
# Subscribe a lambda function
observable.subscribe(lambda value: print('Lambda
Received', value))
```

When the Observable publishes data the lambda function will be invoked. Each data item published will be supplied independently to the function. The output from the above subscription for the previous Observable is:

Lambda Received 2

Lambda Received 3

Lambda Received 5

Lambda Received 7

We can also have used a standard or named function as an Observer:

```
def prime_number_reporter(value):
print('Function Received', value)
# Subscribe a named function
observable.subscribe(prime_number_reporter)
```

Note that it is only the name of the function that is used with the subscribe() method (as this effectively passes a reference to the function into the method).

If we now run this code using the previous Observable we get:

Function Received 2

Function Received 3

Function Received 5

Function Received 7

In actual fact the subscribe() method takes four optional parameters. These are:

- on_next Action to invoke for each data item generated by the Observable.

- on_error Action to invoke upon exceptional termination of the Observable sequence.
- on_completed Action to invoke upon graceful termination of the Observable sequence.
- Observer The object that is to receive notifications. You may subscribe using an Observer or callbacks, not both.

Each of the above can be used as positional parameters or as keyword arguments, for example:

```
# Use lambdas to set up all three functions
observable.subscribe(
on_next = lambda value: print('Received
on_next', value), on_error = lambda exp:
print('Error Occurred', exp), on_completed =
lambda: print('Received completed
notification')
)
```

The above code defines three lambda functions that will be called depending upon whether data is supplied by the Observable, if an error occurs or when the datastream is terminated. The output from this is:

Received on_next 2

Received on_next 3

Received on_next 5

Received on_next 7

Received completed notification

Note that the on_error function is not run as no error was

generated in this example.

The final optional parameter to the subscribe() method is an Observer object. An Observer object can implement the Observer protocol which has the following methods on_next(), on_completed() and on_error(), for example:

```
class PrimeNumberObserver:
def on_next(self, value):
print('Object Received', value)
def on_completed(self):
print('Data Stream Completed')
def on_error(self, error):
print('Error Occurred', error)
```

Instances of this class can now be used as an Observer via the subscribe() method:

```
# Subscribe an Observer object
observable.subscribe(PrimeNumberObserver())
```

The output from this example using the previous Observable is:

Object Received 2

Object Received 3

Object Received 5

Object Received 7

Data Stream Completed

Note that the on_completed() method is also called; however the **on_error()** method is not called as there were no exceptions generated.

The Observer class must ensure that the methods implemented adhere to the Observer protocol (i.e. That the signatures of the on_next(), on_completed () and on_error() methods are correct).

Multiple Subscribers/Observers

An Observable can have multiple Observers subscribed to it. In this case each of the Observers is sent all of the data published by the Observable. Multiple Observers can be registered with an Observable by calling the subscribe method multiple times. For example, the following program has four subscribers as well as on_error and on_completed function registered:

```
# Create an observable using data in a list
observable  =  rx.from_list([2,   3,   5,   7])
class PrimeNumberObserver:
""" An Observer class """
def on_next(self,  value):
print('Object Received',  value)
def on_completed(self):
print('Data Stream Completed')
def on_error(self,  error):
print('Error Occurred',  error)
def prime_number_reporter(value):
print('Function Received',  value)
print('Set up Observers / Subscribers')
# Subscribe a lambda function
```

```
observable.subscribe(lambda value:  print('Lambda
Received', value))
# Subscribe a named function
observable.subscribe(prime_number_reporter)
# Subscribe an Observerobject
observable.subscribe(PrimeNumberObserver())
# Use lambdas to set up all three functions
observable.subscribe(
on_next=lambda value:  print('Received on_next',
value), on_error=lambda exp:  print('Error
Occurred',  exp), on_completed=lambda:
print('Received completed
notification')
)
```

The output from this program is:

Create the Observable object Set up Observers / Subscribers Lambda Received 2

Lambda Received 3

Lambda Received 5

Lambda Received 7

Function Received 2

Function Received 3

Function Received 5

Function Received 7

Object Received 2

Object Received 3

Object Received 5

Object Received 7

Data Stream Completed

Received on_next 2

Received on_next 3

Received on__next 5

Received on__next 7

Received completed notification

Note how each of the subscribers is sent all of the data before the next subscriber is sent their data (this is the default single threaded RxPy behavior).

Subjects in RxPy

A subject is both an Observer and an Observable. This allows a subject to receive an item of data and then to republish that data or data derived from it.

For example, imagine a subject that receives stock market price data published by an external(to the organization receiving the data) source. This subject might add a timestamp and source location to the data before republishing it to other internal Observers. However, there is a subtle difference that should be noted between a Subject and a plain Observable. A subscription to an Observable will cause an independent execution of the Observable when data is published. Notice how in the previous section all the messages were sent to a specific Observer before the next Observer was sent any data at all.

A Subject shares the publication action with all of the subscribers and they will therefore all receive the same data item in a chain before the next data item. In the class hierarchy the Subject class is a direct subclass of the Observer class.

603

The following example creates a Subject that enriches the data it receives by adding a timestamp to each data item. It then republishes the data item to any Observers that have subscribed to it.

```python
import rx
from rx.subjects import Subject
from datetime import datetime
source = rx.from_list([2, 3, 5, 7])
class TimeStampSubject(Subject):
def on_next(self, value): print('Subject
Received', value) super().on_next((value,
datetime.now()))
def on_completed(self):
print('Data Stream Completed')
super().on_completed()
def on_error(self, error):
print('In Subject- Error Occurred', error)
super().on_error(error)
def prime_number_reporter(value):
print('Function Received', value)
print('Set up')
# Create the Subject
subject = TimeStampSubject()
# Set up multiple subscribers for the subject
subject.subscribe(prime_number_reporter)
subject.subscribe(lambda value: print('Lambda
Received', value))
subject.subscribe(
on_next = lambda value: print('Received
on_next',value), on_error = lambda exp:
print('Error Occurred', exp), on_completed =
lambda: print('Received completed
notification')
)
# Subscribethe Subject to the Observable source
```

```
source.subscribe(subject)
```

print(**'Done'**)

Note that in the above program the Observers are added to the Subject before the Subject is added to the source Observable. This ensures that the Observers are subscribed before the Subject starts to receive data published by the Observable. If the Subject was subscribed to the Observable before the Observers were subscribed to the Subject, then all the data could have been published before the Observers were registered with the Subject.

The output from this program is:

```
Set up
  Subject Received 2
  Function Received (2, datetime.datetime(2019, 5, 21, 17,
0, 2,
  196372))
  Lambda Received (2, datetime.datetime(2019, 5, 21, 17,
0, 2,
  196372))
  Received on_next (2, datetime.datetime(2019, 5, 21, 17,
0, 2,
  196372))
  Subject Received 3
  Function Received (3, datetime.datetime(2019, 5, 21, 17,
0, 2,
```

196439))
Lambda Received (3, datetime.datetime(2019, 5, 21, 17, 0, 2,
  196439))
Received on_next (3, datetime.datetime(2019, 5, 21, 17, 0, 2,
  196439))
Subject Received 5
Function Received (5, datetime.datetime(2019, 5, 21, 17, 0, 2,
  196494))
Lambda Received (5, datetime.datetime(2019, 5, 21, 17, 0, 2,
  196494))
Received on_next (5, datetime.datetime(2019, 5, 21, 17, 0, 2,
  196494))
Subject Received 7
Function Received (7, datetime.datetime(2019, 5, 21, 17, 0, 2,
  196548))
Lambda Received (7, datetime.datetime(2019, 5, 21, 17, 0, 2,
  196548))
Received on_next (7, datetime.datetime(2019, 5, 21, 17, 0, 2,
  196548))
Data Stream Completed Received
completed notification
Done

As can be seen from this output the numbers 2, 3, 5 and 7 are received by all of the Observers once the Subject has added the timestamp.

Observer Concurrency

By default RxPy uses a single threaded model; that is Observables and Observers execute in the same thread of execution. However, this is only the default as it is the simplest approach.

It is possible to indicate that when a Observer subscribes to an Observable that it should run in a separate thread using the scheduler keyword parameter on the subscribe() method. This keyword is given an appropriate scheduler such as the rx.concurrency.NewThreadScheduler. This scheduler will ensure that the Observer runs in a separate thread.

To see the difference look at the following two programs. The main difference between the programs is the use of specific schedulers:

```
import rx
Observable =  rx.from_list([2, 3,  5])
observable.subscribe(lambda v: print('Lambda1
Received', v)) observable.subscribe(lambda v:
print('Lambda2 Received', v))
observable.subscribe(lambda v: print('Lambda3
Received', v))
```

The output from this first version is given below:

```
Lambda1 Received 2
    Lambda1 Received 3
    Lambda1 Received 5
    Lambda2 Received 2
    Lambda2 Received 3
    Lambda2 Received 5
    Lambda3 Received 2
    Lambda3 Received 3
    Lambda3 Received 5
```

The subscribe() method takes an optional keyword parameter called scheduler that allows a scheduler object to be provided. Now if we specify a few different schedulers we will see that the effect is to run the Observers concurrently with the resulting output being interwoven:

```
import rx
from rx.concurrency import NewThreadScheduler,
ThreadPoolScheduler, ImmediateScheduler
Observable =  rx.from_list([2, 3,   5])
observable.subscribe(lambda v: print('Lambda1
Received', v), scheduler=ThreadPoolScheduler(3))
observable.subscribe(lambda v: print('Lambda2
Received', v), scheduler=ImmediateScheduler())
observable.subscribe(lambda v: print('Lambda3
Received', v), scheduler=NewThreadScheduler())
# As the Observable runs in a separate thread need
# ensure that the main thread does not terminate
input('Press enterto finish')
```

Note that we have to ensure that the main thread running the program does not terminate (as all the Observables are now running in their own threads) by waiting for user input. The output from this version is:

```
Lambda2 Received 2
    Lambda1 Received 2
    Lambda2 Received 3
    Lambda2 Received 5
    Lambda1 Received 3
    Lambda1 Received 5
    Press enter to finish
    Lambda3 Received 2
    Lambda3 Received 3
    Lambda3 Received 5
```

By default the scheduler keyword on the subscribe() method defaults to None indicating that the current thread will be used for the subscription to the Observable.

Available Schedulers

To support different scheduling strategies the RxPy library provides two modules that supply different schedulers; the rx.concurrency and rx. currency.mainloopscheduler. The modules contain a variety of schedulers including those listed below.

The following schedulers are available in the rx.concurrency module:

- ImmediateScheduler This schedules an action for immediate execution.
- CurrentThreadScheduler This schedules activity for the current thread.
- TimeoutScheduler This scheduler works via a timed callback.
- NewThreadSchedulercreates a scheduler for each unit of work on a separate thread.
- ThreadPoolScheduler. This is a scheduler that utilizes a thread pool to execute work. This scheduler can act as a way of throttling the amount of work carried out concurrently.

The rx.concurrency.mainloopschduler module also defines the following schedulers:

- IOLoopScheduler A scheduler that schedules work via the Tornado I/O main event loop.
- PyGameScheduler A scheduler that schedules works for PyGame.
- WxScheduler A schedulerfor a wxPython event loop.

Try

Given the following set of tuples representing Stock/Equity prices:

```
stocks = (('APPL', 12.45), ('IBM', 15.55),
('MSFT', 5.66), ('APPL', 13.33))
```

Write a program that will create an Observable based on the stocks data. Next subscribe three different observers to the Observable. The first should print out the stock price, the second should print out the name of the stock and the third should print out the entire tuple.

RxPy Operators

Introduction

In this chapter we will look at the types of operator provided by RxPy that can be applied to the data emitted by an Observable.

Reactive Programming Operators

Behind the interaction between an Observable and an Observer is a data stream. That is the Observable supplies a data stream to an Observer that consumes/ processes that stream. It is possible to apply an operator to this data stream that can be used to to filter, transform and generally refine how and when the data is supplied to the Observer.

The operators are mostly defined in the rx.operators module, for example rx.operators.average(). However it is common to use an alias for this such that the operators module is called op, such as **from** rx **import** operators **as** op. This allows for a short hand form to be used when referencing an operator, such as op.average().

Many of the RxPy operators execute a function which is applied to each of the data items produced by an Observable. Others can be used to create an initial Observable (indeed you have already seen these operators in the form of the from_list() operator).Another set of operators can be used to generate a result based on data produced by the Observable (such as the sum() operator).

In fact RxPy provides a wide variety of operators and these operators can be categorized as follows:

- Creational,
- Transformational,
- Combinatorial,
- Filters,
- Error handlers,
- Conditional and Boolean operators,
- Mathematical,
- Connectable.

Examples of some of these categories are presented in the rest of this section.

Piping Operators

To apply an operator other than a creational operator to an Observable it is necessary to create a pipe. A Pipe is essentially a series of one or more operations that can be applied to the data stream generated by the Observable. The result of applying the pipe is that a new data stream is generated that represents the results produced following the application of each operator in turn. This is illustrated below:

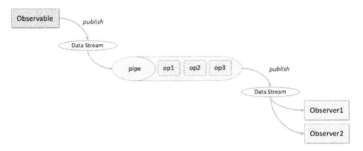

To create a pipe the Observable.pipe() method is used. This method takes a comma delimited list of one or more operators and returns a data stream. Observers can then subscribe to the pipe's data stream. This can be seen in the examples given in the rest of this chapter for transformations, filters, mathematical operators etc.

Creational Operators

You have already seen an example of a creational operator in the examples presented earlier in this chapter. This is because the rx.from_list() operator is an example of a creational operator. It is used to create a new Observable based on data held in a list like structure.

A more generic version of from_list() is the from_() operator. This operator takes an iterable and generates an Observable based on the data provided by the iterable. Any object that implements the iterable protocol can be used including user defined types. There is also an operator from_iterable(). All three operators do the same thing and you can choose which to use based on which provides the most semantic meaning in your context.

All three of the following statements have the same effect:

```
source  =  rx.from_([2,  3,  5,  7])
source  =  rx.from_iterable([2,  3,  5,  7])
source  =  rx.from_list([2,  3,  5,  7])
```

This is illustrated pictorially below:

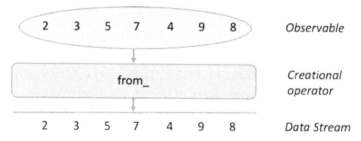

Another creational operator is the rx.range() operator. This operator generates an observable for a range of integer numbers. The range can be specified with our without a starting value and with or within an increment. However the maxi- mum value in the range must always be provided, for example:

```
obs1  =  rx.range(10) obs2  =  rx.range(0,  10)
obs3  =  rx.range(0,  10,  1)
```

Transformational Operators

There are several transformational operators defined in the rx.operators module including rx.operators.map() and rx.operators.flat_map(). The rx.operators.map() operator applies a function to each data item generated by an Observable.

The rx.operators.flat_map() operator also applies a function to each data item but then applies a flatten operation to the result.For example, if the result is a list of lists then flat_map will flatten this into a single list. In this section we will focus on the rx.operators.map() operator.

The rx.operators.map() operator allows a function to be applied to all data items generated by an Observable.The result of this function is then returned as the result of the map() operators Observable. The function is typically used to perform some form of transformation to the data supplied to it. This could be adding one to all integer values, converting the format of the data from XML to JSON,enriching the data with additional information such as the time the data was acquired and who the data was supplied by etc.

In the example given below we are transforming the set of integer values supplied by the original Observable into strings. In the diagram these strings include quotes around them to highlight they are in fact a string:

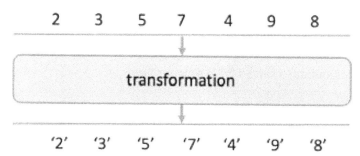

This is typical of the use of a transformation operator; that is to change the data from one format to another or to add information to the data.

The code used to implement this scenario is given below. Note the use of the pipe() method to apply the operator to the data stream generated by the Observable:

```
# Apply a transformation to a data source to
convert
# integers into strings
import rx
from rx  import operators  as op
# Set up a source with a map function
source  =  rx.from_list([2,  3,  5,  7]).pipe(
op.map(lambda value:  "'" +  str(value)  +  "'")
)
# Subscribe a lambda function
source.subscribe(lambda value:  print('Lambda
Received', value,
' is a string ', isinstance(value,  str)))
```

The output from this program is:

Lambda Received '2' is a string True
Lambda Received '3' is a string True
Lambda Received '5' is a string True
Lambda Received '7' is a string True

Combinatorial Operators

Combinatorial operators combine together multiple data items in some way. One example of a combinatorial operator is the rx.merge() operator. This operator merges the data produced by two Observables into a single Observable data stream. For example:

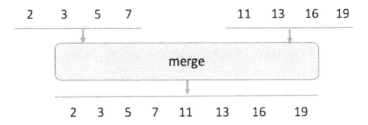

In the above diagram two Observables are represented by the sequence 2, 3, 5, 7 and the sequence 11, 13, 16, 19. These Observables are supplied to the merge operator that generates a single Observable that will supply data generated from both of the original Observables. This is an example of an operator that does not take a function but instead takes two Observables.

The code representing the above scenario is given below:

```
# An example illustratinghow to merge two data
sources
import rx
# Set up two sources
source1 = rx.from_list([2,  3,  5,  7])
source2 = rx.from_list([10,  11,  12])
# Merge two sources into one
rx.merge(source1,  source2)\
.subscribe(lambda v:  print(v,  end=','))
```

Notice that in this case we have subscribed directly to the Observable returned by the merge() operator and have not stored this in an intermediate variable (this was a design decision and either approach is acceptable).

```
# An example illustratinghow to merge two data
sources
import rx
# Set up two sources
source1 = rx.from_list([2,  3,  5,  7])
source2 = rx.from_list([10,  11,  12])
# Merge two sources into one
rx.merge(source1,  source2)\
.subscribe(lambda v:  print(v,  end=','))
```

Notice that in this case we have subscribed directly to the Observable returned by the merge() operator and have not stored this in an intermediate variable (this was a design decision and either approach is acceptable).

The output from this program is presented below:

2,3,5,7,10,11,12,

Notice from the output the way in which the data held in the original Observables is intertwined in the output of the Observable generated by the merge() operator.

Filtering Operators

There are several operators in this category including rx.op-erators.filter (), rx.operators.first(), rx.operators.last()and rx.opera- tors.distinct(). The filter() operator only allows those data items to pass through that pass some test expression defined by the function passed into the filter. This function must return True or False. Any data item that causes the function to return True is allowed to pass through the filter.

For example, let us assume that the function passed into filter() is designed to only allow even numbers through. If the data stream contains the numbers 2, 3, 5,7, 4, 9 and 8 then the filter() will only emit the numbers 2, 4 and 8. This is illustrated below:

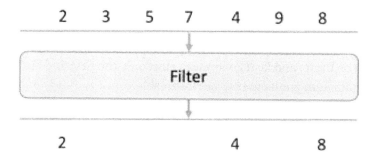

The following code implements the above scenario:

```
# Filter source for even numbers
import rx
from rx  import operators  as op
# Set up a source with a filter
source  =  rx.from_list([2,  3,  5,  7,  4,  9,
8]).pipe(
op.filter(lambda value:  value  %  2  ==  0)
)
# Subscribea lambda function
source.subscribe(lambda value:  print('Lambda
Received',  value))
```

In the above code the rx.operators.filter() operator takes a lambda function that will verify if the current value is even or not (note this could have been a named function or a method on an object etc.). It is applied to the data stream generated by the Observable using the pipe() method. The output generated by this example is:

Lambda Received 2

Lambda Received 4
Lambda Received 8

The first() and last() operators emit only the first and last data item published by the Observable.

The distinct() operator suppresses duplicate items being published by the Observable. For example, in the following list used as the data for the Observable, the numbers 2 and 3 are duplicated:

```
# Use distinctto suppress duplicates
source  =  rx.from_list([2,  3,  5,  2,  4,  3,
2]).pipe(
op.distinct()
)
# Subscribea lambda function
source.subscribe(lambda value:  print('Received',
 value))
```

However, when the output is generated by the program all duplicates have been suppressed:

Received 2

Received 3

Received 5

Received 4

Mathematical Operators

Mathematical and aggregate operators perform calculations on the data stream provided by an Observable. For example, the rx.operators.average() operator can be used to calculate the average of a set of numbers published by an Observable. Similarly rx.operators.max() can select the maximum value, rx.operators.min() the minimum value and rx.operators.sum() will total all the numbers published etc.

An example using the rx.operators.sum() operator is given blow:

```
# Example of summing all the values in a data
stream
import rx
from rx  import operators  as op
# Set up a source and apply sum
rx.from_list([2,  3,  5,  7]).pipe(
op.sum()
).subscribe(lambda v:  print(v))
```

The output from the rx.operators.sum() operator is the total of the data items published by the Observable (in this case the total of 2, 3, 5 and 7). The Observer function that is subscribed to the rx.operators.sum() operators Observable will print out this value:

17

However, in some cases it may be useful to be notified of the intermediate running total as well as the final value so that other operators down the chain can react to these subtotals. This can be achieved using the rx.operators.scan() operator. The rx.operators.scan() operator is actually a transformational operator but can be used in this case to provide a mathematical operation. The scan() operator applies a function to each data item published by an Observable and generates its own data item for each value received. Each generated value is passed to the next invocation of the scan() function as well as being published to the scan() operators Observable data stream. The running total can thus be generated from the previous sub total and the new value obtained.This is shown below:

```
import rx
from rx  import operators  as op
# Rolling or incremental sum
rx.from_([2,  3,  5,  7]).pipe(
op.scan(lambda subtotal,  i:  subtotal+i)
).subscribe(lambda v:  print(v))
```

The output from this example is:

```
2
  5
  10
  17
```

This means that each subtotal is published as well as the final total.

Chaining Operators

An interesting aspect of the RxPy approach to data stream processing is that it is possible to apply multiple operators to the data stream produced by an Observable.

The operators discussed earlier actually return another Observable. This new Observable can supply its own data stream based on the original data stream and the result of applying the operator.This allows another operator to be applied in sequence to the data produced by the new Observable. This allows the operators to be chained together to provide sophisticated processing of the data published by the original Observable.

For example, we might first start off by filtering the output from an Observable such that only certain data items are published.We might then apply a transformation in the form of a map() operator to that data, as shown below:

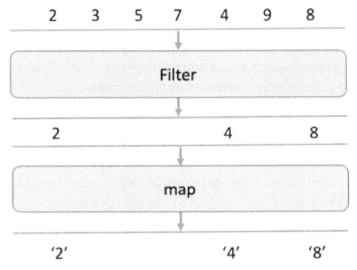

Note the the order in which we have applied the operators; we first filter out data that is not of interest and then apply the transformation. This is more efficient than apply the operators the other way around as in the above example we do not need to transform the odd values. It is therefore common to try and push the filter operators as high up the chain as possible.

The code used to generate the chained set of operators is given below. In this case we have used lambda functions to define the filter() function and the map () function. The operators are applied to the Observable obtained from the list supplied. The data stream generated by the Observable is processed by each of the operators defined in the pipe. As there are now two operators the pipe contains both operators and acts a pipe down which the data flows.

The list used as the initial source of the Observables data

contains a sequence of event and odd numbers. The filter() function selects only even numbers and the map() function transforms the integer values into strings. We then subscribe an Observer function to the Observable produced by the transformational map() operator.

```
# Example of chainingoperators together
import rx
from rx  import operators  as op
# Set up a source with a filter
source  =  rx.from_list([2,  3,  5,  7,  4,  9,
8])
pipe  =  source.pipe(
op.filter(lambda value:  value  %  2  ==  0),
op.map(lambda value:  "'"+  str(value)  +  "'")
)
# Subscribe a lambda function
pipe.subscribe(lambda value:  print('Received',
value))
```

The output from this application is given below:

Received '2' Received '4' Received '8'

This makes it clear that only the three even numbers (2, 4 and 8) are allowed through to the map() function.

Online Resources

See the following online resources for information on RxPy:

- https://rxpy.readthedocs.io/en/latest/ Documentation for the RxPy library.
- https://rxpy.readthedocs.io/en/latest/operators.html Lists of the available RxPy operators.

Try

Given the following set of tuples representing Stock/Equity prices:

```
stocks = (('APPL', 12.45), ('IBM', 15.55),
('MSFT', 5.66), ('APPL', 13.33))
```

Provide solutions to the following:

- Select all the 'APPL' stocks
- Select all stocks with a price over 15.00
- Find the average price of all 'APPL' stocks.

Now use the second set of tuples and merge them with the first set of stock prices:

```
stocks2 = (('GOOG', 8.95), ('APPL', 7.65),
('APPL', 12.45), ('MSFT', 5.66), ('GOOG',
7.56), ('IBM', 12.76))
```

Convert each tuple into a list and calculate how much 25 shares in that stock would be, print this out as the result).

- Find the highest value stock.
- Find the lowest value stock.
- Only publish unique data times (I.e. Suppress duplicates).

Introduction to Sockets and Web Services

Introduction

In the following two chapters we will explore socket based and web service approaches to inter process communications. These processes may be running on the same computer or different computers on the same local area network or may be geographically far apart. In all cases information is sent by one program running in one process to another program running in a separate process via internet sockets. This chapter introduces the core concepts involved in network programming.

Sockets

Sockets, or rather Internet Protocol (IP) sockets provide a programming interface to the network protocol stack that is managed by the underlying operating system. Using such an API means that the programmer is abstracted away from the low level details of how data is exchanged between process on (potentially) different computers and can instead focus on the higher level aspects of their solution.

There are a number of different types of IP socket available, however the focus in this book is on Stream Sockets. A stream socket uses the Transmission Control Protocol (TCP) to send messages.Such a socket is often referred to as a TCP/IP socket.

TCP provides for ordered and reliable transmission of data across the connection between two devices (or hosts). This can be important as TCP guarantees that for every message sent; that every message will not only arrive at the receiving host but that the messages will arrive in the correct order.

A common alternative to the TCP is the User Data gram Protocol (or UDP). UDP does not provide any delivery guarantees (that is messages can be lost or may arrive out of order). However, UDP is a simpler protocol and can be particularly useful for broadcast systems, where multiple clients may need to receive the data published by a server host (particularly if data loss is not an issue).

Web Services

A Web Service is a service offered by a host computer that can be invoked by a remote client using the Hypertext Transfer Protocol (HTTP). HTTP can be run over any re-liable stream transport protocol, although it is typically used over TCP/IP. It was originally designed to allow data to be transferred between a HTTP server and a web browser so that the data could be presented in a human readable form to a user. However, when used with a web service it is used to support program to program communication between a client and a server using machine-readable data formats. Currently this format is most typically JSON (Java ScriptObject Notation) although in the past XML (eXtensible Markup Language) was often used.

Addressing Services

Every device (host) connected to the internet has a unique identity (we are ignoring private networks here). This unique identity is represented as an IP address. Using an IP address we can connect a socket to a specific host anywhere on the internet. It is therefore possible to connect to a whole range of device types in this way from printers to cash tills to fridges as well as servers, mainframes and PCs etc.

IP addresses have a common format such as 144.124.16.237. An IP version 4 address is always a set of four numbers separated by full stops. Each number can be in the range 0–255, so the full range of IP addresses is from 0.0.0.0 to 255.255.255.255.

An IP address can be divided up into two parts; the part indicating the network on which the host is connected and the host's ID, for example:

Network ID

144.124.16 .237

Host ID

Thus:

- The Network ID elements of the IP address identifies the specific network on which the host is currently located.
- The Host ID is the part of the IP address that specifies a specific device on the network (such as your computer).

On any given network there may be multiple hosts, each with their own host ID but with a shared network ID. For example, on a private home network there may be:

- 192.168.1.1 Jasmine's laptop.
- 192.168.1.2 Adam's PC
- 192.168.1.3 Home Printer
- 192.168.1.4 Smart TV

In many ways the network id and host id elements of an IP address are like the postal address for a house on a street. The street may have a name, for example Coleridge Avenue and there may be multiple houses on the street. Each house has a unique number; thus 10 Coleridge Avenue is uniquely differentiated from 20 Coleridge Avenue by the house number.

At this point you may be wondering where the URLs you see in your web browser come into play (such as www.bbc .co.uk). These are textual names that actually map to an IP address. The mapping is performed by something called a Domain Name System (or DNS) server. A DNS server acts as a lookup service to provide the actual IP address for a particular textual URL name.The presence of an English textual version of a host address is because humans are better at remembering (a hopefully) meaningful name rather than what might appear to be a random sequence of numbers.

There are several web sites that can be used to see these mappings (and one is given at the end of this chapter). Some examples of how the English textual name maps to an IP address are given below:

- www.aber.ac.uk maps to 144.124.16.237
- www.uwe.ac.uk maps to 164.11.132.96
- www.bbc.net.uk maps to 212.58.249.213
- www.gov.uk maps to 151.101.188.144

Note that these mappings were correct at the time of writing; they can change as new entries can be provided to the DNS servers causing a particular textual name to map to a different physical host.

Localhost

There is a special IP address which is usually available on a host computer and is very useful for developers and testers. This is the IP address:

127.0.0.1

It is also known as localhost which is often easier to remember. Localhost (and 127.0.0.1) is used to refer to the computer you are currently on when a program is run; that is it is your local host computer (hence the name localhost).

For example, if you start up a socket server on your local computer and want a client socket program, running on the same computer, to connect to the server program; you can tell it to do so by getting it to connect to localhost.

This is particularly useful when either you don't know the IP address of your local computer or because the code may be run on multiple different computers each of which will have their own IP address. This is particularly common if you are writing test code that will be used by developers when running their own tests on different developer (host) machines.

We will be using localhost in the next two chapters as a way of specifying where to look for a server program.

Port Numbers

Each internet device/host can typically support multiple processes. It is therefore necessary to ensure that each process has its own channel of communications. To do this each host has available to it multiple ports that a program can connect too. For example port 80 is often reserved for HTTP web servers, while port 25 is reserved for SMTP servers. This means that if a client wants to connect to a HTTP server on a particular computer then it must specify port 80 not port 25 on that host.

A port number is written after the IP address of the host and separated from the address by a colon, for example:

· www.aber.ac.uk:80 indicates port 80 on the host machine which will typically be running a HTTP server, in this case for Aberystwyth University.

· localhost:143 this indicates that you wish to connect to port 143 which is typically reserved for an IMAP (Internet Message Access Protocol) server on your local machine.

· www.uwe.ac.uk:25 this indicates port 25 on a host running at the University of the West of England, Bristol. Port 25 is usually reserved for SMTP (Simple Mail Transfer Protocol) servers.

Port numbers in the IP system are 16 bit numbers in the range 0–65 536. Generally, port numbers below 1024 are reserved for predefined services (which means that you should avoid using them unless you wish to communicate with one of those services such as telnet, SMTP mail, ftp etc.). Therefore it is typically to choose a port number above 1024 when setting up your won services.

IPv4 Versus IPv6

What we have described in this chapter in terms of IP addresses is in fact based on the Internet Protocol version 4 (aka IPv4). This version of the Internet Protocol was developed during the 1970s and published by the IETF (Internet Engineering Task Force) in September 1981 (replacing an earlier definition published in January 1980). This version of the standard uses 32 binary bits for each element of the host address (hence the range of 0 to 255 for each of there parts of the address). This provides a total of 4.29 billion possible unique addresses. This seemed a huge amount in 1981 and certainly enough for what was imagined at the time for the internet.

Since 1981 the internet has become the backbone to not only the World Wide Web itself, but also to the concept of the Internet of Things (in which every possible device might be connected to the internet from your fridge, to your central heating system to your toaster). This potential explosion in internet addressable devices/ hosts lead in the mid 1990 as to concerns about the potential lack of internet addresses using IPv4. The IETF therefore designed a new version of the Internet Protocol; Internet Protocol version 6 (or IPv6). This was ratified as an Internet Standard in July 2017.

IPv6 uses a 128 bit address for each element in a hosts address. It also uses eight number groups (rather than 4) which are separated by a colon. Each number group has four hexadecimal digits.

The following illustrates what an IPv6 address looks like:

2001:0DB8:AC10:FE01:EF69:B5ED:DD57:2CLE

Uptake of the IPv6 protocol has been slower than was originally expected, this is in part because the IPv4 and IPv6 have not been designed to be interoperable but also because the utilization of the IPv4 addresses has not been as fast as many originally feared (partly due to the use of private networks). However, over time this is likely to change as more organizations move over to using the IPv6.

38.8 Sockets and Web Services in Python

The next two chapters discuss how sockets and web services can be implemented in Python. The first chapter discusses both general sockets and HTTP server sockets. The second chapter looks at how the Flask library can be used to create web services that run over HTTP using TCP/IP sockets.

Online Resources

See the following online resources for information

- `https://en.wikipedia.org/wiki/Network_socket` Wikipedia page on Sockets.
- https://en.wikipedia.org/wiki/Web_service Wikipedia page on Web Services.
- https://codebeautify.org/website-to-ip-addressProvides mappings from URLs to

IP addresses.

- https://en.wikipedia.org/wiki/IPv4 Wikipedia page on IPv4.
- https://en.wikipedia.org/wiki/IPv6 Wikipedia page on IPv6.
- https://www.techopedia.com/definition/28503/dns-server For an introduction to DNS.

Sockets in Python

Introduction

A Socket is an end point in a communication link between separate processes. In Python sockets are objects which provide a way of exchanging information between two processes in a straightforward and platform independent manner.

In this chapter we will introduce the basic idea of socket communications and then presents a simple socket server and client application.

Socket to Socket Communication

When two operating system level processes wish to communicate,they can do so via sockets. Each process has a socket which is connected to the others socket. One process can then write information out to the socket, while the second process can read information in from the socket.

Associated with each socket are two streams, one for input and one for output. Thus, to pass information from one process to another, you write that information out to the output stream of one socket object and read it from the input stream of another socket object (assuming the two sockets are connected).

Several different types of sockets are available, however in this chapter we will focus on TCP/IP sockets. Such a socket is a connection-oriented socket that will provide a guarantee of delivery of data (or notification of the failure to deliver the data). TCP/IP, or the Transmission Control Protocol/Internet Protocol, is a suite of communication protocols used to interconnect network devices on the internet or in a private intranet.TCP/IP actually specifies how data is exchanged between programs over the internet by providing end-to-end communications that identify how the data should be broken down into packets, addressed, transmitted, routed and received at the destination.

Setting Up a Connection

To set up the connection, one process must be running a program that is waiting for a connection while the other must try to connect up to the first program.The first is referred to as a server socket while the second just as a socket.

For the second process to connect to the first (the server socket) it must know what machine the first is running on and which port it is connected to.

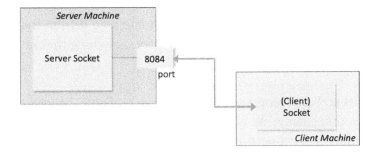

For example, in the above diagram the server socket connects to port 8084. In turn the client socket connects to the machine on which the server is executing and to port number 8084 on that machine.

Nothing happens until the server socket accepts the connection. At that point the sockets are connected, and the socket streams are bound to each other. This means that the server's output stream is connected to the Client socket input stream and vice versa.

An Example Client Server Application

The System Structure

The above diagram illustrates the basic structure of the system we are trying to build.There will be a server object running on one machine and a client object running on another. The client will connect up to the server using sockets in order to obtain information.

The actual application being implemented in this example, is an address book look up application. The addresses of employees of a company are held in a dictionary. This dictionary is set up in the server program but could equally be held in a database etc. When a client connects up to the server it can obtain an employees' office address.

Implementing the Server Application

We shall describe the server application first. This is the Python application pro- gram that will service requests from client applications. To do this it must provide a server socket for clients to connect to. This is done by first binding a server socket to a port on the server machine. The server program must then listen for incoming connections. The listing presents the source code for the Server program.

```
import socket
def main():
# Setup names and offices
addresses = {'JOHN': 'C45',
'DENISE': 'C44',
'PHOEBE': 'D52',
'ADAM': 'B23'}
print('Starting Server')
print('Create the socket')
sock = socket.socket(socket.AF_INET,
socket.SOCK_STREAM)
print('Bind the socket to the port')
server_address = (socket.gethostname(),
8084)
print('Starting up on', server_address)
```

```
sock.bind(server_address)
# specifies the number of connections
allowed print('Listen forincoming connections')
sock.listen(1)
while True:
print('Waiting for a connection')
connection, client_address =
sock.accept()
try:
print('Connection from',
client_address)
while True:
data =
connection.recv(1024).decode()
print('Received: ', data)
if data:
key = str(data).upper() response =
addresses[key] print('sending data back
to the client: ', response)
connection.sendall(
response.encode())
else:
print('No more data from',
client_address)
finally:
break
connection.close()
if_name_=='_main_':
main()
```

The Server in the above listing sets up the addresses to contain a Dictionary of the names and addresses.

It then waits for a client to connect to it. This is done by creating a socket and binding it to a specific port (in this case port 8084) using:

```
print('Create the socket')
sock = socket.socket(socket.AF_INET,
socket.SOCK_STREAM) print('Bind the socket to the
port') server_address = (socket.gethostname(),
8084)
```

The construction of the socket object is discussed in more detail in the next section. Next the server listens for a connection from a client. Note that the sock. listen() method takes the value 1 indicating that it will handle one connection at a time.

An infinite loop is then set up to run the server. When a connection is made from a client, both the connection and the client address are made available. While there is data available from the client, it is read using the recv function. Note that the data received from the client is assumed to be a string. This is then used as a key to look the address up in the address Dictionary.

Once the address is obtained it can be sent back to the client. In Python 3 it is necessary to decode() and encoded() the string format to the raw data transmitted via the socket streams.Note you should always close a socket when you have finished with it.

Socket Types and Domains

When we created the socket class above, we passed in two arguments to the socket constructor:

```
socket(socket.AF_INET, socket.SOCK_STREAM)
```

To understand the two values passed into the socket() constructor it is necessary to understand that Sockets are characterized according to two properties; their domain and their type.

The domain of a socket essentially defines the communications protocols that are used to transfer the data from one process to another. It also incorporates how sockets are named (so that they can be referred to when establishing the communication).

Two standard domains are available on Unix systems; these are AF_UNIX which represents intra system communications, where data is moved from process to process through kernel memory buffers. AF_INET represents communication using the TCP/IP protocol suite; in which processes may be on the same machine or on different machines.

- A socket's type indicates how the data is transferred through the socket. There are essentially two options here:
- Data gram which sockets support a message-based model where no connection is involved, and communication is not guaranteed to be reliable.

- Stream sockets that support a virtual circuit model, where data is exchanged as a byte stream and the connection is reliable.

Depending on the domain, further socket types may be available, such as those that support message passing on a reliable connection.

Implementing the Client Application

The client application is essentially a very simple program that creates a link to the server application. To do this it creates a socket object that connects to the servers' host machine, and in our case this socket is connected to port 8084.

Once a connection has been made the client can then send the encoded message string to the server. The server will then send back a response which the client must decode. It then closes the connection.

The implementation of the client is given below:

```python
import socket
def main():
print('Starting Client')
print('Create a TCP/IP socket')
sock = socket.socket(socket.AF_INET,
socket.SOCK_STREAM) print('Connect  the  socket
to  the  server  port')server_address =
(socket.gethostname(),
8084)
```

```
print('Connecting to: ',  server_address)
sock.connect(server_address) print('Connected to
server')
try:
print('Send data')message  =  'John'
print('Sending: ',  message)
sock.send(message.encode())
data = sock.recv(1024).decode()
print('Received from server: ',  data)
finally:
print('Closing socket')
sock.close()
if_name_=='_main_':
main()
```

The output from the two programs needs to be considered together.

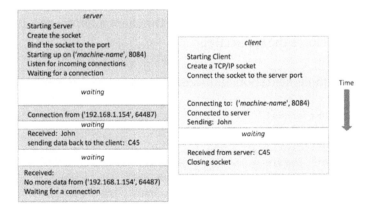

As you can see from this diagram, the server waits for a connection from the client. When the client connects to the server; the server waits to receive data from the client. At this point the client must wait for data to be sent to it from the server. The server then sets up the response data and sends it back to the client. The client receives this and prints it out and closes the connection. In the mean time, the server has been waiting to see if there is any more data from the client; as the client closes the connection the server knows that the client has finished and returns to waiting for the next connection.

The Socket server Module

In the above example, the server code is more complex than the client; and this is for a single threaded server; life can become much more complicated if the server is expected to be a multi-threaded server (that is a server that can handle multiple requests from different clients at the same time).

However, the server socket module provides a more con-venient, object-oriented approach to creating a server. Much of the boiler plate code needed in such applications is defined in classes, with the developer only having to provide their own classes or override methods to define the specific functionality required.

There are five different server classes defined in the socket server module.

- BaseServer is the root of the Server class hierarchy; it is not really intended to be instantiated and used directly. Instead it is extended by TCP Server and other classes.

- TCPServer uses TCP/IP sockets to communicate and is probably the most commonly used type of socket server.
- UDPServer provides access to data gram sockets.
- UnixStreamServer and UnixDatagramServer use Unix-domain sockets and are only available on Unix platforms.

Responsibility for processing a request is split between a server class and a request handler class. The server deals with the communication issues (listening on a socket and port, accepting connections, etc.) and the request handler deals with the request issues (interpreting incoming data, processing it, sending data back to the client).

This division of responsibility means that in many cases you can simply use one of the existing server classes without any modifications and provide a custom request handler class for it to work with.

The following example defines a request handler that is plugged into the TCPServer when it is constructed. The request handler defines a method handle() that will be expected to handle the request processing.

```
import socketserver
class
MyTCPHandler(socketserver.BaseRequestHandler): """
The  RequestHandler  class  for  the  server. """
def  init  (self,  request,  client_address,
```

```
server):
print('Setup names and offices')
self.addresses = {'JOHN': 'C45',
'DENISE': 'C44',
'PHOEBE': 'D52',
'ADAM': 'B23'}
super(). init (request, client_address,
server)
def handle(self):
print('In Handle')
# self.request is the TCP socket connected
# to the client
data = self.request.recv(1024).decode()
print('data received:', data)key =
str(data).upper() response =
self.addresses[key] print('response:', response)
# Send the result back to the client
self.request.sendall(response.encode())
def main():
print('Starting server')server_address =
('localhost', 8084)print('Creating server')
server =
socketserver.TCPServer(server_address,
MyTCPHandler)
print('Activating server')
server.serve_forever()
if_name_== '_main_':
main()
```

Note that the previous client application does not need to change at all; the server changes are hidden from the client. However, this is still a single threaded server. We can very simply make it into a multi-threaded server (one that can deal with multiple requests concurrently) by mixing the socket server. ThreadingMixIn into the TCPServer. This

651

can be done by defining a new class that is nothing more than a class that extends both

ThreadingMixIn and TCPServer and creating an instance of this new class instead of the TCPServer directly. For example:

```
class ThreadedEchoServer(
socketserver.ThreadingMixIn,
socketserver.TCPServer):
pass
def main():
print('Starting')
address = ('localhost', 8084)
server = ThreadedEchoServer(address,
MyTCPHandler)
print('Activating server')
server.serve_forever()
Infact you do not even need to create your own
class (such as the ThreadedEchoServer) as the
socketserver.ThreadingTCPServer has been
provided as a default mixing of the TCPServer
and the ThreadingMixIn classes. We could
therefore just write:
def main():
print('Starting')
address = ('localhost', 8084)
server = socketserver.ThreadedEchoServer(address,
MyTCPHandler)
print('Activating server')
server.serve_forever()
```

HTTP Server

In addition to the TCPServer you also have available a http.server. HTTPServer; this can be used in a similar manner to the TCPServer, but is used to create servers that respond to the HTTP protocol used by web browsers. In other words it can be used to create a very simple Web Server (although it should be noted that it is really only suitable for creating test web servers as it only implements very basic security checks).

It is probably worth a short aside to illustrate how a web server and a web browser interact. The following diagram illustrates the basic interactions:

In the above diagram the user is using a browser (such as Chrome, IE or Safari) to access a web server. The browser is running on their local machine (which could be a PC, a Mac, a Linux box, an iPad, a Smart Phone etc.).

To access the web server they enter a URL (Universal Resource Locator) address into their browser. It also indicates that they want to connect up to port 8080 (rather than the default port 80 used for HTTP connections). The remote machine receives this request and determines what to do with it. If there is no program monitoring port 8080 it will reject the request. In our case we have a

Python Program (which is actually the web server program) listening to that port and it is passed the request. It will then handle this request and generate a response message which will be sent back to the browser on the users local machine.The response will indicate which version of the HTTP protocol it supports, whether everything went OK or not (this is the 200 code in the above diagram – you may have seen the code 404 indicating that a web page was not found etc.). The browser on the local machine then renders the data as a web page or handles the data as appropriate etc.

To create a simple Python web server the http.server.HT TPServer can be used directly or can be sub classed along with the socketserver. ThreadingMixIn to create a multi-threaded web server, for example:

```
class ThreadingHTTPServer(ThreadingMixIn,
HTTPServer): """Simple  multi-threaded  HTTP
server  """
pass
```

Since Python 3.7 the http.server module now provides exactly this class as a built in facility and it is thus no longer necessary to define it yourself (see http.server.ThreadingH TTPServer).

To handle HTTP requests you must implement one of the HTTP request methods such as do_GET(), or do_POST(). Each of these maps to a type of HTTP request, for example:

- do_GET() maps to a HTTP Get request that is generated if you type a web address into the URL bar of a web browser or
- do_POST() maps to a HTTP Post request that is used for example, when a form on a web page is used to submit data to a web server.

The do_GET(self) or do_POST(self)method must then handle any input supplied with the request and generate any appropriate responses back to the browser. This means that it must follow the HTTP protocol.

The following short program creates a simple web server that will generate a welcome message and the current time as a response to a GET request. It does this by using the datetime module to create a time stamp of the date and time using the today() function. This is converted into a byte array using the UTF-8 character encoding (UTF-8 is the most widely used way to represent text within web pages). We need a byte array as that is what will be executed by the write() method later on.

Having done this there are various items of meta data that need to be set up so that the browser knows what data it is about to receive.This meta data is known as header data and can including the type of content being sent and the amount of data (content) being transmitted. In our very simple case we need to tell it that we are sending it plain text (rather than the HTML used to describe a typical web page) via the 'Content-type' header information. We also need to tell it how much data we are sending using the content length.

We can then indicate that we have finished defining the header information and are now sending the actual data.

The data itself is sent via the wfile attribute inherited from the Base HTTPRequestHandler. There are infact two related attributes rfile and wfile:

- rfile this is an input stream that allows you to read input data (which is not being used in this example).
- wfile holds the output stream that can be used to write (send) data to the browser. This object provides a method write() that takes a byte-like object that is written out to (eventually) the browser.

A main() method is used to set up the HTTP server which follows the pattern used for the TCPServer; however the client of this server will be a web browser.

from http.server import BaseHTTPRequestHandler, ThreadingHTTPServer from datetime import datetime

```
class
MyHttpRequestHandler(BaseHTTPRequestHandler):
"""Very simple requesthandler. Only supports
GET."""
def do_GET(self):
print("do_GET() starting to process request")
welcome_msg = 'Hello From Server at ' +
str(datetime.today())
byte_msg = bytes(welcome_msg, 'utf-8')
self.send_response(200)
self.send_header("Content-type", 'text/plain;
charset-
```

```
utf-8')
self.send_header('Content-length',
str(len(byte_msg)))
self.end_headers()
print('do_GET() replying with message')
self.wfile.write(byte_msg)
def main():
print('Setting up server')
server_address = ('localhost', 8080)
httpd = ThreadingHTTPServer(server_address,
MyHttpRequestHandler)
print('Activating HTTP server')
httpd.serve_forever()
if_name_=='_main_':
main()
```

Once the server is up and running, it is possible to connect to the server using a browser and by entering an appropriate web address into the browsers' URL field. This means that in your browser (assuming it is running on the same machine as the above program) you only need to type into the URL bar http://local- host:8080 (this indicates you want to use the http protocol to connect up to the local machine at port 8080).

When you do this you should see the welcome message with the current date and time:

Web Services in Python

Introduction

This chapter looks at RESTful web services as implemented using the Flask framework.

RESTful Services

REST stands for Representational State Transfer and was a termed coined by Roy Fielding in his Ph.D. to describe the lightweight, resource-oriented architectural style that underpins the web. Fielding, one of the principle authors of HTTP, was looking for a way of generalizing the operation of HTTP and the web. The generalized the supply of web pages as a form of data supplied on demand to a client where the client holds the current state of an exchange. Based on this state information the client requests the next item of relevant data sending all information necessary to identify the information to be supplied with the request. Thus the requests are independent and not part of an ongoing stateful conversation (hence state transfer).

It should be noted that although Fielding was aiming to

create a way of describing the pattern of behavior within the web, he also had an eye on producing lighter weight web based services (than those using either proprietary Enterprise Integration frameworks or SOAP based services). These lighter weight HTTP based web services have become very popular and are now widely used in many areas. Systems which follow these principles are termed RESTful services.

A key aspect of a RESTful service is that all interactions between a client (whether some JavaScript running in a browser or a standalone application) are done using simple HTTP based operations. HTTP supports four operations these are HTTP Get, HTTP Post, HTTP Put and HTTP Delete. These can be used as verbs to indicate the type of action being requested. Typically these are used as follows:

- retrieve information (HTTP Get),
- create information (HTTP Post),
- update information (HTTP Put),
- delete information (HTTP Delete).

It should be noted that REST is not a standard in the way that HTML is a standard. Rather it is a design pattern that can be used to create web applications that can be invoked over HTTP and that give meaning to the use of Get, Post, Put and Delete HTTP operations with respect to a specific resource (or type of data).

The advantage of using RESTful services as a technology,

compared to some other approaches (such as SOAP based services which can also be invoked over HTTP) is that

- the implementations tend to be simpler,
- the maintenance easier,
- they run over standard HTTP and HTTPS protocols and
- do not require expensive infrastructures and licenses to use.

This means that there is lower server and server side costs. There is little vendor or technology dependency and clients do not need to know anything about the implementation details or technologies being used to create the services.

A RESTful API

1. A RESTful API is one in which you must first determine the key concepts or resources being represented or managed.
2. These might be books, products in a shop, room bookings in hotels etc. For example a bookstore related service might provide information on resources such as books, CDs, DVDs, etc. Within this service books are just one type of resource. We will ignore the other resources such as DVDs and CDs etc.
3. Based on the idea of a book as a resource we will identify suitable URLs for these RESTful services. Note that although URLs are frequently used to describe a web page—that is just one type of resource. For example, we might develop a resource such as

/bookservice/book

from this we could develop a URL based API, such as
/bookservice/book/<isbn>

Where ISBN (the International Standard Book Number) indicates a unique number to be used to identify a specific book whose details will be returned using this URL.

We also need to design the representation or formats that the service can supply. These could include plain text, JSON, XML etc. JSON standards for the JavaScript Object Notation and is a concise way to describe data that is to be transferred from a service running on a server to a client running in a browser. This is the format we will use in the next section. As part of this we might identify a series of operations to be provided by our services based on the type of HTTP Method used to invoke our service and the contents of the URL provided. For example, for a simple Book Service this might be:

- GET /book/<isbn>—used to retrieve a book for a given ISBN.
- GET /book/list—used to retrieve all current books in JSON format.
- POST /book (JSON in body of the message)—which supports creating a new book.
- PUT /book (JSON in body of message)—used to update the data held on an existing Book.
- DELETE /book/<isbn>—used to indicate that we would like a specific book deleted from the list of books held.

Note that the parameter isbn in the above URLs actually forms part of the URL path.

Python Web Frameworks

There are very many frameworks and libraries available in Python that will allow you to create JSON based web services; and the shear number of options available to you can be overwhelming.For example, you might consider

- Flask,
- Django,
- Web2py and
- CherryPy to name just a few.

These frameworks and libraries offer different sets of facilities and levels of sophistication. For example Django is a full-stack web framework; that is it is aimed at developing not just web services but full blown web sites. However, for our purposes this is probably overkill and the Django Rest interface is only part of a much larger infrastructure. That does not mean of course that we could not use Django to create our bookshop services; however there are simpler options available. The web2py is another full stack web framework which we will also discount for the same reason.

In contrast Flask and CherryPy are considered non full-stack frameworks (although you can create a full stack web application using them). This means that they are lighter weight and quicker to get started with. CherryPy was original rather more focused on providing a remote function call facility that allowed functions to be invoked over HTTP; however this has been extended to provide more REST like facilities. In this chapter we will focus on Flask as it is one of the most widely used frameworks for light weight RESTful services in Python.

Flask

Flask is a web development framework for Python. It describes itself as a micro framework for Python which is somewhat confusing; to the point where there is a page dedicated to this on their web site that explains what it means and what the implications are of this for Flask. According to Flask, the micro in its description relates to its primary aim of keeping the core of Flask simple but extensible. Unlike Django it doesn't include facilities aimed at helping you integrate your application with a database for example. Instead Flask focuses on the core functionality required of a web service framework and allows extension to be used, as and when required, for additional functionality.

Flask is also a convention over configuration framework; that is if you follow the standard conventions then you will not need to deal with much additional configuration information (although if you wish to follow a different set of conventions then you can provide configuration information to change the defaults). As most people will (at least initially)follow these conventions it makes it very easy to get something up and running very quickly.

Hello World in Flask

As is traditional in all programming languages we will start of with a simple 'Hello World' style application.This application will allow us to create a very simple web service that maps a particular URL to a function that will return JSON format data. We will use the JSON data format as it is very widely used within web-based services.

Using JSON

JSON standards for JavaScript ObjectNotation; it is a light weight data-interchange format that is also easy for humans to read and write. Although it is derived from a subset of the JavaScript programming language; it is in fact completely language independent and many languages and frameworks now support automatically processing of their own formats into and from JSON. This makes it ideal for RESTful web services.

JSON is actually built on some basic structures:

- A collection of name/value pairs in which the name and value are separated buy a colon ':' and each pair can be separated by a comma ','.
- An ordered list of values that are encompassed in square brackets ('[]').

This makes it very easy to build up structures that represent any set of data, for example a book with an ISBN, a title,

665

author and price could be represented by:

```
{
"author": "Phoebe Cooke", "isbn": 2,
"price": 12.99, "title": "Java"
}
```

In turn a list of books can be represented by a comma separated set of books within square brackets. For example:

```
[ {"author": "Gryff Smith","isbn": 1, "price":
10.99, "title": "XML"},
{"author": "Phoebe Cooke", "isbn":2, "price":
12.99, "title": "Java"}
{"author": "Jason Procter", "isbn": 3, "price":
11.55, "title": "C#"}]
```

Implementing a Flask Web Service

There are several steps involved in creating a Flask web service, these are:

1. Import flask.
2. Initialize the Flask application.
3. Implement one or more functions (or methods) to support the services you wish to publish.
4. Providing routing information to route from the URL to a function (or method).
5. Start the web service running.

We will look at these steps in the rest of this chapter.

A Simple Service

We will now create our hello world web service. To do this we must first import the flask module. In this example we will use the Flask class and jsonify() function elements of the module.

We then need to create the main application object which is an instance of the Flask class:

```
from flask import Flask, jsonify app =
Flask(__name   )
```

The argument passed into the Flask() constructor is the name of the application's module or package. As this is a simple example we will use the _name_ attribute of the module which in this case will be '_main_'. In larger more complex applications, with multiple packages and modules, then you may need to choose an appropriate package name.

The Flask application object implements the WSGI(Web ServerGateway Interface) standard for Python. This was originally specified in PEP-333 in 2003 and was updated for Python 3 in PEP-3333 published in 2010. It provides a simple convention for how web servers should handle requests to applications. The Flask application object is the element that can route a request for a URL to a Python function.

Providing Routing Information

We can now define routing information for the Flask application object. This information will map a URL to a function. When that URL is, for example, entered into a web browsers URL field, then the Flask application object will receive that request and invoke the appropriate function.

To provide route mapping information we use the @app.route decorator on a function or method. For example, in the following code the @app.route decorator maps the URL /hello to the function welcome() for HTTP Get requests:

@app.route('/hello', methods=[**'GET'**])

```
def welcome():
return jsonify({'msg': 'Hello Flask World'})
```

There are two things to note about this function definition:

- The @app.route decorator is used to declaratively specify the routing information for the function. This means that the URL '/hello' will be mapped to the function welcome(). The decorator also specifies the HTTP method that is supported; in this case GET requests are supported (which is actually the default so it does not need to be included here but is useful from a documentation point of view).

- The second thing is that we are going to return our data using the JSON format; we therefore use the jsonify() function and pass it a Python Dictionary structure with a single key/value pair. In this case the key is 'msg' and the data associated with that key is 'Hello Flask World'. The jsonify() function will convert this Python data structure into an equivalent JSON structure.

Running the Service

We are now ready to run our application. To do this we invoke the run() method of the Flask application object:

```
app.run(debug=True)
```

Optionally this method has a keyword parameter debug that can be set to True; if this is done then when the application is run some debugging information is generated that allows you to see what is happening. This can be useful in development but would not typically be used in production.

The whole program is presented below:

```
from flask import Flask, jsonify app =
Flask(__name   )
@app.route('/hello', methods=['GET'])
def welcome():
return jsonify({'msg': 'Hello Flask World'})
app.run(debug=True)
```

When this program is run the initial output generated is as shown below:

```
* Serving Flask app "hello_flask_world" (lazy
loading)
* Environment: production
WARNING: This is a development server. Do not use
it in a production deployment.
Use a production WSGI server instead.
* Debug mode: on
* Running on http://127.0.0.1:5000/ (Press CTRL+C
to quit)
* Restarting with stat
* Debugger is active!
* Debugger PIN: 274-630-732
```

Of course we don't see any output from our own program yet. This is because we have not invoked the welcome() function via the /hello URL.

Invoking the Service

We will use a web browser to access the web service. To do this we must enter the full URL that will route the request to our running application and to the welcome() function.

The URL is actually comprised of two elements, the first part is the machine on which the application is running and the port that it is using to listen for requests. This is actually listed in the above output—look at the line starting 'Running on'. This means that the URL must start with http://127.0.0.1:5000. This indicates that the application is running on the computer with the IP address 127.0.0.1 and listening on port 5000. We could of course also use localhost instead of 127.0.0.1.

The remainder of the URL must then provide the information that will allow Flask to route from the computer and port to the functions we want to run. Thus the full URL is http://127.0.0.1:5000/hello and thus is used in the web browser shown below:

As you can see the result returned is the text we supplied to the jsonify()function but now in plain JSON format and displayed within the Web Browser. You should also be able to see in the console output that a request was received by the Flask framework for the GET request mapped to the /hello URL:

127.0.0.1 - - [23/May/2019 11:09:40] "GET /hello HTTP/1.1" 200

-

One useful feature of this approach is that if you make a change to your program then the Flask framework will notice this change when running in development modeand can restart the web service with the code changes deployed. If you do this you will see that the output notifies you of the change:

* Detected change in 'hello_flask_world.py', reloading
* Restarting with stat

This allows changes to be made on the fly and their effect can be immediately seen.

The Final Solution

We can tidy this example up a little by defining a function hat can be used to create the Flask application object and by ensuring that we only run the application if the code is being run as the main module:

```python
from flask importFlask, jsonify, url_for
def create_service():
app = Flask(  name  )
@app.route('/hello', methods=['GET'])
def welcome():
return jsonify({'msg': 'Hello Flask World'})
with app.test_request_context():
print(url_for('welcome'))
return app
if   name
== '  main  ':
app = create_service()
app.run(debug=True)
```

One feature we have added to this program is the use of the test_re- quest_context(). The test request context object returned implements the context manager protocol and thus can be used via a with statement; this is useful for debugging purposes. It can be used to verify the URL used for any functions with routing information specified. In this case the output from the print statement is '/hello' as this is the URL defined by the @app.route decorator.

Bookshop Web Service

Building a Flask Bookshop Service

The previous chapter illustrated the basic structure of a very simple web service application. We are now in a position to explore the creation of a set of web services for something a little more realistic; the bookshop web service application.

In this chapter we will implement the set of web services described earlier in the previous chapter for every simple bookshop. This means that we will define services to handle not just the GET requests but also PUT, POST and DELETE requests for the RESTful bookshop API.

The Design

Before we look at the implementation of the Bookshop RESTful API we will consider what elements we for the services services.

One question that often causes some confusion is how web services relate to traditional design approaches such as object oriented design. The approach adopted here is that the Web Service API provides a way to implement an interface to appropriate functions, objects and methods used to implement the application/ domain model.

This means that we will still have a set of classes that will represent the Bookshop and the Books held within the bookshop. In turn the functions implementing the web services will access the bookshop to retrieve, modify, update and delete the books held by the bookshop.

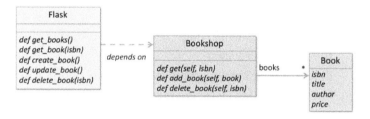

This shows that a Book object will have an isbn, a title, an author and a price attribute.

In turn the Bookshop object will have a books attribute that will hold zero or more Books. The books attribute will actually hold a List as the list of books needs to change dynamically as and when new books are added or old books deleted. The Bookshop will also define three methods that will

- allow a book to be obtained via its isbn,
- allow a book to be added to the list of books and
- enable a book to be deleted (based on its isbn).

675

Routing information will be provided for a set of functions that will invoke appropriate methods on the Bookshop object. The functions to be decorated with @app.route, and the mappings to be used, are listed below:

- get_books() which maps to the /book/list URL using the HTTP Get method request.
- get_book(isbn) which maps to the /book/<isbn> URL where isbn is a URL parameter that will be passed into the function. This will also use the HTTP GET request.
- create_book()which maps to the /book URL using the HTTP Post request.
- update_book() which maps to the /book URL but using the HTTP Put request.
- delete_book() which maps to the /book/<isbn> URL but using the HTTP Delete request.

The Domain Model

The domain model comprises the Book and Bookshop classes. These are presented below.

The Book class is a simple Value type class (that is it is data oriented with no behavior of its own):

```
class Book:
def   init    (self,  isbn,  title,  author,
price):
self.isbn =  isbn self.title  =   title
self.author  =  author self.price  =  price
```

```
def    str    (self):
return self.title  +  ' by ' +  self.author  +  '
@ ' +
str(self.price)
```

The Bookshop class holds a list of books and provides a set of methods to access books, update books and delete books:

```
class Bookshop:
def    init    (self,  books):
self.books  =  books
def get(self,  isbn):
if int(isbn)  >  len(self.books):
abort(404)
return list(filter(lambda b:  b.isbn  ==  isbn,
self.books))[0]
def add_book(self,  book):
self.books.append(book)
def delete_book(self,  isbn):
self.books  =  list(filter(lambda b:  b.isbn  !=
isbn, self.books))
```

In the above code, the books attribute holds the list of books currently available.

The get() method returns a book given a specified ISBN. The add_book() method adds a book object to the list of books. The delete_book() method removes a book based on its ISBN. The bookshop global variable holds the Bookshop object initialized with a default set of books:

```
bookshop = Bookshop(
[Book(1, 'XML', 'Gryff Smith', 10.99), Book(2,
 'Java', 'Phoebe Cooke', 12.99), Book(3,
'Scala', 'Adam Davies', 11.99), Book(4,
'Python', 'Jasmine Byrne', 15.99)])
```

Encoding Books Into JSON

One issue we have is that although the jsonify() function knows how to convert builtin types such as strings,integers, lists, dictionaries etc. into an appropriate JSON format; it does not know how to do this for custom types such as a Book. We therefore need to define some way of converting a Book into an appropriate JSON format.

One way we could do this would be to define a method that can be called to convert an instance of the Book class into a JSON format. We could call this method to_json(). For example:

```
class Book:
"""Represents a book in the bookshop"""
def  init  (self, isbn, title, author,
price):
self.isbn = isbn self.title = title
self.author = author self.price = price
def  str  (self):
return self.title + ' by ' + self.author + '
@ ' +
str(self.price)
def to_json(self):
```

```
return {
'isbn':  self.isbn,
'title':  self.title,
'author':  self.author,
'price':  self.price
}
```

We could now use this with the jsonify() function to convert a book into the JSON format:

```
jsonify({'book':  book.to_json()})
```

This approach certainly works and provides a very lightweight way to convert a book into JSON.

However, the approach presented above does mean that every time we want to jsonify a book we must remember to call the to_json() method. In some cases this means that we will also have to write some slightly convoluted code. For example if we wish to return a list of books from the Bookshop as a JSON list we might write:

```
jsonify({'books':  [b.to_json()  for b  in
bookshop.books]})
```

Here we have used a list comprehension to generate a list containing the JSON versions of the books held in the bookshop. This is starting to look overly complex, easy to forget about and probably error prone. Flask itself uses encoders to encode types into JSON. Flask provides a way of creating your own encoders that can be used to convert a custom type, such as the Book class, into JSON. Such an encoder can automatically be used by the jsonify() function.

To do this we must implement an encoder class; the class will extend the flask. json.JSONEncoder super class. The class must define a method default(self, obj). This method takes an object and returns the JSON representation of that object. We can therefore write an encoder for the Book class as follows:

```
class BookJSONEncoder(JSONEncoder):
def default(self, obj):
if isinstance(obj, Book):
return {
'isbn': obj.isbn,
'title': obj.title,
'author': obj.author,
'price': obj.price
}
else:
return super(BookJSONEncoder, self).default(obj)
```

The default() method in this class checks that the object passed to it is an instance of the class Book and if it is then it will create a JSON version of the Book.This JSON structure is based on the isbn, title, author and price attributes. If it is not an instance of the Book class, then it passes the object up to the parent class.

We can now register this encoder with the Flask application object so that it will be used whenever a Book must be converted into JSON.This is done by assigning the custom encoder to the Flask application object via the app.json_encoder attribute:

```
app  =  Flask(    name    )
app.json_encoder  =  BookJSONEncoder
```

Now if we wish to encode a single book or a list of books the above encoder will be used automatically and thus we do not need to do anything else. Thus our earlier examples can be written to simply by referencing the book or bookshop.books attribute:

```
jsonify({'book':  book})
jsonify({'books':  bookshop.books})
```

Setting Up the GET Services

We can now set up the two services that will support GET requests, these are the

· /book/list and /book<isbn> services.

The functions that these URLs map to are given below:

@app.route('/book/list', methods=[**'GET'**])
  def get_books():

```
return jsonify({'books': bookshop.books})

@app.route('/book/<int:isbn>', methods=['GET'])
    def get_book(isbn):
    book = bookshop.get(isbn)
    return jsonify({'book': book})
```

The first function merely returns the current list of books held by the bookshop in aJSON structure using the key books. The second function takes an isbn number as parameter. This is a URL parameter; in other words part of the URL used to invoke this function is actually dynamic and will be passed into the function. This means that a user can request details of books with different ISBNs just by changing the ISBN element of the URL,for example:

- /book/1 will indicate that we want information on the book with the ISBN 1.
- /book/2 will indicate we want information on the book with ISBN 2.

In Flask to indicate that something is a URL parameter rather than a hard coded element of the URL, we use angle brackets (<>). These surround the URL parameter name and allow the parameter to be passed into the function (using the same name).

In the above example we have also(optionally) indicated the type of the parameter. By default the type will be a string; however we know that the ISBN is in fact an integer and so we have indicated that by prefixing the parameter name with the type int (and separated the type information from the parameter name by a colon':'). There are actually several options available including

- string (the default),
- int (as used above),
- float for positive floating point values,
- uuid for uuid strings and
- path which dislike string but accepts slashes.

We can again use a browser to view the results of calling these services; this time the URLs will be

- http://127.0.0.1:5000/book/list and
- http:/127.0.0.1:5000/book/1

for example:

As you can see from this the book information is returned as a set of key/value pairs in JSON format.

Deleting a Book

The delete a book web service is very similar to the get a book service in that it takes an isbn as a URL path parameter. However, in this case it merely returns an acknowledgment that the book was deleted successfully:

```
@app.route('/book/<int:isbn>', methods=['DELETE'])
    def delete_book(isbn):
    bookshop.delete_book(isbn)
    return jsonify({'result': True})
```

However, we can no longer test this just by using a web browser. This is because the web browser uses the HTTP

Get request method for all URLs entered into the URL field. However, the delete web service is associated with the HTTP Delete request method.

To invoke the delete_book() function we therefore need to ensure that the request that is sent uses the DELETE request method. This can be done from a client that can indicate the type of request method being used. Examples might include another Python program, a JavaScript web site etc.

For testing purposes, we will however use the curl program. This program is available on most Linux and Mac systems and can be easily installed, if it is not already available, on other operating systems.

The curl is a command line tool and library that can be used to send and receive data over the internet. It supports a wide range of protocols and standards and in particular supports HTTP and HTTPS protocols and can be used to send and receive data over HTTP/S using different request methods. For example, to invoke the delete_book() function using the /book/2 URL and the HTTP Delete method we can use curl as follows:

curl http://localhost:5000/book/2 -X DELETE

This indicates that we want to invoke the URL (http://localhost:5000/book/2) and that we wish to use a custom request method(i.e. Not the default GET) which is in the case DELETE (as indicated by the -X option).The result returned by the command is given below indicating that the book was successfully deleted.

```
{
"result": true
}
```

We can verify this by checking the output from the /book/list URL in the web browser:

This confirms that book 2 has been deleted.

Adding a New Book

We also want to support adding a new book to the Bookshop.

The details of a new book could just be added to the URL as URL path parameters; however as the amount of data to be added grows this would become increasingly difficult to maintain and verify. Indeed although historically there was a limit of 2083 characters in Microsoft's Internet Explore (IE) which has theoretically be removed since IE8, in practice there are typically still limits on the size of the URL. Most web servers have a limit of 8 KB (or 8192 bytes) although this is typically configurable. There may also be client side limits (such as those imposed by IE or Apple's Safari (which usually have a 2 KB limit). If the limit is exceeded in either a browser or on the server, then most systems will just truncate the characters outside the limit (in some cases without any warning).

Typically such data is therefore sent in the body of the HTTP request as part of a HTTP Post request. This limit on the same of a Post requests message body is much higher (usually up to 2 GB). This means that it is a much more reliable and safer way to transfer data to a web service. However, it should be noted that this does not mean that the data is any more secure than if it is part of the URL; just that it is sent in a different way. From the point of view of the Python functions that are invoked as the result of a HTTP Post method request it means that the data is not available as a parameter to the URL and thus to the function. Instead, within the function it is necessary to obtain the request object and then to use that to obtain the information held within the body of the request.

A key attribute on the request object, available when a HTTP request contains JSON data, is the request.json attribute. This attribute contains a dictionary like structure holding the values associated with the keys in the JSON data structure.

This is shown below for the create_book() function.

from flask **import** request, abort

```
@app.route('/book',  methods=['POST'])
def create_book():
print('create book')
if not request.json  or not 'isbn' in
request.json:
abort(400)
book  =
Book(request.json['isbn'],request.json['title'],
request.json.get('author',  ""),
float(request.json['price']))
bookshop.add_book(book)
return jsonify({'book':  book}),  201
```

The above function accesses the flask.request object that represents the current HTTP request. The function first checks to see that it contains JSON data and that the ISBN of the book to add, is part of that JSON structure. If it the ISBN is not then the flask.abort() function is called passing in a suitable HTTP response status code. In this case the error code indicates that this was a Bad Request (HTTP Error Code 400).

If however the JSON data is present and does contain an

ISBN number then the values for the keys isbn, title, author and price are obtained. Remember that JSON is a dictionary like structure of keys and values thus treating it in this way makes it easy to extract the data that a JSON structure holds. It also means that we can use both method and key oriented access styles.This is shown above where we use the get() method along with a default value to use, if an author is not specified.

Finally, as we want to treat the price as a floating point number we must use the float() function to convert the string format supplied by JSON into a float. Using the data extracted we can instantiate a new Book instance that can be added to the bookshop. As is common in web services we are returning the newly created book object as the result of creating the book along with the HTTP response status code 201, which indicates the successful creation of a resource.

We can now test this service using the curl command line program:

```
curl  -H  "Content-Type:  application/json"  -X
POST  -d
'{"title":"Read  a  book",
"author":"Bob","isbn":"5",
"price":"3.44"}'  http://localhost:5000/book
```

The options used with this command indicate the type of data being sent in the body of the request (-H) along with the data to include in the body of the request (- d). The result of running this command is:

689

```
{
"book": {
"author": "Bob", "isbn": "5", "price": 3.44,
"title": "Read a book"
}
}
```

Illustrating that the new book by Bob has been added.

Updating a Book

Updating a book that is already held by the bookshop object
is very similar to adding a book except that the HTTP Put
request method is used.

Again the function implementing the required behavior
must use the flask. request object to access the data
submitted along with the PUT request. However, in this
case the ISBN number specified is used to find the book to
be updated, rather than the specifying a completely new
book.

The update_book()function is given below:

```
@app.route('/book', methods=['PUT'])
def update_book():
if not request.json or not 'isbn' in
request.json:
abort(400)
isbn = request.json['isbn'] book =
bookshop.get(isbn) book.title =
request.json['title']
book.author = request.json['author']
```

```
book.price = request.json['price']
return jsonify({'book': book}), 201
```

This function resets the title, author and price of the book retrieved from the bookshop. It again returns the updated book as the result of running the function.

The curl program can again be used to invoke this function, although this time the HTTP Put method must be specified:

```
curl -H "Content-Type: application/json" -X
PUT -d
'{"title":"Read a Python Book", "author":"Bob
Jones","isbn":"5", "price":"3.44"}'
http://localhost:5000/book
```

The output from this command is:

```
{
"book": {
"author": "Bob Jones", "isbn": "5",
"price": "3.44",
"title": "Read a Python Book"
}
}
```

This shows that book 5 has been updated with the new information.

What Happens if We Get It Wrong?

The code presented for the bookshop web services is not particularly defensive, as it is possible to try to add a new book with the same ISBN as an existing one. However, it does check to see that an ISBN number has been supplied with both the create_book()and update_book() functions. However, what happens if an ISBN number is not supplied? In both functions we call the flask.abort() function. By default if this happens an error message will be sent back to the client. For example, in the following command we have forgotten to include the ISBN number:

```
curl  -H  "Content-Type:  application/json"  -X
POST  -d
'{"title":"Read  a  book",  "author":"Tom
Andrews",
"price":"13.24"}'  http://localhost:5000/book
```

This generates the following error output:

```
<!DOCTYPE  HTML  PUBLIC  "-//W3C//DTD  HTML  3.2
Final//EN">
<title>400  Bad  Request</title>
<h1>Bad  Request</h1>
<p>The  browser  (or  proxy)  sent  a  request
that  this  server  could not  understand.</p>
```

The odd thing here is that the error output is in HTML format, which is not what we might have expected since we are creating a web service and working with JSON.The problem is that Flask has default to generating an error HTML web page that it expects to be rendered in a web browser.

We can overcome this by defining our own custom error handler function. This is a function that is decorated with an @app.errorhandler() decorator which provides the response status code that it handles. For example:

```
@app.errorhandler(400)
def not_found(error):
return make_response(jsonify({'book': 'Not
found'}), 400)
```

Now when a 400 code is generated via the flask.abort() function, the not_found() function will be invoked and a JSON response will be generated with the information provided by the flask.make_response()function. For example:

```
curl  -H  "Content-Type:  application/json"  -X
POST  -d
'{"title":"Read  a  book",  "author":"Tom
Andrews",
"price":"13.24"}'  http://localhost:5000/book
```

The output from this command is:

```
{
"book":  "Not  found"
}
```

Bookshop Services Listing

The complete listing for the bookshop web services application is given below:

```
from flask  import Flask,  jsonify,  request,
abort,  make_response
from flask.json  import JSONEncoder
class Book:
def   init    (self,  isbn,  title,  author,
price):
self.isbn = isbn self.title  =  title
self.author = author self.price = price
def   str    (self):
return self.title + ' by ' + self.author + '
@ ' +
str(self.price)
class BookJSONEncoder(JSONEncoder):
def default(self,  obj):
if isinstance(obj,  Book):
return {
'isbn':  obj.isbn,
'title':  obj.title,
'author':  obj.author,
'price':  obj.price
}
else:
return super(BookJSONEncoder,  self).default(obj)
class Bookshop:
def   init    (self,  books):
self.books = books
def get(self,  isbn):
if int(isbn) > len(self.books):
abort(404)
return list(filter(lambda b:  b.isbn == isbn,
self.books))[0]
def add_book(self,  book):
self.books.append(book)
def delete_book(self,  isbn):
self.books = list(filter(lambda b:  b.isbn != 
```

```
isbn, self.books))
bookshop = Bookshop([Book(1, 'XML', 'Gryff
Smith', 10.99), Book(2, 'Java', 'Phoebe
Cooke', 12.99), Book(3, 'Scala', 'Adam
Davies', 11.99), Book(4, 'Python', 'Jasmine
Byrne', 15.99)])
def create_bookshop_service(): app = Flask(
name    ) app.json_encoder = BookJSONEncoder
@app.route('/book/list', methods=['GET'])
def get_books():
return jsonify({'books': bookshop.books})
@app.route('/book/<int:isbn>', methods=['GET'])
def get_book(isbn):
book = bookshop.get(isbn)
return jsonify({'book': book})
@app.route('/book', methods=['POST'])
def create_book():
print('create book')
if not request.json or not 'isbn' in
request.json:
abort(400)
book = Book(request.json['isbn'],
request.json['title'], request.json.get('author',
""), float(request.json['price']))
bookshop.add_book(book)
return jsonify({'book': book}), 201
@app.route('/book', methods=['PUT'])
def update_book():
if not request.json or not 'isbn' in
request.json:
abort(400)
isbn = request.json['isbn'] book =
bookshop.get(isbn) book.title =
request.json['title']
book.author = request.json['author']
book.price = request.json['price']
return jsonify({'book': book}), 201
```

```
@app.route('/book/<int:isbn>',
methods=['DELETE'])
def delete_book(isbn):
bookshop.delete_book(isbn)
return jsonify({'result':  True})
400)
@app.errorhandler(400)
def not_found(error):
return make_response(jsonify({'book':  'Not
found'}),
return app
if_name_=='_main_':
app  =  create_bookshop_service()
app.run(debug=True)
```

Try

The exercises for this chapter involves creating a web service that will provide information on stock market prices. The services to be implemented are:

Get method:

- /stock/list this will return a list of the stocks that can be queried for their price.
- /stock/ticker this will return the current price of the stock indicated by ticker, for example/stock/APPL or/-stock/MSFT.

POST method:

- /stock with the request body containing JSON for a new stock ticker and price, for example {'IBM': 12.55}.

PUT method:

- /stock with the request body containing JSON for an existing stock ticker and price.

DELETE method

- /stock/<ticker> which will result in the stock indicated by the ticker being deleted from the service.

You could initialize the service with a default set of stocks and prices such as
  [('IBM', 12.55), ('APPL', 15.66), ('GOOG', 5.22)].

You can test these services using the curl command line tool.

References

Smith, John. "*Python Programming for Advanced Users: An In-Depth Exploration of Python's Advanced Features and Techniques.*" In this comprehensive volume published by Wiley in 2021, Smith delves into the intricacies of Python, offering advanced users a thorough understanding of the language. Topics include meta classes, decorators, and advanced object-oriented programming, making it an indispensable resource for those seeking to master Python at an advanced level.

Brown, Alice. "*Mastering Python: Advanced Tips and Techniques for the Discerning Programmer.*" Published by O'Reilly Media in 2029, Brown's book is a tour de force of advanced Python programming. It offers in-depth guidance on topics like metaprogramming, multithreading, and advanced data manipulation. With a focus on practical applications, this work empowers programmers to take their Python skills to the next level.

Davis, Richard. "*Effective Python: 90 Specific Ways to Write Better Python Code.*" This authoritative book from Addison-Wesley Professional, released in 2020, goes beyond mere syntax and explores the art of writing elegant and efficient Python code. Davis presents 90 concise, practical tips and techniques, making it an essential reference for those striving to write Python code that is not only functional but also maintainable and elegant.

Johnson, Sarah. "*Python in Practice: Create Better Programs Using Concurrency, Libraries, and Design Patterns.*" Published by Addison-Wesley Professional in 2013, Johnson's work is a treasure trove of knowledge for developers seeking to harness the power of Python in real-world applications. It covers topics like concurrency, third-party libraries, and design patterns to help programmers create robust and efficient software.

White, Robert. "*Fluent Python: Clear, Concise, and Effective Programming.*" O'Reilly Media, 2015. In this book, White provides advanced programmers with insights into Python's idiomatic and expressive features. It offers guidance on writing Pythonic code, understanding data structures, and effectively using Python's dynamic capabilities. This work is indispensable for those looking to write code that truly embodies Python's unique philosophy.

Lewis, Emily. "*Python Cookbook: Recipes for Mastering Python.*" O'Reilly Media, 2013. Lewis's book is a compendium of practical Python recipes that cover a wide range of topics, from data manipulation to network programming. Each recipe offers a hands-on approach to solving real-world problems, making it a valuable resource for advanced Python programmers.

Clark, Michael. "*Python for Data Analysis: Harness the Power of Python for Data Exploration and Analysis.*" Published by O'Reilly Media in 2017, Clark's book is a go-to guide for data professionals and analysts. It provides comprehensive coverage of data analysis using Python, including data wrangling, visualization, and statistical analysis. This resource is essential for anyone looking to master Python in the context of data science and analysis.

Turner, William. "*Python Tricks: A Buffet of Awesome Python Features for the Astute Programmer.*" Published by Dan Bader in 2017, this book is a curated collection of Python tips and techniques. It covers a wide spectrum of Python features and best practices, offering readers a diverse array of skills to enhance their Python proficiency.

King, Laura. "*Advanced Python Programming: Unlock the Full Potential of Python with Advanced Techniques.*" This book, published by Packt Publishing in 2016, is a treasure trove of advanced Python techniques. King explores topics like metaprogramming, functional programming, and concurrent programming to empower Python developers with advanced capabilities.

Roberts, Daniel. "*Mastering Python Design Patterns: Harness the Power of Python for Software Design.*" Published by Packt Publishing in 2016, Roberts' book is a guide to mastering software design patterns in Python. It covers various design patterns, providing in-depth explanations and practical examples for each. This resource is a must-have for those aiming to excel in software architecture and design using

Python.

E. Gamma, R. Helm, R. Johnson, J. Vlissades, *Design patterns: elements of reusable object-oriented software*, Addison-Wesley (1995).

Milton Keynes UK
Ingram Content Group UK Ltd.
UKHW020658271123
433341UK00021B/1774

9 798868 912733